Antrim and Argyll

Some Aspects of the Connections

Antrim and Argyll
Some Aspects of the Connections

Contributors

Stuart Eydmann

Eric J. Graham

Cormac McSparron

Aodán Mac Póilin

Róise Ní Bhaoill

Editor

William Roulston

First published 2018
by Ulster Historical Foundation,
The Corn Exchange,
31 Gordon Street, Belfast, BT1 2LG
www.ancestryireland.com
www.booksireland.org.uk

ISBN: 978-1-909556-63-8

COVER ILLUSTRATION
Excerpt from Speed's map of Scotland, 1610

Department
for Communities
www.communities-ni.gov.uk

Ulster Historical Foundation
Registered with The Charity Commission for Northern Ireland (NIC100280)

Print manufacture by Jellyfish Print Solutions
Text formatting by FPM Publishing
Cover design by J.P. Morrison

Contents

Preface and Acknowledgements

The connections between Ulster and western Scotland, and in particular between County Antrim and Argyll, can be traced back millennia and are reflected in many different ways. The origins of this book can be found in a project commissioned by the Ministerial Advisory Group – Ulster Scots Academy which explored a number of aspects of the relationship between Antrim and Argyll over the millennia. The project, which brought together scholars in a range of disciplines in both Northern Ireland and Scotland, was delivered by the Ulster Historical Foundation and the initial research was carried out in 2014–15. Subsequently, the Department for Communities provided additional support to allow this research to be published, for which we are very grateful.

In their chapter for this book, Dr Róise Ní Bhaoill and Aodán Mac Póilin explore the Gaelic links between Antrim and Argyll, looking at linguistic and literary connections, as well as the evidence of surnames, place-names, folklore and mythology in broadening our understanding of the relationship between the two regions. They highlight an important theme in the development from the twelfth century of the Gaelic clans of Argyll – most of which traced their descent from Ireland – and the development of the Lordship of the Isles, led by the MacDonalds of Islay, one outcome of which was the establishment of a branch of that family in Antrim. Another important link originated in the late thirteenth century when Scottish mercenaries began to be brought to Ireland, initially by Irish lords, but ultimately by every side right up to the end of the sixteenth century and beyond. Many of these Scottish mercenaries, most of whom belonged to clans from Argyll, settled in Ireland. Sadly, Aodán died in December 2016 and his loss was felt deeply by those involved in this sector.

In two substantial chapters Dr Cormac McSparron examines the archaeological and historical evidence for contact between Antrim and Argyll from the prehistoric period to the Early Medieval period. He highlights the fact that during this era there are times when it is difficult not to see the history and archaeology of Antrim, Argyll and Ulster and western Scotland as completely intertwined, almost to the extent of eroding any concept of them having a separate identity. During other periods, however, the regions would appear to be running parallel to each other. In the Mesolithic period the similarities in the tool technologies on either side of the North Channel is such that it must be likely that they had a common origin, but they seem to have developed independently.

In the Neolithic there is evidence for much deeper and more sustained contact between Antrim and Argyll, while there can be no doubting the strong similarity in a number of areas between the Early Bronze Age archaeological remains in Antrim and Argyll and again in the surrounding areas. The Iron Age is more problematic for while there are a number of very large and impressive monumental structures associated with the collective functions of society, there is less evidence for the actual people, with hardly any settlement evidence. The contrast with Argyll and the rest of Scotland at this time could not be greater for here there seems to be no evidence of a similar hiatus in the Scottish settlement record.

With Early Medieval Antrim and Argyll, traditional narrative history explicitly states an origin for the emerging Scottish nation amongst the Irish of Dál Riada. The sea became an obstacle, however, at the very end of the eighth century when the control of the seas, if not actually lost, became contested with the arrival of the Vikings. The difficulty in communications is apparent in the decreasing frequency of entries regarding Scottish affairs in the Irish annals as a North Channel world, for a time, becomes a memory. At the same time the power of the most powerful over-kings in both Scotland and Ireland is increasing. Ireland and Scotland jointly were looking inward, consolidating their monarchical institutions, powerful dynasties striving to emerge as the sole royal family. Yet they were developing in parallel and, for the Scottish in particular, the narrative of the emergence of the leading Scottish dynasties from an Irish aristocracy with long roots, and a highly developed supporting body of genealogy and literature, was of vital importance.

The musical connections between Antrim and Argyll are the subject of Stuart Eydmann's chapter. In approaching his task he acknowledges that it is important to recognise the many factors at play in music change and transmission and to note that explanations are rarely as straightforward as we might like them to be, complexity and contradiction being the norm. Furthermore, music does not exist in isolation, but always reflects and is a reflection of the wider cultural context in which it is created, developed and maintained. It is continually in a state of change, being moulded and shaped by historical, political, economic and social factors. Music is highly portable and can be carried easily from place to place. In addition, it is also infinitely pliable. In his chapter Dr Eydmann ranges far and wide with the author drawing on many different sources in discussing musical instruments – fiddle, accordion, bagpipes, harp, fife, flute and drum – as well as singing – songs in Scots, English and Gaelic. He highlights the linkages and disconnects in the musical heritage of Antrim and Argyll and concludes that this is indeed a field worthy of detailed research and analysis, sharing of findings, and promotion of enhanced understanding.

In his chapter Eric Graham explores the fascinating connections between Argyllshire emigrants to North Carolina and Antrim flaxseed traders. The eighteenth-century links between Antrim and Argyll were mainly maritime-related and from the mid 1760s onwards there was an economic boom in the maritime trades that involved Antrim vessels, captains and merchants. To the fore was the great upsurge in the West Indian rum and sugar voyages, with goods legally landed at Campbeltown in Kintyre for duty purposes before being conveyed to Belfast and Larne. The early 1770s witnessed the largest surge in emigration of tenantry and servants driven out from the Highlands and Islands to the Carolinas and Georgia by the rapid and dramatic rise in rents and the changes in agricultural methods and management imposed by their lairds. Dr Graham examines the response of the authorities in Scotland to this as they tried to understand the reasons for it. He also looks into the deeper origins of the networks linking Antrim and Argyll with North Carolina, drawing attention to the 'Argyll Colony' of 1739.

Others who contributed to the initial project include Pamela Linden, John Edmund and Colin Breen and we acknowledge with gratitude their assistance, and that of others who provided advice and suggestions for avenues of research.

We acknowledge and are grateful to the following institutions and individuals for permission to reproduce illustrations that appear in this book: New York Public Library for the map of the British Isles on page xii; the Deputy Keeper of the Records, the Public Record Office of Northern Ireland, and Viscount Dunluce for the image of the McDonnell genealogy (D2977/5/1/4/3) on page 11; the National Library of Scotland for the title page of *Aird's Selection of Scotch, English, Irish and Foreign Airs* on page 106; the Ulster Archaeological Society for the images on pages 25, 30, 31, 37, 43, 86, which appeared originally in the *Ulster Journal of Archaeology*; William Roulston for the photographs of Dunseverick on page 48 and Art O'Neill's headstone on page 105; Betina Linke for the photograph of Elagh Castle on page 83; and the Library of Congress, Washington DC, for the maps of Scotland on page 142 and North Carolina on page 144.

Abbreviations

JIA	*Journal of Irish Archaeology*
JRSAI	*Journal of the Royal Society of Antiquaries of Ireland*
NLS	National Library of Scotland
NRS	National Records of Scotland
PRIA	*Proceedings of the Royal Irish Academy*
PPS	*Proceedings of the Prehistoric Society*
PRONI	Public Record Office of Northern Ireland
PSAS	*Proceedings of the Society of Antiquaries of Scotland*
SHR	*Scottish Historical Review*
TNA	The National Archives (London)
UJA	*Ulster Journal of Archaeology*

Notes on Contributors

Stuart Eydmann is a researcher and writer on musical traditions and is a long-standing member of the Scottish music group, The Whistlebinkies. He has taught historical studies at the Open University and the Royal Scottish Academy of Music and Drama and he was a Post-Doctoral Research Fellow and then Traditional Artist in Residence at the Department of Celtic and Scottish Studies, University of Edinburgh, where he undertook commissioned research on Ulster-Scots musical traditions. He was a member of the Scottish Culture Minister's Working Group on the Traditional Arts that reported in 2010 and is currently a Tutor at Edinburgh College of Art, University of Edinburgh. His recent publications include a history of the harp in modern Scotland, the biography of Scottish Gaelic singer Dolina MacLennan and various studies on traditional music revivals.

Eric Graham was born in Ayrshire and is a graduate of Strathclyde and Exeter universities where he studied Scottish and Maritime History. His doctoral thesis provided the basis of his book, *A Maritime History of Scotland* (1650–1790). He is the author of a number of other books and has been widely published in learned journals. As a founding member of the Early Scottish Maritime History Exchange (ESME), Eric is committed to widening the appeal of Scottish maritime history. Eric is an Honorary Post-Doctoral Research Fellow, Scottish Centre for the Diaspora, University of Edinburgh.

Aodán Mac Póilin was Director of the ULTACH Trust. He wrote and lectured extensively on cultural and linguistic politics. He was Irish-language editor of the literary magazine *Krino*, co-editor of Padraic Fiacc's *Ruined Pages: New Selected Poems* (1994/2012) and *Bás in Éirinn – May You Die in Ireland* (2011), and edited and contributed to *The Irish Language in Northern Ireland* (1997). He was chairperson of the first Irish-medium school in Northern Ireland and a founding member of Iomairt Cholmcille, which promotes the shared culture and linguistic heritage of Ireland and Scotland.

Cormac McSparron graduated with a BA in Archaeology and Modern History from Queen's University Belfast, an MPhil from QUB entitled 'The Medieval Coarse Pottery of Ulster' and a PhD from QUB entitled 'Statistical analysis of the Single Burial Tradition in Early Bronze Age Ireland and some implications for social structure'. He worked for the Environment and Heritage Service on excavation and post-excavation projects from 1991 to 1995 and was active in private sector rescue archaeology from 1997 to 2001 before joining the Centre for Archaeological Fieldwork as a Fieldwork Director in 2002. He has directed and published a number of important excavations of varying types and periods and has a wide range of research interests.

Róise Ní Bhaoill works for the ULTACH Trust in Belfast. She is the author of a number of publications for learners of Irish, including *Taisce Focal, Little Stories for Big People* (2007) and *Ceol Leat! Songs and Rhymes for Young Children* (2016). She co-edited *Gaelic-medium Education Provision: Northern Ireland, the Republic of Ireland, Scotland and the Isle of Man* (2003) and *Bás in Éirinn – May You Die in Ireland* (2011). She also edited *Ulster Gaelic Voices, Bailiúchan Doegen 1931* (2010).

Excerpt from *The British Isles, comprehending Great Britain and Ireland; with the adjacent islands*, 1786 (New York Public Library)

I

Argyll and Antrim: Gaelic Connections

Aodán Mac Póilin and Róise Ní Bhaoill

Territorial place-names are something of a minefield, and while Gaelic links between modern Antrim and modern Argyll go back to at least AD 500, 1,500 years ago Argyll did not exist and Antrim meant something else entirely. St Mochaoi is said to have founded a monastery at *Aondruim* towards the end of the fifth century, but this was Nendrum in County Down. Another early monastery was that of *Aontreibh*, misspelled occasionally as *Oentruimh* and *Aentruim*, Latinised as 'Antrima' or 'Aontroma', and ultimately anglicised as Antrim (the modern Irish is *Aontroim*). By the fourteenth century the Normans had divided modern County Antrim into three counties, Twescard (*Tuaisceart* – the north), including north Antrim and a portion of north Derry, 'the county of the town of Carrickfergus' to the south-east, still a residual administrative unit in 1891, and, finally, Antrim to the south-west (approximating to the baronies of south and north Antrim). Modern County Antrim was not established until the reign of Queen Elizabeth the First.

Argyll, *Oirear Gael* in modern Irish, *Earra Gàidheal* in Scottish Gaelic, means 'the coast (or region or frontier) of the Gael'. Whatever the early people of Argyll called themselves, they did not call themselves Gaels, as this term is an import from the Welsh *Gwyddll*, probably brought to Ireland by Christian missionaries as a generic term for the inhabitants of Ireland. By the seventh century it had been adopted by the locals, who may not have known that it was actually an insult, meaning something like 'the wild man of the woods'. The place-name does not appear in the written evidence until the end of the twelfth century when the diocese of Argyll was separated from that of Dunkeld.[1] The Hebrides were, at that time, under Norse control, and in the twelfth century the southern Hebrides from Mull to Islay, as well as Bute and Arann, belonged to the diocese of the Isles, until 1472 subject to the ecclesiastical province of Trondheim in Norway.

Argyll's borders expanded and contracted from its permanent core, Kintyre and the immediate mainland to the north and east. The rugged mountains of *Droim Alban* appear to have formed its eastern border; in fact the watershed which runs through the mountains from Loch Lomond to the Great Glen corresponds closely to the present eastern limits of Argyll.

This natural barrier was notoriously difficult to traverse by land, as the following fourteenth-century description by John of Fordun shows:

> Impassable as they are on horseback, save in very few places, they can hardly be crossed even on foot, both on account of the snow always lying on them, except in summer-time only, and by reason of the boulders torn off the beetling crags, and the deep hollows in their midst.[2]

To the north, briefly, Argyll extended well up the western coast: 'Charters dating back to the 13th and 14th centuries refer to "North Argyle" – the western coastlands from Kintail northwards to Gairloch and Lochbroom.'[3] (Loch Broom is where the Ullapool ferry to Lewis departs).

In 1708, the region was divided into two Westminster parliamentary constituencies, Buteshire (Bute and Arann) and Argyllshire (later Argyll and then Argyll and Bute). By this time, southern Hebridean islands such as Mull, Islay, Jura and Tyree were incorporated into the concept of 'Argyll'. In 1890, Argyll became a local government county (losing the Small Isles to Inverness-shire), but was split in 1975 between the Strathclyde and Highland Regions, much of the northern part of Argyll going to Highland. The Strathclyde part was reorganised as the local government district of Argyll and Bute. For convenience, however, we will use the modern terms here, but including areas associated with historic Argyll and Scottish Dál Riada (Arann and Bute, and parts of modern Lochaber in and around Fort William) which are not technically in modern Argyll.

Gaelic links between Antrim and Argyll lasted well into the modern period. As late as 1881, 65 per cent of the population of Argyll was Gaelic-speaking, and clusters of native speakers of Argyll Gaelic survived until the twenty-first century. Gaelic faded from Antrim somewhat earlier, but the Ordnance Survey memoirs show a vibrant Gaelic culture in the Glens of Antrim before the Famine, 43 per cent of Rathlin Islanders were Gaelic-speaking in 1901, and there were still native speakers of Antrim Gaelic in the second half of the twentieth century. The Antrim and Argyll dialects of Gaelic were linguistically very close.

As it is impossible to summarise one and a half millennia of the history of any region in a few pages, this account will do no more than touch on a number of themes. Geography played a major role in the historical and cultural development of the people of the region. At the dawn of recorded history the Gaelic kingdom of Dál Riada straddled the mainland of both sides of the Sea of Moyle and the islands between, and although its origins remain tantalisingly obscure, Dál Riada was to have enormous symbolic importance for Scottish identity and the Scottish crown.

One of the most interesting things about this relationship was the extent to which, for much of this period, the cultural orientation of Gaelic Scotland, and Argyll in particular, was towards Ireland. Not only did Scottish kings trace their genealogy to Ireland, the Gaelic clans of Argyll traced – or invented – Irish progenitors, and poets and harpers from Ireland included Gaelic Scotland in their itineraries.

Another important theme was the emergence of the Gaelic-speaking Lordship of the Isles (1336–1493) led by the MacDonalds of Islay, one outcome of which was the establishment of a branch of that family in Antrim, for long active in the Gaelic worlds of both Ireland and Scotland. A further important link was the introduction of galloglasses and redshanks, Scottish mercenaries mainly from Argyll, to Ireland between the thirteenth and sixteenth centuries.

During the reign of James VI and I, the Highlands and Islands of Scotland came increasingly under the direct control of centralised governments in Edinburgh and later London. Plantations of Lowland Scots in Ulster and Kintyre, and the deliberate insertion of an ultra-loyal Gaelic clan, the Campbells, between Clan Donald South in Scotland and the McDonnells of Antrim, utterly changed the political and indeed religious dynamic of Argyll. However, cultural traditions were slower to change and echoes of an older sensibility can still be identified hundreds of years later. A quick scan of the first lines of the folktales compiled by Campbell of Islay in the second half of the nineteenth century throws up a remarkable proportion of stories set in Ireland: 'Fionn was going to marry Grainne, the daughter of the King of Carmag [King Cormac] in Eirinn', 'There were two brothers once in Eirinn', 'There was at some time a young king in Eirinn'.[4]

The archipelago

An archipelago is defined as a chain or cluster of islands or an island-abounding sea. Essentially, in a period when travel by sea was often easier than travel by land, mainland Argyll and Antrim – peripheral areas of large islands – were linked by the island archipelago of the southern Hebrides. This distinctive region has to be understood as much as a seascape as a landscape. In the legend *The Children of Lir*, Fionnuala and her three brothers, who had been turned into swans by their stepmother, spent three hundred years on the turbulent Sea of Moyle '*idir Éirinn agus Albain*' – between Ireland and Scotland. One phrase in the story, '*crioslach an chuain*' – the [land-]girdled sea, vividly evokes a sailor's view of the ever-changing necklace of islands and headlands and peninsulas that stud the horizon.

An unconventional look at this archipelago may help us to consider Dál Riada as an ancient kingdom unified by sea rather than land. Before the development of modern maps, where north is always to the top, directions were more fluid. In the Gaelic tradition, for example, you go 'down north'

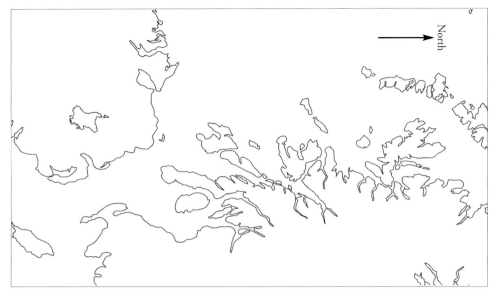

and 'up south'. The map above follows neither convention, but for those completely disorientated, Inishowen is in the top left-hand corner.

Names have been deliberately left off this map, in part to remind us that, 1,500 years ago, few of our modern place-names existed. 'Scotia' meant Ireland, and the Grampians were named from a sixteenth-century typographical error based on a reference by Tacitus to a battle with the Picts at the unidentified mountain of Mons Graupius.

We do not know when Gaelic was introduced to the islands and mainland of western Scotland. In the second half of the sixth century Colm Cille had to have an interpreter when he went among the Picts beyond the mountains, but it appears that those who lived west of the mountains were already Irish-speaking. While tradition dates the founding of Dál Riada to about the year AD 500, it is now generally assumed that settlers from Ireland had been making their home on the Scottish coast for some time – possibly centuries – before this, and the Irish version of the founding of Scottish Dál Riada is best interpreted as the extension of the power of a ruling elite from Gaelic-speaking Ireland to an existing Gaelic speaking community across the Sea of Moyle.

Recently, Ewan Campbell has argued that a Gaelic-speaking community could have been established in Scotland for much longer than has been hitherto believed, citing, among other arguments, the absence of any trace in Argyll place-names of a linguistic substratum deriving from Pictish or Brythonic (a Celtic language related to Welsh, spoken in much of southern Scotland). Campbell concludes that 'the people inhabiting Argyll maintained a regional identity from at least the Iron Age through to the Medieval period and that throughout this period they were Gaelic speakers'.[5] Campbell's use of the term 'Iron Age' is unsatisfyingly vague – it is usually reckoned to have begun in Ireland about 500 BC and to have ended about AD 400, while in some estimates it began in Britain several centuries earlier and ended with the Roman invasion. Estimates for the introduction of Irish to Ireland are even more various; the consensus suggests a date between 500 and 300 BC, although recently some scholars have postulated a date as early as 1800 BC.

Dál Riada: legend and history

In a subject mired in controversy and speculation, a small number of statements are accepted as having a sound historical basis. The first is that the kingdom of Dál Riada existed in the second half of the first millennium AD. The second is that it existed for some time on both sides of the Sea of Moyle until it was broken up in the seventh century. The third is that Scottish Dál Riada was an integral part of the Gaelic-speaking world before it fell under Norse control. The fourth is that since the ninth century all of the monarchs of Scotland traced their ancestry to Dál Riada, and, ultimately, to Ireland.

There are plenty of accounts in Gaelic and Latin of the origins of Dál Riada, but those accounts form a largely impenetrable and contradictory tangle of history and pseudo-history, myths and legends, genealogies both fanciful and real, and downright lies. The lies performed an important role in their time. They were created over many centuries by or on behalf of a hereditary ruling class whose legitimacy depended on a long-tailed aristocratic lineage. This aristocratic class revered tradition and precedent, or what it believed to be tradition and precedent, but was not immune from the temptation to invent or elaborate its claims to a noble ancestry. As a result, while even late material may – indeed is likely to – contain authentic elements of genuine history or genuine tradition, these can be difficult to disaggregate from the rest.

Even the lies are useful and can provide important historic evidence. A twelfth-century fabrication about a fifth-century event may not tell much about the fifth century, but it can tell a great deal about the twelfth, and it can exert enormous influence on the politics of the centuries that follow. The motives of those who invented an aristocratic or a royal heritage, the self-image of those who claimed that heritage, and the acceptance of these inventions by broader society can be just as important as any objective truth.

The eleventh-century *Annals of Tigernach* (deriving in part from much earlier annals) and written mostly in Latin, traces the founding of Scottish Dál Riada to the year AD 501: 'Fergus Mór mac Eirc, with the people of Dál Riata, held part of Britain, and he died there'.[6] There is a much earlier reference to Erc, the father of Fergus. In the middle of the seventh century, a monk called Beccán on the Scottish island of Iona wrote a poem in Irish

Map of Dál Riada, *c.* AD 600

in praise of Colm Cille which includes a reference to how Colm Cille, having left Ireland for Iona, 'pierced the midnight / of Erc's region',[7] a clear reference to Scottish Dál Riada. The earliest reference to Dál Riada to which a date can be ascribed is in the *Life of Colm Cille* by Adomnán (Eunan in English), written in Latin AD *c.* 690. Adomnán refers to the *Korkureti*, which in modern Irish would be Corca Riada – the descendants of Riada. The term 'corca' as a tribal or territorial designation, is interchangeable with 'dál'. The Venerable Bede, drawing on some Gaelic source, used the term 'dál' in and around 730, explaining that *Dalreudini* meant the division or dynasty of Reuda. He departs from surviving Gaelic sources by naming Riada rather than Fergus mac Eirc as the leader of the invasion (as well as indicating that the Irish invaders displaced the Picts):

> In process of time, Britain, besides the Britons and the Picts, received a third nation the Scots, who, migrating from Ireland under their leader, Reuda, either by fair means, or by force of arms, secured to themselves those settlements among the Picts which they still possess.

These accounts came considerably later than the events they refer to, Beccán's by up to 150 years, Adomnán's by just under 200 years and Bede's by more than 200. For all that, most authorities accept that the names Erc and Dál Riada were established well before they were recorded in the seventh and eighth centuries. Almost everything else is still being debated by scholars. Fergus mac Eirc may not have existed (not even the oldest Irish sources claim that he ruled all of Dál Riada), the origins of Dál Riada in Ireland remain obscure, and the Reuda mentioned by Bede, if he existed, may never have set foot in Scotland. One other important tradition has rarely been seriously challenged. Because of the unanimity of the sources, (Ewan Campbell being a notable exception), it is generally agreed that the jumping-off point for the establishment of Scottish Dál Riada was the small kingdom of Dál Riada in what we now call north Antrim.

It is also generally agreed that much of the genuine history of Dál Riada is overshadowed by the power-politics of later periods. In the seventh century the Uí Néill, descendants of Niall of the Nine Hostages, aiming for political hegemony, began to build a new origin-myth to provide a sense of racial unity within Ireland's ruling elites. This origin-myth, usually described nowadays as pseudo-history, merging genuine tradition with bits and pieces of classical and biblical learning and whatever fictions were necessary to fill in the gaps, eventually came to be accepted – with local variations – as the true history of the Irish people, and, by extension, the people of Scottish Dál Riada.

While the broad narrative framework was accepted, the origins of Dál Riada created as much controversy among Medieval Gaelic scholars as among modern academics, ensuring that the genealogies are enormously difficult to navigate. One account traces Dál Riada to Conn of the Hundred Battles, ancestor of Niall of the Nine Hostages, another to Eoghan, Conn's great rival, and yet another traces the lineage to the second-century king of Munster Conaire Mór. All of these figures, except for Niall, who flourished in the fourth and fifth centuries, are mythical, and represent different early population groups; Connachta (from Conn), Eoghanacht (from Eoghan) and Érainn (to which Conaire Mór belonged). Modern scholarship leans towards the Érainn, identified in Ptolemy's map in Munster, but known to have branches in north Connacht, the midlands and the north. Conaire was later claimed by the Uí Néill, who shoe-horned him into their own genealogy as a son or son-in-law of Conn of the Hundred Battles.

Another name to be conjured with is that of Colla Uais, putative ancestor of Fergus Mac Eirc and the McDonnells. One version of the legend involves three brothers, the Three Collas, who were related in some way to Niall of the Nine Hostages (the sources disagree on what the relationship was). As part of the Uí Néill expansion north, they conquered southern and central Ulster during Niall's lifetime. One of them, Colla Uais, pushed even further north, and established a dynasty in north-east Ulster. In another version the Three Collas preceded Niall by a century. They had made a bid for the high-kingship and been forced to flee to Scotland, from whence they returned and were tasked by the new high-king (whose father they had killed) with expanding north into Ulster.

Fergus mac Eirc: legends

In a late seventh-century Latin hagiography of St Patrick, the author, Tíreachán, has him visiting the north Antrim coast, and mentions *Buas fluium* and *Dún Sebuirgi*, the Bush River and Dunseverick. Patrick's role in Tíreachán's account is limited to founding churches and saving souls, but the saint was later enlisted in the cause of promoting the dynasty of Fergus mac Eirc. The ninth-century *Tripartite Life of St Patrick* has him visiting Dál Riada where he 'found welcome in the land of the twelve sons of Erc', giving his blessing to Dunseverick and promising that the descendants of Fergus mac Eirc would rule over Pictland in Scotland.[8] It is probably no coincidence that this 'prophecy' appeared when Kenneth mac Alpin, claiming descent from Fergus, had been elected king of both the Gaels and the Picts in the middle of the ninth century.

Legend has it that Fergus sailed first to Kintyre, landing in Macrihanish Bay. The mountain that overlooks the bay is still called Tír Fergus – the land of Fergus. Fergus is also commemorated in a place-name in Ireland. Although the *Annals of Tigernach* have him dying in Scotland, George Hill records an alternative tradition that he died at Carrickfergus and was buried at Monkstown on the north shore of Belfast Lough. One source of this story is Boece's 1527, *Historia Gentis Scotorum* (History of the Scottish People):

> Finally, being summoned by the elders of Ireland, so that he might use his advice and authority to settle a quarrel that had arisen in their public meetings about the choosing of a king, he did not only put an end to it, but did so utterly. And this was his final act in this life. They say that, while making the crossing from Ireland to Albion, he was caught in a storm and was wind-driven onto a crag, and died, after having reigned more than twenty-five years, and that the name of Crag Fergus was given to this place.[9]

Fergus mac Eirc and the kings of Scotland

What could have been an obscure little Gaelic colony in Scottish Dál Riada came to have enormous symbolic importance, mainly because, since Kenneth mac Alpin, all Scottish monarchs, including Norman families such as the Bruces and Stuarts, have claimed descent from Fergus mac Eirc. This tradition survived the merging of the Crowns of Scotland and England under James the VI and I; indeed, the present Queen traces her descent from Fergus mac Eirc and Niall of the Nine Hostages.

Following the ninth-century accession of the Dalriadic kings, Gaelic became the language of the governing elite and spread rapidly. It extended to the north coast, south into areas such as Galloway and modem Ayrshire and in parts of the central belt, and east into parts of Perthshire, Aberdeenshire and Fife. However, Gaelic was never the sole language of Scotland: Pictish was spoken in the east, Brythonic (a form of early Welsh) in the south, Anglo-Saxon was making inroads in the south-east, and Norse was establishing itself in the northern and Western Isles. Pictish, Brythonic and Norse eventually disappeared, and Gaelic has retreated to the Highlands and western islands.

The development of the Scottish clans

The rise of the Dalriadic kings of Scotland coincided with the Viking incursions, so that the new Scottish kingdom lost control of the islands, which were renamed, and are still called, *na hInse Gall* – the isles of the foreigners/Vikings. The western seaboard remained a contested area, and it is likely that the term Argyll developed to distinguish the mainland of former Dál Riada from the Viking-dominated islands. The society that emerged resisted the domination of the emerging centralised kingdoms of both Norway and Scotland, as well as occasional Irish interventions, giving rise to a largely independent Kingdom of the Isles in the twelfth century. The leader of this movement, Somerled, took the ambiguous title of 'Regulus' of the Hebrides and Kintyre. Although he briefly ruled both the

Outer Hebrides and Isle of Man, his main power base was in the islands of what is now Argyll – he was killed trying to expand on to the mainland. His descendants were more successful, one branch, the MacDougalls, eventually controlling Lorne, the northern part of mainland Argyll, and taking the title Lords of Argyll in the thirteenth and early fourteenth centuries.

Norse does not appear to have displaced Gaelic even in the islands, and most of the hybrid Viking/Gaelic clans that dominated the Western Isles after the collapse of the Norse empire in the twelfth century went to great lengths to ensure an Irish Gaelic ancestry. Somerled's mother was acknowledged to have been of Norse extraction, but, with a father called Giolla Bríde and a grandfather called Giolla Adomnáin, it was long presumed that his paternal background was Gaelic. On documentary evidence, Eoin Mac Néill disputed Somerled's claim to a Gaelic male ancestry, and recent genealogical studies have indicated that Somerled's male descendants belong to a Norwegian haplogroup. Nevertheless, Somerled belonged to the Gaelic world, and founded a Gaelic-speaking dynasty: his son Dughall gave rise to the Clan MacDougall, his grandson Domhnall was the ancestor of the Clan Donald, his great-grandson Alastair established his own line of McAlisters, and there are plenty of other clans such as McCullough, MacSorley, MacEachern with more or less legitimate claim on him as an ancestor.

Somerled's own genealogy below is one version of many. Approximate dates have been added, and the attentive reader will note the gap between Fergus mac Eirc and the ninth century ancestor with the profoundly un-Gaelic name Godfrey, a gap filled by various genealogists with a variety of imaginative antecedents:

> **Colla Uais** (AD *c.* 330)
> Eochaidh
> Erc
> Carthend
> **Erc**
> **Fergus** (AD *c.* 500)
> Godfrey (AD *c.* 830)
> Maine
> Niallgusa
> Suibne
> Mearrdha
> Solam
> Giolla Adomnan
> Giolla Bríde
> **Somerled** (AD *c.* 1150)

The genealogy, in English and Irish, of the fourth earl of Antrim, 1704
(PRONI, D2977/5/1/4/3)

For much of the middle ages, following Somerled's precedent, Scottish clans both in Argyll and beyond found it expedient to be of Irish descent. MacLeans, Sweeneys, MacNeils, MacGregors and Lamonts all claimed descent from Fergus mac Eirc. Clan MacFarlane claimed descent from Corc mac Lugaid, King of Munster. Further east, the Buchanans, MacCauslands, MacMillans and Munros claimed descent from the Ó Catháins of Derry, the MacKenzies claimed descent from the Ó Beoláins.

Of course, the cultural hegemony and high status of Gaelic Ireland did not survive, and some clans covered their bets by inventing alternative genealogies. The Campbells, for example, were notoriously flexible. Although they cited several Irish ancestors, Lugaid son of Ith son of Mil of Spain, Diarmuid Ó Duibhne and Fergus Leith Berg son of Nemed, they invented ancestors such as King Arthur and Brutus as alternatives to their Irish inventions. They also claimed Norman descent from the family of Beauchamp (beautiful field) translated into Italian as Campo Bello. This may have been considered to be an improvement on the Gaelic Cam-béal, which means 'crooked mouth'.

McDonnells of Antrim

Throughout this account, we will follow the convention of anglicising the clan name *Mac Dhomhnuill* as McDonnell in Ireland and MacDonald in Scotland. The MacDonalds of Islay had been one of the more obscure clans descended from Somerled, but were blessed with a great deal of luck. They took the side of Robert the Bruce against their relations, the powerful MacDougall clan, and were rewarded with extensive lands on mainland

Argyll. After Robert the Bruce died in 1329, John the Good (Eoin Math) MacDonald of Islay managed to expand his territories through more good luck, and by marrying two heiresses, one of them the daughter of King Robert II. By the time he died in 1386, he had gained control of all of the southern Hebrides and much of the Argyll mainland and is known to history as the first Lord of the Isles.

Branches of the MacDonalds of Islay were established in other parts of the Highlands, on the islands of Mull, Skye, Jura and Arran, on Kintyre and various other parts of the mainland. Inevitably, their expansionist policies involved the Lords of the Isles in a dizzying complex of power struggles in which wars, diplomacy, constantly shifting alliances and dynastic marriages with other clans in Scotland, and in Ireland with the O'Kanes, Magennises, O'Donnells, O'Neills of Clandeboy and O'Neills of Tyrone, as well as Gaelicised Norman families such as the Savages and Burkes.

They ran out of luck in 1493, when the Lordship of the Isles was abolished, and all the lands held directly by MacDonald of Islay forfeited to the Crown. While other branches of Clan Donald, Clanranald, Glengarry, Sleat, Keppoch, Lochalsh, Glencoe and Ardnamurchan, survived and sometimes thrived, the Islay MacDonalds spent the sixteenth century embroiled in a long power struggle with the MacLeans. As a result they failed to take account of the rising power of the Campbells, a once obscure Argyll clan, who were not only consistent supporters of the Scottish Crown, but were the first of the major Highland clans to adopt the reformed faith. By 1607 King James VI and I had handed over control of Isla and Kintyre to the Campbells. Although a minor branch of the family, the MacDonalds of Dunnyveg, did not last much longer in Islay than the main branch, they did manage to hold on to lands in Ireland they had inherited through marriage into the Bisset family of Antrim at the end of the fourteenth century.

Their position was somewhat anomalous. At one level they had inherited a unified Gaelic world-view that could allow an Irish bardic poet to describe the last Lord of the Isles as having 'the sovereignty of the Gael' and 'the sovereignty of Ireland and Scotland'. But under the Tudors and Stuarts this Gaelic world was not only in decline and becoming increasingly fragmented, it was also being pulled ever farther apart by two centralising jurisdictions, even under the Stuarts, who controlled them both. Gaelic Ireland and Gaelic Scotland did, however, continue to overlap where the southern Hebrides met Argyll and Antrim. This common Gaelic world, as well as the dual Scottish and Irish worlds of the Antrim McDonnells will be explored here through examples from the sixteenth and seventeenth centuries.

The killing of Shane O'Neill: manuscript evidence

Like many northern Gaelic leaders, Shane O'Neill had married into Gaelic Scotland in pursuit of alliances and mercenaries. One of his three wives was the daughter of James MacDonald of Dunnyveg, and at the time of his death he had a MacLean wife and was contemplating marrying his mistress, a Campbell by birth.[10] In 1565 he had defeated the McDonnells at Glentaisie, and captured James MacDonald, who died in his custody. However, by 1567 he was in difficulties in his wars with the English and he 'was driven to such straightness and extreem exigent, that the 2nd day of June, 1567 ... therefore took his journey towards the Scotts'.[11] The McDonnell 'Scotts', or 'Albanaigh' as the Irish sources had it, met him at a parley at Cushendun and killed him.

The McDonnells clearly felt obliged to justify their actions. In 1996 Caoimhín Breathnach published a sixteenth-century collection of stories,[12] arguing that the McDonnells commissioned these modernised versions of older tales to defend the killing of Shane O'Neill. In one story, 'The Violent Death of Conn of the Hundred Battles' (putative ancestor of both the O'Neills and the McDonnells), Conn died because, although a great and in many ways a good king, one unworthy action had brought about his downfall. The intended parallel between the case of Conn and that of Shane O'Neill is in this case easy to work out.

Rather less obvious is the reworking of an eighth-century tale, 'The Story of Mac Dá Thó's Pig', which describes a boasting contest between the men of Ulster and those of Connacht as to who would carve a ceremonial pig at a banquet. In the oldest version, the Connacht hero, Cet mac Magach, dismisses the claim of the last of a series of challenges from Ulstermen by citing an earlier victory at the Ulster-Connacht border: 'you came away with a spear through your throat ... so that Cumscraid the Stammerer is your nickname ever since'.

In the sixteenth-century version, this encounter is transposed to north Antrim, and numerous place-names, including Carey, Duncarbit, Dunworry and Knocklayd, which are or can be assumed to be related to the Battle of Glentaisie, are cited. The symbolic importance of the story is that after this last incident, the tables are turned on Cet by an Ulster hero, Conall Cearnach, who, it happens, is associated in some traditions with north Antrim.

Gaelic literature in Ireland and Scotland were often drawn on mythology – a poem celebrating the sword of one of the Lords of the Isles is, for example, compared to those of Fionn mac Cumhaill, Oscar, Cúchulainn and Conall Cearnach. However, mythological texts from as early as the eighth century were also used in legal tracts as exemplars for knotty legal issues. In this case, an elaborate moral defence of the killing of Shane O'Neill through references to mythology drew on another, very old, cultural thread of the common Gaelic world.

Attempts by Randal Arannach to buy Islay and Kintyre

While the MacDonalds were losing their grip on Islay, Randal Arannach McDonnell, a cousin of the MacDonalds of Dunnyveg, was engaged in building an alternative power-base that, by the early seventeenth century, made him the greatest Gaelic landowner in Ulster, eventually owning more than three hundred thousand acres from Larne to Coleraine. Coincidentally, all of this territory had at one time or another been associated with Dál Riada.

The 'Arannach' appended to Randal's name reflected the fact that he had been fostered as a child with the Stewarts on the Scottish island of Arann, tucked in behind Kintyre, and with a mixed population of lowlanders and Gaelic-speaking Highlanders. Randal managed to maintain his lands without getting into debt, in the process, in spite of being himself a Catholic, bringing in large numbers of Presbyterian lowland Scots as tenants.

Randall managed to obtain a lease of Islay for a number of years, but failed to establish a permanent presence.[13] In 1608 he actually bought the island from Angus MacDonald of Dunnyveg, the then chief. By this time, of course, James VI of Scotland had also become James I of England, and although James had confirmed Randal Arannach in his possessions in Antrim shortly after the Union of the Two Crowns in 1603, he was not a bit keen to see the resurgence of the MacDonald South in Scotland. James forbade the purchase, and Islay, formerly the epicentre of MacDonald power, went to the Campbells.

In 1635, with James safely in his grave, Randal, with initial support from Charles I, attempted to purchase Kintyre from James Campbell, who had run into debt. The sale was bitterly opposed by Campbell's elder brother, the future Duke of Argyll, who blocked it although money had already passed hands. The following year Randal died, and although his son, another Randal, attempted to regain Kintyre by force of arms during the Covenanting and Civil Wars, he too failed.

Captain Sorley's adventures and manuscripts

The third example relates to a cousin of Randal Arannach. Like Randal, Captain Sorley McDonnell was a grandson of the famous Sorley Boy, and like him he was born in Dunluce Castle, but was the losing side in the ruthless internecine strife from which Randal Arannach emerged victorious. Following the Flight of the Earls, Sorley became involved in a plot in 1615 along with:

> ... other malcontents, the sons and nephews of exiled or imprisoned Maguires, O'Neills, O'Donnells and O'Cathans, and the reports written after the collapse of their plans give curious glimpses into their lives. They made their way to each other's

houses with their personal band of retainers – armed men, rhymers, chaplains, fools, dwarves and scribes are mentioned – where they settled down for several days' plotting and drinking.[14]

The plot was not entirely unrealistic, particularly if the plotters succeeded in launching simultaneous rebellions in Ireland and Scotland, but collapsed in farce when Rory Óg O'Cathan got drunk at a wedding in Coleraine and after threatening other (planter) guests, was locked out of the house where he ranted throughout the night. Among his rantings were the details of the plot. All the most prominent plotters were rounded up, except for Sorley and another O'Cathan, who were parleying near Ballycastle with Sorley's kinsman Colla Ciotach McDonnell. Sorley escaped to Scotland with his twenty or so retainers.

The Scottish part of the plot went ahead. The Islay MacDonalds recovered Islay, Jura, Cononsay and Kintyre, but were eventually driven back by the Campbells to the tip of Kintyre. Sorley escaped from there to the Glens, from where he descended on Larne, seized a ship belonging to Sir Thomas Phillips (who had recently expropriated Coleraine from Randal Arannach) and sailed back to Scotland to rejoin the MacDonald rebellion. By this time the rebellion had been crushed, and Sorley was pursued all over the Western Isles by three ships sent by Phillips. Sorley finally escaped by capturing a French ship, leaving the French crew on his own ship to be pursued by Phillips, and sailing for the Netherlands with clansmen he had gathered en route. Eventually, he became captain of a company of musketeers serving Spain in O'Neill's Irish regiment in Flanders, and lived out the rest of his life as a professional soldier, dying in 1632.

Sorley was a minor, if interesting, historical figure, but a major cultural one. The Low Countries were full of Irish exiles, including soldiers waiting for an opportunity to return to Ireland, Counter-Reformation clergy in the Irish College in Louvain (Leuven), and a number of scribes. Sorley commissioned at least two manuscripts. One of these is a collection of Bardic poetry relating to many of the northern Gaelic families. This contains no McDonnell material at all, suggesting that whatever material Sorley had commissioned relating to his own family has been lost.

The other manuscript, *Duanaire Finn*, a large collection of Fenian lays, is of enormous importance, its published version filling two volumes of poetry and one of notes. Its real importance is not in its size, but in the range of material, some of which – on linguistic grounds – can be traced to the thirteenth century, and some of which is likely to have been taken down from oral recitation. Many of the poems in the collection are to be found nowhere else. A note, in which one of the scribes apologises for not having more material, shows that it is an original compilation and not a copy of some other manuscript.

Galloglasses and redshanks

The McDonnells of Antrim were the main suppliers of Scottish mercenaries to Ireland between the thirteenth and the sixteenth centuries. Lightly armed mercenaries introduced in the sixteenth century were called redshanks (presumably with reference to their bare legs). The earlier, more significant, and heavily-armed mercenaries were known as galloglasses, in Irish gall-óglaigh ('warriors from the Innse Gall' – the islands of the Vikings – the Gaelic term for the Hebrides). Most redshanks and all the early galloglasses came from the southern Hebrides or the Argyll mainland. G. A. Hayes McCoy has explained that the English, with a standing, professional and disciplined army, were at an enormous advantage in fighting the native Irish, for whom war was a seasonal and largely amateur affair. The professional galloglasses to a large extent redressed this imbalance, to such an extent, in fact, that the English also began to employ them.[15]

Many of the galloglass families bypassed Antrim; the Sweeneys from Kintyre, for example, went straight to north Donegal, and expanded south, setting up branches of the family in various parts of Donegal and County Cork. We will be ignoring galloglass families such as McCabe, McCallion and McGirr, which settled elsewhere, and concentrate on those which can be found in significant numbers, or in a significant proportion, in Antrim. Hayes McCoy also identified the names of specific redshank bands who came at different times, particularly during the sixteenth century: MacLeans from Ardmanach, Jura and Morven, MacDonalds from Loch Indaal, the Rinns of Jura and the Paps of Jura; Campbells from Argyll, MacQuarries from Ulva and MacKays from Kintyre. He cautioned, however, that many of these did not stay in Ireland.[16]

Evidence from surnames

Some Scottish Gaelic surnames are surprisingly concentrated in Antrim. A number, such as McDonnell, McAlister, McDowell and McNeill, are well documented galloglass names from Argyll. However, a galloglass name may not necessarily mean a galloglass origin. The constant to-ing and fro-ing of people between Antrim and Argyll, both pre- and post Plantation, brought many Argyll surnames to Antrim, including settlers who came on the invitation of Randal Arannach McDonnell, as well as Gaelic-speaking Episcopalians who left Scotland in protest at the establishment of the Presbyterian Church under William of Orange, or people who simply married across the sheugh. The following account does no more than scratch the surface of the subject.

A number of family names with Argyll roots are particularly associated with County Antrim. In the 1901 census, 92 per cent of those in Ireland bearing the surname McCambridge (Mac Ambróis), 91 per cent of

McKillops (Mac Fhilib). In addition, 88 per cent of those called McConachie, McConachy or McConaghie (Mac Dhonnchaidh), and 79 per cent with the name McKendry (Mac Eanruig) or its variants McHendry, McKendrick or McHenry, lived in Antrim.

Other Argyll surnames are particularly common in Antrim and the adjoining counties of Down and Derry. For example, McCaughan (Mac Eachain) is remarkably concentrated in north-east Ulster, with 70 per cent in Antrim with another 24 per cent in Derry. Antrim accounts for 56 per cent and Down and Derry for a further 25 per cent of people called McAlister (Mac Alastair) and its variants. McNeill (Mac Néill), 53 per cent of whom lived in Antrim, is also an Argyll name, as is McDowell (Mac Dubhghaill) and its variants, 46 per cent of whom were in Antrim, with a further 29 per cent in County Down.

A high proportion of those bearing the name McKay (Mac Aoidh), but this surname is complex. It may represent another Scottish clan (Mac Dhai) or be a variant of an Irish surname. The surname McMullan/McMillen (Mac Maoláin), with 54 per cent in Antrim and a further 28 per cent in County Down can also be of both Irish and Scottish origin, but in both these cases, Scottish origin probably accounts for most of those in Antrim.

These and other Argyll surnames in Antrim, such as McKane, McCloy, Campbell, McKinney, McQuilkin and McCurdy, would be worth further study. It would be particularly important to disaggregate the figures for Belfast, which drew people from all over Ireland, from the rest of the county, and to look at the range of anglicisations. It would also be worth

McDONNELL, McDONALD, McCONNELL, DONNELL/DONALD/DONALDSON
1901 CENSUS (COUNTIES WITH 600 PLUS)

		McDonnell MacDonnell	McDonald MacDonald	McConnell	Donnell Donald Donaldson
Antrim	3,026	584	854	1,043	545
Down	1,812	177	400	784	451
Mayo	1,618	1,506	98	14	
Tyrone	1,093	145	326	378	244
Armagh	1,038	168	386	246	238
Cork	776	531	184	15	46
Cavan	720	94	515	93	18
Donegal	701	57	85	414	145
Louth	691	367	269	42	13
Derry	667	82	159	204	222
Dublin	2,486	1,355	898	142	91
Ireland	21,941	8,658	7,255	3,667	2,361

investigating those Irish names such as Ó Brollacháin, Ó Miadhaigh, Mac Mhuirich that finished up in Argyll.

The McDonnell surname requires particular attention. A quick scan of the 1901 census will surprise many by revealing that there are nearly three times as many with the name McDonnell in Mayo as in Antrim. To some extent, this merely reflects the fact that many branches of the clan settled in various parts of Ireland. It also reflects the vagaries of the anglicisation process. In Gaelic, the initial 'D' of *Mac Dhomhnuill* is aspirated, forming a guttural sound that is easily swamped by the 'c' of 'mac'. What an English-speaker hears, then, is more like McConnell, an anglicised form particularly prevalent in Ulster. Once we figure in McConnell and other variants, we find twice as many people with the clan name in Antrim than in Mayo.

Some religious issues

The Campbells of Argyll were the first Highland clan to embrace Presbyterianism, and most other Highland clans followed suit, although some initially inclined towards the episcopalianism out of loyalty to the Stuarts. It has been argued that the early conversion of Argyll led to a much more relaxed version of Presbyterianism than that which later manifested itself in the Outer Hebrides. Most of the Scottish MacDonalds eventually became Protestant, but Randal Arannach McDonnell of Antrim spearheaded a counter-reformation movement in Scotland from Ballycastle, which had some success, particular in South Uist and Barra.

The first book ever published in Gaelic – in 1567 – was a translation of Knox's *Book of Common Order*, by John Carswell, bishop of Argyll, made, according to the preface, for 'the men of Ireland and Scotland'. It was written in Classical Irish, a standard form of the language developed since the twelfth century for the bardic poetry of both Ireland and Scotland. Only an occasional slip into the vernacular reveals that the translator had been a Scottish Gael.

Probably because of the proximity of Gaelic-speaking Protestant Argyll, there were significant communities of Protestant Gaelic-speakers in north-east Ulster during the seventeenth and eighteenth and indeed nineteenth centuries. The following quotations are from a pamphlet written in 1712:

> I met many of the inhabitants, especially in the Baronies of Glenarm, Dunluce and Killconway, who could not speak the English tongue; and asking them in Irish what religion they professed, they answered they were Presbyterians, upon which I asked them further, how they could understand their minister preaching; to that they answered, he always preached in Irish.[17]

After 1691, when Presbyterianism became the established church in Scotland, Ireland became a refuge for Scottish Episcopalians, some of whom settled in Antrim:

> At their first going over, they went to Church, but not understanding the Divine Service celebrated there, they soon went over to the communion of the Church of Rome, only for the Benefit of such Exhortations, as the Popish priests usually gave their congregations in Irish. And when they were asked the Reason, why they did so? They said, 'It was better to be of their Religion, than none at all'.

According to the pamphlet, when a Gaelic-speaking minister was appointed '… he hath not only brought back to our Church, such Highlanders as had lapsed into Popery, but hath also converted many of the Natives of Ireland.'

The existence of a vibrant Gaelic-speaking Protestant community a few miles away across the sea, and a number of Protestant Irish-speaking communities in north-east Ulster, may go some way to explain the highly tolerance of the Protestant middle class in Belfast towards the language in the late eighteenth and early nineteenth centuries. Almost uniquely in Ireland, this class gave rise to the first language revival movement in Ireland, the Belfast Gaelic Society of 1828, which renamed itself the Ulster Gaelic Society in 1830.

Conclusion

In many ways, north-east Ulster and Argyll was where Gaelic Ireland and Gaelic Scotland met, blended and interacted in a complex relationship lasting one and a half thousand years. This essay does no more than touch on a small number of themes relating to this long association, all of which could benefit from further exploration.

Notes

1 Angus MacMillan, 'The emergence and early governance of Argyll' in J. Derrick McClure, John M. Kirk, Margaret C. Storrie (ed.), *A Land that Lies Westward: Language and Culture in Islay and Argyll* (Edinburgh, 2009), pp 104–05.

2 (*Brevis Descriptio regni Scotice) John of Fordun's Chronicle of the Scottish Nation*, vol. 4 (London, 1872).

3 'Preface' in John R. Baldwin (ed.), *Peoples and Settlement in North-West Ross* (Edinburgh, 1994), p. vii.

4 J. F. Campbell, *Popular Tales of the West Highlands*, vol. 2 (1860-61; reprinted Edinburgh, 1994), pp 243, 337, 373.

5 Ewan Campbell, 'Were the Scots Irish?', *Antiquity*, 75 (2001), pp 285–92.

6 '*Feargus Mor mac Earca cum gente Dal Riada partem Britaniae tenuit, et ibi mortuus est.*' Other annals give slightly different dates, including 498, 500.

7 '*to-réd midnocht / migne Ercae*' in T. E. Clancy and Gilbert Márkus, *Iona: The Earliest Poetry of a Celtic Monastery* (Edinburgh, 1995), pp 146–7.

8 David N. Dumville, 'Ireland and North Britain in the Earlier Middle Ages: Contexts for Míniugud Senchasa Fher n-Alban' in Colm Ó Baoill and Nancy R. McGuire (eds), *Rannsachadh na Gàidhlig 2000* (Aberdeen, 2002), pp 189–90.

9 http://www.philological.bham.ac.uk/boece/1e.html.

10 The Campbell mistress was the widow of James MacDonald – which made her stepmother to O'Neill's first wife. She was also a half-sister to the 4th earl of Argyll, who had once been married to the MacLean wife.

11 George Hill, *An Historical Account of the Macdonnells of Antrim* (Belfast, 1873), pp 144–5.

12 Caoimhín Breathnach, *Patronage, Politics and Prose: Ceasacht Inghine Guile; Sgéala Muide Meic Dhá Thó; Oideadh Chuinn Chéadchathaigh* (Maynooth, 1996).

13 Hill, *Historical Account of the Macdonnells*, pp 229–30.

14 Hector McDonnell, *The Wild Geese of the Antrim MacDonnells* (Dublin, 1996), p. 24.

15 G. A. Hayes McCoy, *Scots Mercenary Forces in Ireland, 1565–1603* (Dublin, 1937), p. 23.

16 Ibid., p. 13.

17 John Richardson, *A Short History of the Attempts to Convert the Popish Natives of Ireland to the Established Religion* (London, 1712).

2

Argyll and Antrim in the Prehistoric Era

Cormac McSparron

Introduction

It is almost a cliché of archaeological writing to note that only a few miles of water separate the County Antrim coast from the southern tip of the Kintyre peninsula. Like many things generally held to be apparent its full significance is not always fully thought through or discussed. This essay attempts, at least in part, to address this deficiency by discussing the archaeology of Antrim and Argyll with specific reference to each other, as if they were parts of the same region rather than, as archaeology usually considers them, parts of two different countries. Of course modern political or administrative boundaries do not always reflect the distribution of archaeological sites or historical phenomena and where appropriate the discussion will go beyond Antrim and Argyll as required.

We will look at the evidence of each archaeological era in its chronological order in this and the succeeding chapter and then attempt to draw together common themes using a *longue durée* approach of looking past individual events or personalities and attempting to see the long term cycles or structures which are influencing history. The conclusion is reached that in general the history and archaeology of Antrim and Argyll show that interrelationships have frequently been very close, at times almost completely intertwined. It is apparent that this is also true for Ulster and western Scotland and at times for most or even the whole of Ireland and Scotland. There have been episodes of interruptions in this close relationship, however. In the Later Neolithic and also in the Iron Age there may be episodes where the close interrelationships between Antrim and Argyll became dislocated, although alternative interpretations of both the Late Neolithic and Iron Age interrupts are possible. However, in both these cases apparent dislocation was followed by an intense interrelationship once more as close geographical proximity, and a sea that can unify as much as divide, began once more to draw the regions together. Another episode of interruption in the smooth relationship of Antrim and Argyll was the Viking era, where centuries of interaction in the North Channel were shattered by the arrival of Norse plunderers. Unlike earlier episodes of interruption this one is documented allowing us to see that this

Key

1 Mount Sandel
2 Cushendun
3 Bay Farm
4 Ballygalley
5 Ballyharry
6 Aghalislone
7 Ballinderry Road
8 Bush
9 Ardnadam
10 Kingarth
11 Beacharra
12 Ballymacaldrick
13 Tamnyrankin
14 Knockoneill
15 Port Charlotte
16 Tievebulliagh
17 Brockley
18 Aughategan, south Argyll
19 Aughenhonen, near Campbeltown
20 Aghnacreebeg
21 Giant's Ring, Ballynahatty
22 Ballymeanoch
23 Poltalloch
24 Kilmartin
25 Castle Mahon
26 Ballynoe
27 Knockdhu
28 Cul a' Bhaile
29 An Sithean
30 Stronoiller
31 Culcharron
32 Claggan
33 Corrstown
34 Ballyprior Beg
35 Townparks
36 McIlwhans Hill
37 Dunadd
38 Dunseverick
39 Dunmull
40 The Giant's Sconce
41 Ederline
42 Dun Mor Vaul

Map of Prehistoric era

interruption was caused by invaders from across the sea. Ireland and Scotland for a time turned inward, possibly helping to stimulate the gradual accumulation of royal power and authority by an ever decreasing number of important dynasties in both countries. However, despite this increasing concern with their own affairs, until the end of the Early Medieval period their royal institutions seem to run on parallel lines, with similar customs of kingship and succession. Even in the Later Medieval period, when Scotland formed a more centralised form of kingship, something which the appearance of the Normans frustrated in Ireland, the kings of Scotland still defined themselves within an ideological and cultural milieu which was essentially Irish.

The oscillating nature of the relationship between Antrim and Argyll, the closest point of contact between the two great landmasses of these islands, is perhaps best illustrated by a piece of historical irony. The event which caused the interruption in the close relationship between the two regions in the Early Medieval period, the arrival of the Vikings, led to the formation of a maritime kingdom, which would in time evolve into the Lordship of the Isles, an institution which ensured that the cultural closeness of parts of Antrim and Ulster with the Highlands and Islands of Scotland lasted through the Later Medieval period still to be felt today.

Post-glacial Antrim and Argyll

There is no *certain* evidence for human populations in either Ireland or Scotland before the end of the last Ice Age. There were warm periods between glaciations, called interstadials, often lasting thousands of years, when human settlement would have been possible and it is perhaps even likely that there were populations of humans in Ireland and Scotland in these warm periods. Peter Woodman has found evidence for large mammal fauna, including woolly mammoth, hyena, horse and reindeer from caves in Cork and Waterford dating to the last interstadial, which would support this.[1] However, if there were human populations in Ireland or Scotland at this stage, no trace has yet been found of their settlements, with just a couple of stone tools of poor provenance to hint at their presence. The glaciers from the last Ice Age finally began to retreat about 18,000 years ago. This process took several thousand years and it is likely that it was not complete until about 13,000 years ago.[2] The immediate post-glacial environment would not have been particularly attractive for human settlement; the ground surface would have been rock and clay with only a thin covering of humus and plants gradually accumulating. The first plants to recolonise the land after the glacial retreat were likely to be mosses, and grasses followed by dwarf shrubs and then tree species like birch. For several thousand years after the glacial retreat temperatures would have been somewhat colder than current. At this stage a number of animal species colonised Ireland including reindeer, elk, bears, wolves and hares, with a similar process happening in Scotland.[3] To date no evidence of immediate post-glacial human settlement has been found in Ireland, but recent excavations at Howburn, Lanarkshire, in south central Scotland, suggest that there may have been human populations living there about 12,000 years ago.[4] About 11,000 years ago the climate became sharply colder again, although not quite as cold as an Ice Age, in an episode called the Younger Dryas, leading to the extinction of many of the larger mammal species, possibly also seriously affecting any human populations living in Ireland and Scotland.[5] Finally, by about 10,000 years ago the North Atlantic Drift (the Gulf Stream) began to circulate warm water to north-west Europe, rapidly warming the local climate to a temperature similar to modern levels, although Woodman has noted how poorly dated the emergence of the North Atlantic Drift actually is.[6]

The Mesolithic in Antrim and Argyll

With the beginnings of the circulation of warm water to our shores the environment was much more favourable for human settlement. Not only was the climate more comfortable for humans, but rich seas teamed with marine life which settlers could exploit.[7] The earliest human communities in both Ireland and Scotland after the return of consistently milder climactic conditions were hunters and gatherers, and occupy an era which archaeologists call the Mesolithic or Middle Stone Age. We know from anthropological studies of hunter-gatherer groups that these early colonists would have had a rich culture with a wide variety of tools and a complex social life. However, after such a long time period, save in the most exceptional cases, only scant remains of their culture survive, usually just flint tools, which has caused some archaeologists in the past to attribute an overly colourless and parsimonious existence to them.

In Ireland the earliest known Mesolithic settlement is at Mount Sandel, County Londonderry. Remains of a hut, storage pits and a large amount of food waste, including evidence for fish such as salmon, trout and eels, various types of bird, wild boar and a variety of plant foods like crab apple and hazelnuts was discovered.[8] A characteristic type of very small, very sharp flint tools, called microlithis were found, multiple microliths being embedded into bone or wood to make composite blades or projectiles. Radiocarbon dates from Mount Sandel have shown that the site was occupied from about 7800 BC.[9]

In Scotland the earliest Mesolithic occupation evidence comes from the Western Isles, Arran, Islay, Jura and Rhum[10] where similar microliths have been found in deposits which are generally assumed to be Early Mesolithic, broadly contemporary with Mount Sandel, based on an examination of the artefact types, but which have provided few reliable radiocarbon dates.

In Ireland there seems to have been a change in the type of Mesolithic flint tools around 6000 BC, which may be indicative of wider changes in society. Composite tools made from microliths appear to have given way to a flint tool type typified by much larger, superficially cruder, flint tools, described as 'broad bladed' tool technology by archaeologists. These broad bladed flints take the form of quite large flint flakes and blades usually hafted onto a wooden handle. Unfortunately, although quite a few Late Mesolithic sites have been found, to date no certain occupation sites have been discovered. A large number of these Late Mesolithic sites have been found in County Antrim. At Cushendun Hallam Movius uncovered deep deposits of Later Mesolithic artefacts, as he did at Larne, leading to him suggesting that the term Larnian be applied to the Late Mesolithic broad bladed flint technology and associated culture of Ireland.[11] At Castle Carra, Cushendun, Declan Hurl of the NIEA, uncovered during a number of small excavations from 1995 to 2006, a series of deep deposits rich in charcoal, charred hazelnut shells and broad bladed flint tools, with no evidence of flint manufacture waste.[12] At Bay Farm, Carnlough a flint knapping site was discovered, with large quantities of flint waste and some completed artefacts.[13] Flint tools and the possible remains of a temporary settlement site were found at Newferry, on the shores of the Lower Bann.[14] Woodman has suggested that there was a relatively small group occupying County Antrim during the Late Mesolithic period, roughly between 6000 and 4000 BC, and that they had no fixed, permanent home, but rather a base camp where they spent some time each year and a series of temporary camps to which they moved to exploit various food and raw material resources.

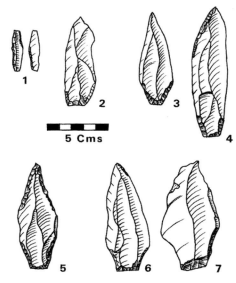

Mesolithic flint tools from Newferry

In the west of Scotland, concentrated on the coast and the Inner Hebrides, there are a number of Mesolithic sites where broad bladed flint technology has been found also. These sites are all what archaeologists describe as 'shell midden' sites, where the intensive exploitation of coastal shell fish has resulted in the build-up of a large dump of shells. Traditionally these sites have been viewed as being later than the microlith bearing sites, and derived from the Irish 'Larnian' broad bladed technology, what Movius called 'Obanian'.[15] There are differences, however, between the Obanian and the Larnian technologies. Most notable is the presence of bone and antler objects in the Scottish Obanian, such as barbed points made from antler, and their absence from the Irish Larnian assemblages.[16]

One important question is the source of the flint for the western Scottish Mesolithic. It has been suggested that County Antrim flint has been widely used and that the size and number of the flint nodules required is in excess of the occasional small nodule of coastal flint which could be carried by seaweed to Argyll.[17] This implies that there *was* regular movement of people across the North Channel to obtain or trade in flint. This does not tally, however, with the evidence of the artefacts, especially the contrasts between the Obanian and Larnian flint types, which while similar and possibly having shared origins, do not have the high degree of similarity one would expect between groups in regular close contact.

It is possible that there may be some evidence of a meeting of material culture in Kintyre, here there seem to be some 'Obanian' flints which compare more closely with Irish analogues. A number of Kintyre flints conform to the classic 'Bann Flake' form common in the Larnian flint tradition.[18] The possibility of flint being brought from Antrim and then being distributed through western Scotland by means of trade and exchange from Larnian communities in Kintyre could explain some of the wider comparisons and contrasts in the Antrim and Argyll Mesolithic.

There has been an expectation that Mesolithic societies would be likely to have only had simple rituals, especially rituals of death and burial, because of a general expectation amongst archaeologists that hunter-gatherer communities must be small, egalitarian and quite simple. This view has been overturned in recent years by the finding of a series of four Early Mesolithic cremation burials in County Limerick, on the left bank of the River Shannon at Castleconnell.[19] The burials took the form of a large pit, which originally contained a post at its centre, accompanied by a very fine polished stone axe, flint microliths and cremated human remains. Radiocarbon dates suggested that these cremations dated to the Early Mesolithic. There has been no replication of these results elsewhere in Ireland, Scotland or the rest of Britain, although given the probable low density of the Mesolithic population we would be unlikely to find them frequently. Nevertheless, it does demonstrate just how much we do not understand about early hunter-gatherer communities and how much we may have underestimated their social complexity.

The Early Neolithic period in Antrim and Argyll

At the end of the Mesolithic period there was an enormous change in society and technology which archaeologists have called the Neolithic, or New Stone Age. This was the era of the emergence of farming and an economy based on the growing or crops and/or the husbandry of animals, as opposed to an economy based solely on the procurement of wild food resources. The Neolithic is more than a simple economic shift, however. It is a complete transformation in the way of thinking about the world. Mesolithic hunter-gatherers largely adapted to suit their environment whilst Neolithic farmers were more capable of adapting their environment to suit them. The way this change happened is uncertain, however, and how and when it happened has been hotly debated by archaeologists in recent years.

The earliest farmers

There are some hints that Mesolithic communities may have been moving in the direction of farming in the centuries leading up to 4000 BC. At Ferriter's Cove in County Kerry, Peter Woodman found a cattle bone, which was radiocarbon dated to 4495 to 4165 BC, at a temporary settlement site which was used by Mesolithic hunter-gatherers on a seasonal basis.[20] This has been interpreted as evidence of contact between hunter-gatherer groups and farming communities, although there is very little evidence for farming groups in Ireland at this early date and it is possible that the contact happened outside Ireland.

When solid evidence for farming communities does appear in Ireland and Scotland they are *very* different from the earlier Mesolithic hunter-gatherer communities. Their technology is different, they use different flint tool manufacture techniques which result in more crafted flints in a wider range of forms than Mesolithic flint tools, and they make pots. They live in permanent settlements, with wooden rectangular houses, and they bury their dead in substantial stone tombs. The Early Neolithic farmers left a much greater mark on the landscape, they cut down trees and made fields. Environmental evidence from ancient deposits bogs and lake bottoms shows a decline of tree pollen and an increase in grasses at this time showing that the landscape was becoming less wooded.[21] There has been considerable work on dating this emergence of the Neolithic in Ireland and Britain in recent years. Until recently the emergence of the Irish Neolithic had been estimated, based on radiocarbon dating at around 4000 BC. New and more sophisticated analyses of radiocarbon dates, using mathematical modelling, have shown that the earliest Neolithic houses and Neolithic farming emerged in Ireland around 3720 BC and spread rapidly across the whole of Ireland.[22] The same happened in Britain at this time with Scotland being reached by Neolithic farmers at approximately the same time as Ireland.[23]

Early Neolithic settlements

In recent decades archaeological excavations have found the remains of many Early Neolithic settlements in Ireland and Scotland. Quite a number of wooden Neolithic houses of this era have been uncovered during excavations in County Antrim. Two Neolithic houses were uncovered at Ballygalley and at Island Magee a number of Neolithic houses have been found at Ballyharry townland.[24] Single Neolithic houses have been found at Aghalislone and Ballinderry Road, both on the outskirts of Lisburn, and Bush, County Antrim.[25] All of these sites have been uncovered by archaeological investigations in advance of commercial development, demonstrating the value of this kind of work. The density of Neolithic settlement in County Antrim is replicated in other parts of both Northern Ireland and the Republic of Ireland where a large amount of development led archaeological investigation has taken place in recent decades.

Almost as interesting as the rapid appearance of Neolithic houses across Ireland is their equally rapid disappearance. It seems as if there is intensive occupation in scattered small settlements of rectangular houses throughout the whole of Ireland for about a century after the initial emergence of the Neolithic. After about 3600 BC, however, there is very little evidence of continuing Neolithic settlement in fixed communities. The environmental record shows that cultivation continues to be intensive for several more centuries based mostly around cereal cultivations supplemented by wild resources; it is just that the settlements are missing.[26] It has been speculated that the Neolithic community begins to live a more mobile existence, in less archaeologically visible structures; alternatively, it may be that houses cluster together in village settlements for defence, reducing their visibility to archaeological investigations on developments such as road construction, relative to scattered settlements of one or two houses.[27]

In Britain, until recently, with the exception of a few sites in the west, there was only fragmentary evidence for the sort of settled Neolithic found in Ireland causing some archaeologists to reject the settled Neolithic theory for Britain (and by extension Ireland) and suggest a highly mobile Neolithic of small scale cultivation moving year on year to new locations, with seasonal gatherings at large Neolithic enclosures, called causewayed camps or causewayed enclosures by archaeologists.[28]

In the last few years, however, there have been increasing numbers of Early Neolithic settlements found in southern Britain, many of them rectangular houses. A large interdisciplinary research programme has recently looked at the dating evidence for the Early Neolithic settlement record of the entirety of Britain and Ireland.[29] It has confirmed the dating of the emergence of the Neolithic in Ireland and found evidence of Neolithic settlement in south-eastern England about a century earlier than in Ireland. The researchers have suggested a progression of Neolithic farmers across Britain and Ireland spreading from south-east England. Other researchers have suggested that the first Irish and western British Neolithic farmers are colonists from Brittany.[30]

In western Scotland there are a few Neolithic settlement sites which bear comparison with Irish sites. At Ardnadam, Cowall, several successive phases of an oval timber Neolithic house were excavated dating to between 3699 and 3342 BC.[31] Excavations in advance of a quarry extension have revealed a sub-rectangular timber house along with Early Neolithic pottery and stone tools at Kingarth, on the Isle of Bute.[32] Although not a house, a horizon of Neolithic settlement, comprised of flint tools, hazelnut shells and charcoal, was found beneath the chambered cairn at Port Charlotte, Islay, reminiscent of the Neolithic house found beneath the court tomb at Ballyglass, County Mayo.[33] Radiocarbon dates suggest the occupation dated to between 3779 and 3542 BC.[34] These dates are compatible with an emergence of Neolithic farming communities in Argyll at a broadly similar time period to the Irish Neolithic.

New colonists or just new ideas?
Evidence for a change in the diet consistent with a change from a hunting and gathering based economy to an agricultural one is also provided by laboratory analysis of the bones of deceased humans from this era. Schulting and Richards, using isotope data from human remains coupled with radiocarbon dates, suggest a sudden change in the diet on the west coast of Scotland from a primarily maritime diet to a largely terrestrial diet.[35] The change in diet is so great and so sudden that these authors suggest that the arrival of a new population group must be given serious consideration.[36] From the radiocarbon dating of the human remains in their study a date of around 3800 BC is suggested for this dietary change, although the authors acknowledge the poor resolution of some of the dating evidence; allowing for this, their evidence is compatible with the other dating evidence for the emergence of the Neolithic in the rest of Scotland and Ireland.[37]

The question of whether Antrim and Argyll shared a Neolithic colonising event from Brittany or whether colonists made their way from south-east England, to Argyll and then Ireland is not yet settled. What does seem probable is that the radical break observed in both regions around 3700 BC or slightly before is not likely to be the result of indigenous innovation. There must have been an element of outside influence, in all probability a migration or series of migrations of agriculturalists from continental Europe.

The first monuments

A major element of the Early Neolithic in Antrim and Argyll, and more widely in Ireland and Scotland, is the appearance of large stone tombs in both regions at about the same time as the appearance of evidence for Neolithic settlement or agriculture. On both sides of the North Channel area there is considerable similarity in the tomb type, what Stuart Piggott called the Clyde/Carlingford tombs, although this term is used less frequently now the Scottish tombs having been subsumed into the wider chambered tomb type, which are mostly found in western Scotland in Argyll, Galloway and Wigtownshire, and the Irish tombs into the court tomb type.[38] Nevertheless, while not identical, the tombs on either side of the north Irish Sea region show considerable similarity in form and in the ritual used in Early Neolithic burial. At Beacharra in Kintyre a chambered tomb was excavated which had a forecourt area, reminiscent of an Irish court tomb, and three burial chambers.[39] The pottery within the tomb, called Beacharra Ware by Childe, has strong affinities with pottery found in Ulster, in particular the Beacharra B ware which Arthur ApSimon has identified as being essentially the same type of pottery found in Irish court tombs where it is usually called Ballyutoag style pottery.[40] The main artefacts found from chambered tombs are flint arrowheads and/or flint plano-convex knives. Both of these types of artefacts have been found in Ulster court tombs; arrowheads were found in the burial chamber at Ballymacaldrick by Oliver Davies and plano-convex knives were found at Knockoneill and Tamnyrankin, both in east County Londonderry, and at the portal tomb (a related form to the court tomb) at Tirnony, County Londonderry.[41]

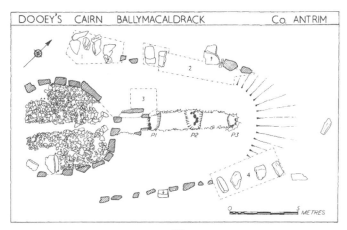

Ballymacaldrick court tomb
page 31, Neolithic pottery from Ballymacaldrick

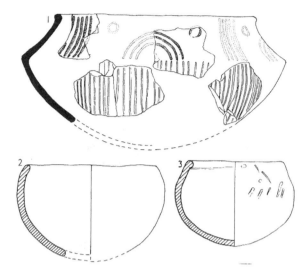

The remains of both cremations and inhumations have been found in the tombs, the burial ritual apparently emphasising the communal with apparently little emphasis on the individuality of corpses. While it seems likely that the tombs could not be the resting place of the entire community, the lack of emphasis on the individual probably indicates that these were *not* simply burial places of chiefs or leaders. These monuments probably had multiple functions as well as burial, including establishing ownership of the land by a specific group, ensuring the lands continued fertility and the continuance of the social order.

A new analysis of the best quality radiocarbon dates for Irish court tombs has suggested that their initial phase of use was between 3700 and 3570 BC, which closely matches the period of emergence of the first Neolithic settlements in Ireland.[42] No similar dating programme has yet been carried out for the chambered tombs of Scotland, but what radiocarbon dating that has been carried out, such as the dating of the Port Charlotte chambered cairn on Islay, indicates that they are broadly contemporary with the Irish court tombs.[43]

Trade and exchange between Antrim and Argyll in the Early Neolithic
There is evidence for movement of raw materials and artefacts across the North Channel during this era. Two sites in County Antrim, Tievebulliagh, outside Cushendun, and Brockley on Rathlin Island, are sources of a very special fine grained basic igneous rock called porcellanite which is used for the manufacture of polished stone axes. Porcellanite axes are most common in the north-eastern quarter of Ireland, but outside this area they are most frequently encountered in Argyll and north-east Scotland with a smattering through the rest of Britain and Ireland.

31

There is also a significant body of evidence to say that County Antrim flint was being used in Scotland in the Neolithic. Recent work at Aughategan, south Argyll, has demonstrated that the flint from an Early Neolithic occupation horizon there is from Antrim, while work by Saville has shown that Antrim flint is common in western Scotland being found at Aughenhonen, near Campbeltown, and at a number of other sites also.[44]

Contrasting with the movement of Antrim flint and polished stone axes to western Scotland and beyond, there is evidence for Scottish pitchstone in Antrim. Pitchstone is a very hard natural glass, quite similar to obsidian. It not only looks exotic compared to flint, although much harder to work into a tool, but would have provided a much sharper cutting edge compared with flint, possibly making it suitable for surgical tools.[45] It has been found now in significant quantities at a number of east Antrim sites, most frequently at the two Neolithic houses excavated at Ballygalley.[46] Scientific analysis of the pitchstone has now confirmed its Scottish provenance, suggesting it originates on Arran.

Collectively the stone axes, and especially the flint and pitchstone, demonstrate sustained and regular contacts across the North Channel. The exchange of artefacts or raw materials may take two forms, trade relations and gift exchange. With trading relations, if there is a need for raw materials and complementary sources in two regions then you may get trade. There is a need in Scotland for flint; there is little good flint in Scotland for making flint tools, also there is no equivalent stone of the sharpness of pitchstone in Ireland. This seems like a good candidate for a trading relationship. On the other hand, because of the availability of sources suitable for making polished stone axes in Scotland it seems that there is not so much a need for trade in axes; yet we regularly find axes of County Antrim porcellanite in Argyll and further afield in Scotland. However, porcellanite, the material used to make Antrim axes, is, when polished, rather attractive and would have had at least considerable value as an exotic item, even if one not necessarily superior in a functional sense. It is the kind of object appropriate for a gift-exchange relationship where a gift is given, or an exchange of gifts is made, at a significant time, such as at a marriage or treaty, creating a mutual obligement and cementing alliances for the future.

The Middle and Late Neolithic in Antrim and Argyll

As the Neolithic progressed new tomb types appeared in both Scotland and Ireland. From Shetland to the south-east of Ireland a new type or burial cairn emerged with a long passage which was differentiated in height and width from the larger chamber/s which it led to, archaeologists call tombs of this type passage tombs.

Passage tombs of Ireland and Scotland

There are several groups of these passage tombs across the western parts of these islands, two of the best known and most impressive are in the Orkneys and in the Boyne Valley. At Mae's Howe in Orkney there is a large passage tomb composed of an approximately circular cairn, 45m in diameter and 7m high, with an 11m long passage composed of stone slabs, leading to a rectangular chamber 4.5m square constructed entirely from dry stones, with a corbelled ceiling extending to a height of 4.5m. The entrance passage is aligned with Midwinter's sunset when light enters the tomb. It is part of a cluster of similar monuments, many decorated with the picked rock carvings which have become known as passage tomb art. Both inhumation and cremation were carried out and the remains of food offerings have been found in the tombs along with pottery and stone mace heads.[47] The tombs in the Boyne Valley have many similarities to the Orkney types. They share a basic form with the Orkney graves, but are even more massive; Newgrange has a diameter of 76m, and has kerb stones decorated with passage tomb art around the base of the mound. Like Mae's Howe, Newgrange is aligned on the sun, but here the sun enters the passage at Midwinter sunrise. The primary burial ritual is cremation and finds found with the burials include pottery, mushroom-headed bone pins and decorated stone objects similar to the Orkney mace heads. Other groups of passage tombs are found throughout Ireland, excluding Munster. There is a small group of passage tombs in north and north-east Antrim, clustered close to the coast. None of these tombs have been archaeologically excavated.

There are fewer passage tombs from Argyll. One very interesting example at Aghnacreebeg, Lorn, has been closely studied. It is a multi-phase monument, being initially a simple chamber in a cairn, without external passage, which then had a separate passage tomb inserted into the cairn.[48] The passage tomb revealed finds of flint knives and round-bottomed Neolithic vessels. The pottery, Beacharra Ware, which was mentioned above in relation to the slightly earlier Clyde-Carlingford tombs, bears close comparison with some Irish Neolithic pottery and is also very similar to certain Breton Neolithic vessels, which has caused some archaeologists to look to Brittany as a potential origin for the first Irish and Scottish farming communities.[49]

Unfortunately not as much work has yet been carried out on passage tomb dating as has for court tombs. What dating evidence there is seems to suggest that passage tombs may be slightly later than Irish court tombs and Scottish chambered tombs, perhaps starting around 3300 BC.[50]

Fields but no houses?

There little direct evidence for settlement in Ulster or the west of Scotland, or more widely in Ireland and Scotland during the Middle and Late Neolithic. As noted above Neolithic houses apparently disappear from the archaeological record by about 3600 BC, although whether this is a real disappearance or whether it is simply that the nature of settlement changes in a way that makes it difficult for archaeologists to find, is uncertain.[51] There does seem to be some kind of change in the nature of Neolithic agriculture, possibly occasioned by environmental decline,[52] at about the time of the appearance of passage tombs (about 3300 BC or a little later) in Ireland, leading to a decrease in cereal production, although cereal crops were still grown, with an increase in the use of wild foodstuffs and a degree of re-forestation. Similar processes seem to have been happening at the same time in Scotland.[53]

Later Neolithic non-funerary and funerary rituals

The Later Neolithic, after about 3100 BC, seems to be marked in both Ireland and Scotland by changes in ritual. In both new ritual structures appear in the form of henges. These are large circular enclosures, sometimes, as at the Giant's Ring, Ballynahatty, near Belfast, surrounding an earlier monument, in this case an earlier passage tomb. Although they sometimes enclose funerary monuments they frequently do not, or the funerary monument does not appear to be central to the ritual use of the site. Henges are typically found on low-lying ground, often near water. Although it was thought for many years that they were very rare in Ulster, with one known in County Down and one in County Tyrone,[54] in recent years more have been found and today at least nine are recorded in the Northern Ireland Sites and Monuments Record, three in Down, four in Fermanagh and two in Tyrone; there are none from County Antrim, however. There are only two known from Argyll in the Royal Commission on the Ancient and Historic Monuments of Scotland database, although others are known from the rest of Scotland.

In Ireland burial ritual also saw some changes with a new type of megalithic tomb, the wedge tomb, consisting of a covered passage contained within a well-defined wedge shaped cairn, mostly found in western Ireland, but with some in north Ulster and 11 known examples from County Antrim. These tombs are very late in the megalithic tomb tradition with Brindley and Lanting suggesting they are first built about 2500 BC, which is at the very cusp of the beginning of the Early Bronze Age.[55] In fact, Beaker pottery, usually associated with the spread of metalworking technology in Europe, is frequently found in wedge tombs, although this ritual use of Beaker pottery is different from the classic Beaker burials found in Scotland and in much of north-western Europe (see below). The wedge tomb ritual is, like that of the earlier megaliths, an essentially collective one, whereas the classic Beaker burial can be viewed a statement of individuality. Beaker pottery has also been occasionally found in Scotland placed into Chambered Cairns, in the Irish manner.

The Early Bronze Age

The Bronze Age is a time of enormous change in both Antrim and Argyll, as in the rest of Britain and Ireland. Completely new technologies of copper, bronze and gold working appear along with new burial practices, perhaps suggesting more emphasis on the individual in community ritual, yet all the time with apparently great continuity with the past. Some archaeologists distinguish a separate Copper Age or Chalcolithic, distinct from the Bronze Age. The actual date for the commencement of bronze, as opposed to copper, is uncertain some suggesting that the gap between the two may be very short, so in this essay the more conventional practice of subsuming the Copper Age into the Early Bronze Age is followed.

New burials of the Early Bronze Age

At about the time of the emergence of copper and bronze working in Scotland and Ireland there is a shift in the burial ritual away from the collective burial of the dead in large monumental megalithic tombs towards a burial ritual where individuals or small groups are buried in smaller graves. These graves are usually stone-lined boxes set into the earth, called cists, or sometimes just simple pits dug into the ground. Individual burials of this type appeared in Britain before they appeared in Ireland, were they were usually accompanied by a pottery vessel called a Beaker and are consequently called Beaker burials by archaeologists, a burial type found widely across the northern parts of western Europe. While 'classic' Beaker burials are unknown from any part of Ireland, they are known from Scotland, with quite a few in Argyll.[56] The 'classic' Beaker burial takes the form of the crouched inhumation of an individual within a stone-lined cist or a pit in the ground, accompanied by a Beaker pot and covered by a capstone. Sometimes the pit or cist burial is covered by a mound called a barrow, although frequently smaller barrows have been removed by agricultural improvements.

All of the Argyll beaker burials were contained within cists. Two of these Argyll Beaker burials, at Ballymeanoch and Poltalloch, were part of larger cemeteries and were accompanied by other cists; however, in these other burials the body was accompanied by a different type of pottery vessel called a Food Vessel. The Food Vessel is in many respects the successor to the Beaker Pot and the burial ritual of the two types is similar, the placement of a single or very small group of human remains (initially unburnt remains, but as time goes by cremation becomes more common) in a pit or cist frequently, but not always, accompanied by a Food Vessel and sometimes other grave goods. This burial rite of placement in a cist accompanied by a Food Vessel, is very common all over Ireland also where it is subdivided into a number of sub-groups, all of which are found in Antrim.[57] In general, the burial ritual in Antrim and Argyll, and for that matter the rest of Ireland and Scotland, is similar in most aspects at this time, the type of disposal of the remains, the size, shape of the burial holder, the accompanying pottery and other grave goods, such as bronze objects like knives, or even daggers and occasionally stone jewellery. In Ireland Food Vessels began accompanying burials within cists in the decades after 2200 BC.[58] It seems likely that the Food Vessel burials begin at about the same time in Scotland. There is evidence that Irish merchants were trading copper into Scotland at this time. The emergence of Food Vessels accompanying burials in Ireland and Scotland may have originated with the mixing of the Beaker burial traditions of Scotland with those of Irish copper traders, resulting in a new hybrid burial practice, found widely in both countries in succeeding centuries.

While new ritual practices were percolating into Ireland, there was still some ritual continuity with earlier times. Although this new burial rite emphasised the individual over the collective, it would be a mistake to see it as a complete break with the past. Earlier megalithic tombs became incorporated into the new ritual with cists and pits containing burials frequently being placed into the cairns covering earlier megalithic tombs, showing a desire on the part of the users of these new graves to emphasise continuity with earlier generations possibly emphasising traditional ownership of lands by those adopting new burial fashions.

The burial ritual in both Antrim and Argyll changes with time. Gradually cremation becomes the dominant method of disposal of the body and later, from about 1900 to 1600 BC the cremated remains begin to be inserted into decorated burial urns rather than simply accompanied by a funerary vessel. In Antrim and Argyll the urns take two main forms, Cordoned and Collared Urns.[59] Both urns are significantly larger than the earlier funerary vessels and, while generally decorated, are less intensely decorated than the earlier vessels. The Cordoned Urns are so called because of two applied clay strips which partition the vessel into three broad zones, while the Collared Urns are so called because of the narrowing in the upper mid body and accompanying overhanging rim. The Cordoned Urn is most commonly found in Scotland, particularly the east, with a few known from Wales, none from England. It is also frequently found in Ireland, especially in Ulster. The Collared Urn is a form found all over Britain and is also found in Ireland, but less commonly. The Collared and Cordoned Urns tend to be found with a 'richer' assemblage of artefacts than the earlier Food Vessel burials, this may reflect a society which is becoming more materially wealthy and possibly more hierarchical with the emergence of the first true aristocracies and chiefs. A variant of the urn tradition, the Encrusted Urn, which may display greater continuity with earlier Food Vessel burial practices, is commonly found across Ireland and more occasionally in Scotland.[60]

The introduction of metallurgy

There are other changes which affected both Antrim and Argyll equally at this time. The introduction of metallurgy is an enormous innovation. The earliest evidence for metallurgy in Ireland

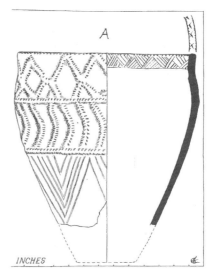

Encrusted urn from Kilskeery, County Tyrone

or Britain comes from Ross Island, County Kerry, which has been dated to approximately 2400 BC from excavations of an occupation site with Beaker pottery, close to an ancient copper mine.[61] It is probable that copper and bronze technology rapidly spread through Ireland and Britain, the Beaker package of pottery and an individual burial ritual possibly in its wake, although, as mentioned above, this package seems to take a slightly different form in Ireland than in Britain. The interrelationships between metallurgy, burial ritual and the use and presence of Beaker pottery have not yet been resolved satisfactorily by archaeologists.

The earliest copper objects to be made in Ireland were simple copper flat axes made in a simple one-piece stone mould. Gold working seems to have appeared at about the same time, or slightly later. The magnificent lunulae typify Irish Early Bronze Age gold working. These are large thin crescent moon shaped pieces of jewellery in the form of a gold collar. Although found across western Europe, most have been found in Ireland. As with many objects from the Early Irish Bronze, the dating of lunulae is difficult, although Taylor has suggested a date in the range 2200 to 1900.[62] It has recently been suggested that the lunulae, rather than being a lunar symbol as their shape would suggest, is actually a representation of a solar boat, carrying the sun on its journey through the sky.[63] This is based upon Iberian and Scandinavian Early Bronze Age representations of boats accompanying the sun.

Non-funerary rituals of the Early Bronze Age

Community rituals seem to show significant change in the Early Bronze Age. The ceremonial henge structures of the Late Neolithic seem to have been evolved into the stone circle; they both are ritual enclosures, but the change is one of material, from an earthen bank to stone. These are found all over Ireland and Britain with a spectacular grouping of stone circles and henges in a landscape already peppered by Neolithic and Early Bronze Age burial and ritual monuments in Kilmartin Glen, Argyll. Although there are no definite stone circles surviving in Antrim today, there are some accounts of now lost or destroyed stone circles, mainly from the Ordnance Survey Memoirs, although it is difficult to test the veracity of these sites without significant fieldwork. Stone circles are found in considerable numbers in west Ulster, however.[64] The exact usage of these monuments is obscure, although their romantic appearance has led to much imaginative speculation. It is, however, possible to make some assumptions about them. They are in the main large; a significant group could either assemble within them or around the outside of them. This suggests that they could have been used for collective purposes where all, or at least a significant part of the community, may have been present. What limited excavation that has been carried out, such as at Castlemahon, County Down, has revealed that the interior of stone circles is very clean, with little or no evidence of use, and with only a few, clearly ritual archaeological features found (such as the presence of a fire pit and the burial of a cremated child at the very centre of the Castlemahon circle).[65] This shows that they were treated with respect, much as we today might treat a church. In a number of cases, such as the stone circle at Ballynoe, County Down, the circle appears to enclose an earlier megalithic tomb; this has been observed for the Orcadian and Boyne passage tombs also. This suggests that the stone circle may be able to ritually mark off certain areas, or possibly contain spiritual forces. In some cases the surrounding of the earlier tomb by a stone circle has been interpreted as a sort of de-commissioning act or even an act of domination by new beliefs of older ways.

Ballynoe stone circle, County Down

Early Bronze Age settlements

There are few examples of Early Bronze Age houses or settlement sites in Ulster, or elsewhere in Ireland. This is perplexing, especially given the rate of discovery of other types of monuments from the rescue excavations of the last two decades. The reasons for this are unclear; again, it may simply be that Early Bronze Age houses are located in areas not typically chosen for modern development, such as upland areas. One of the few locations where there appears to be direct evidence of Early Bronze Age settlement is at Knockdhu, County Antrim. Here Philip Macdonald of the Centre for Archaeological Fieldwork, Queen's University Belfast, found a number of round house sites which have been radiocarbon dated to approximately 1900 BC,[66] within the Early Bronze Age, with a few slightly earlier Early Bronze Age dates being found elsewhere on this site. There are large numbers of similar hut or house sites, mainly unexcavated, known from upland locations all over Ireland. The results from Knockdhu would suggest that some of these may well date to the Early Bronze Age. There are Early Bronze Age houses known from Argyll such as the sand dune house at Ardnave, Islay.[67] There are also hut circle sites in more inland, and sometimes upland, locations in Argyll, although those few that have been excavated to date, such as Cul a' Bhaile on Jura and An Sithean, Islay, are later.[68] Given the number (134) of hut circle sites in Argyll and the presence of upland Early Bronze Age settlement in adjacent areas, some of these hut circle sites must be Early Bronze Age. At Lintshie Gutter, Lanarkshire, located on a hill in west central Scotland, there is a collection of 31 hut circles in what the Royal Commission on the Ancient and Historic Monuments of Scotland call an 'unenclosed platform settlement'.[69] Excavations there revealed that the hut circles date mainly to the Early Bronze Age, which broadly contemporary with the hut circles excavated by Macdonald at Knockdhu.

One area of contrast between the Late Neolithic and Early Bronze Age in Antrim and Argyll is in the profusion of rock art in Argyll. Although there are a few examples of cup marked and cup and ring marked stones from Antrim, and a few more in County Down, there are at least 49 sites with cup and ring marked stones in Argyll. There are other locations in Ireland where the concentration of cup and ring marked stones is closer to the density of that in Argyll, for instance Kerry, where over 40 examples of cup and ring marked stones are known from the Iveragh peninsula alone.[70] The profusion of rock art in Argyll and its relative absence in east Ulster may be more to do with the type of landscape and the availability of flat exposed outcrops of rock at the desired locations and altitudes that fitted the purpose of the builders.

When looked at as a whole the archaeological record of the Early Bronze Age in Antrim and Argyll is suggestively similar. The similarities in the burial record alone between Scotland and Ireland in the Early Bronze

Age is such that, with no other evidence available, an archaeologist would be likely to suggest two very similar societies, with similar customs, social structure, and probably regular contact, such as trading and intermarriage in the closest geographically situated parts, namely Antrim and Argyll. When other evidence is taken into account, such as the possibility suggested by Knockdhu, County Antrim, that in Antrim, at least, there is an upland Early Bronze Age settlement pattern, similar to that found in parts of Scotland, then the possibility of very close Early Bronze Age interactions across the North Channel is strengthened. There are some contrasts in the archaeological record, the absence of rock art, or stone circles from Antrim for instance, both of which are common in Argyll, but these absences may simply reflect the differing landscape and topography of the two regions and their subsequent land use history.

The Later Bronze Age

Later Bronze Age metalwork

The Irish Bronze Age has been one of the most visible archaeological eras in British and Irish prehistory because of the huge amount of fine bronze-work, gold-work and other craft objects found which date from that era, much of it deposited deliberately in watery places and rivers as a deliberate ritual act. In what archaeologists sometimes call the Middle Bronze Age, around about 1500 BC, bronze tools, such as axes, become much more sophisticated in their construction, heralding a new phase in the Irish Bronze Age.[71] New decorative gold work appears, like gold torques, and the so-called 'dress fastners' and 'sleeve fastners', containing far more weight of gold within them than the gold lunulae of the Early Bronze Age. This is also the time of the appearance of the first swords in the Irish archaeological record. As the Late Bronze Age continues, this process of ritual deposition in watery places accelerates, with large numbers of bronze objects being deliberately deposited in bogs. Highly developed short swords, spears, various types of axe and other tools, as well as more ritualistic objects like horns, sheet bronze, riveted cauldrons, buckets, and unusual pendants, called crotals, said to resemble bulls' testicles, all appear at this time and have been recovered, frequently in excellent condition, from bogs and rivers. The hint from the increasing amounts of weaponry is that this is a hierarchical warrior society is compounded by the finding of both bronze and leather shields. Even larger and heavier gold objects also seem to be being deliberately deposited in ritual acts. These gold objects, gorgets, and the so-called dress fasteners and sleeve fasteners, and their frequent deposition, seems almost spendthrift, even in the context of ritual or dedicatory deposits by a wealthy gold mining and working society.

Scottish metalwork is broadly similar and follows the same developmental path as Irish metalwork during the Bronze Age, beginning with the simple flat axes and daggers of the Early Bronze Age, developing into flanged axes and halberds in the Middle Bronze Age and, like in Ireland, a wide range of Bronze Age tools and weapons, including swords in the Late Bronze Age.[72] Like Ireland, much of this metal work is found because of ritual deposition. In parallel with this, gold objects, following many of the same forms and utilising the same decorative styles, are found in Scotland as in Ireland. The finding of three Late Bronze Age gold bracelets of Irish style at Islay is cited as a likely example of an Irish merchant in Scotland.[73] These similarities of form and style in the metalwork of the Bronze Age are visible in the entirety of the bronze and gold from Scotland and Ireland. In fact, across the whole of western Europe there seem to be similar trends and forms visible in the bronze tools and weapons.

Later Bronze Age burial in Antrim and Argyll

Burial ritual evolves consistently in Ireland and Scotland through the Bronze Age. In Ireland, as mentioned above, in the latter part of the Early Bronze Age, after 1900 BC, the cist with the food vessel was joined by the pit and funerary urn; urn burials eventually becoming the dominant ritual. In Scotland a similar process happened. By approximately 1400 BC the decorated funerary urn had been in Ireland replaced by a much plainer urn and the cremation itself becomes more tokenistic, with only a small portion of the cremated remains actually being interred in the urn. In the Late Bronze Age and Iron Age that follows the urn is abandoned altogether and the burial ritual generally consists of a quantity of cremated remains, without funerary vessel, often surrounded by a small circular ditch, possibly, in some cases, capped by a mound of earth derived from the spoil of the ditch and referred to by archaeologists as a barrow.

In Argyll the Middle and Later Bronze Age funerary rituals continue to be reminiscent of Irish burial rituals, but with differences. Firstly, especially in the Later Bronze Age, there is less evidence of burial, of any type, in the Scottish archaeological record. In Argyll there are a number of simple cremations reminiscent of Irish cremations of this period, but instead of being surrounded by a shallow ditch and possibly an earthen mound or barrow they are surrounded by a low cairn of stones within which an earthen mound is built; examples of this type of burial have been found at Stronoiller, Lorn, Culcharron, Lorn and Claggan, Morvern.[74]

The absence of many Late Bronze Age burials from Scotland may simply be because they have not been found yet, however. The full extent of Late Bronze Age burial, in very simple cremations, in Ireland has only become apparent in recent years with large scale developer-funded archaeological excavations on major industrial or infrastructure renewal projects. In earlier years the greater visibility, to the non-professional archaeologist, of the Earlier Bronze Age burials meant that when encountered by chance on a farm or construction site it was recognised for what it was. Much infrastructural development work in Scotland was carried out in the 1960s and 1970s, in the era before large scale rescue archaeology, rather than in the 1990s and after, as in Northern Ireland and the Republic of Ireland.

Later Bronze Age settlement
In the past fifteen years the study of the Irish Later Bronze Age has been revolutionised by one site: Corrstown, Portrush, County Londonderry.[75] This site has established that on the north Ulster coast a large village-sized settlement, organised around a central roadway, flourished for several generations between 1360 and 1150 BC. Estimates of the size of the population of the village suggest it is likely that it had a population of 200 to 300 persons with up to 70 houses permanently occupied at one time. The scale of settlement is unprecedented for prehistoric Ireland, or for that matter any Neolithic or Bronze Age settlement in Ireland or Britain. There is no shortage of other settlement evidence for this era, with two recently excavated Late Bronze Age settlements found at Ballyprior Beg, Island Magee, County Antrim, and Townparks, near Antrim Town.[76] Similar individual or small clusters of Later Bronze Age round houses have been found across Ireland, but nowhere on the scale of the village at Corrstown.

Argyll and the rest of Scotland likewise have plenty of evidence of Late Bronze Age settlement, but there is, as yet, no evidence of large scale settlements like Corrstown. At Cul a' Bhaile on Jura and at An Sithean on Islay there are Late Bronze Age settlements, but they are just small clusters of houses; the larger of the two excavated sites, An Sithean, has eight houses.[77] There are of course larger clusters of hut sites which are unexcavated, many of which may be Late Bronze Age, although it is unlikely that any of the known sites is as large as the Corrstown settlement.

Some of the Late Bronze Age Irish settlements appear to have had enclosures surrounding the houses, possibly to keep livestock contained as much as to provide defence, although any sort of stout wall or fence can have some defensive capability. At McIlwhans Hill, County Antrim, near Belfast, evidence for a Late Bronze Age oval stone enclosure containing two houses, dating between 1050 and 500 BC was found.[78] This site also had some evidence for some earlier, pre-enclosure, Early Bronze Age activity destroyed by the later construction there. Contemporary settlements in Argyll still seem unenclosed, but there is evidence from the excavation at Dryburn Bridge in south-east Scotland of an oval palisaded enclosure with several round houses which was in use sometime between 800 and 400

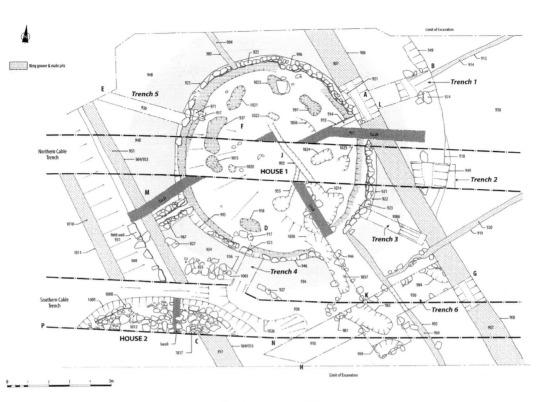

Ballyprior Beg round house,
Island Magee, County Antrim

BC, the nature of the radiocarbon dates making more precision impossible. Superficially at least, the McIlwhans and Dryburn Bridge structures seem similar.

There is also in the Later Bronze Age Irish archaeological record an episode of construction of much larger enclosures, which would certainly have had some defensive capability, if only for show, which are called hill forts. These were very large circular ditch and bank enclosures, frequently surrounding the entire top of a hill, sometimes with multiple enclosing ditch and bank systems. In the case of Haughey's Fort in County Armagh the outermost, of three, enclosures has a diameter in excess of 300m.[79] Haughey's Fort was intensively used from about 1100 to 900 BC and there is evidence for both settlement and craft activity. A similar enclosed fort was also dug at Knockdhu, County Antrim, by Philip Macdonald of Queen's University Belfast, which, as we have seen, had an earlier Bronze Age, pre-enclosure phase also. There a natural mountain peninsula was cut off at one end by a series of banks and ditches to make a type of hill fort called a promontory fort. Macdonald's excavations there suggested that the site was enclosed sometime between 1500 and 1000 BC with Late Bronze occupation possibly continuing as late as 630 BC.[80] These are major constructions involving the ability to organise and utilise a large workforce, probably by a small wealthy elite. In Scotland the archaeological record suggests similar developments. A number of hilltop sites, such as Traprain Law, East Lothian, seem to have been enclosed in banks and ditches in the Late Bronze Age, possibly commencing around 1000 BC.[81]

In Ireland there is a further intensification of agricultural activity after 1000 BC. The increase in agricultural activity is visible from pollen evidence, and it is matched an apparent increase in the amount of human settlement, although this may be an artefact of the decentralisation of previously village-based settlements, such as Corrstown mentioned above.[82] In Ireland, after 600 BC there seems to be less pressure on the land, possibly an indicator of declining population, and only limited evidence of woodland clearance and agriculture by the fourth century BC.[83] This decline in agricultural activity in Ireland is clearly of great importance and it may be key to understanding some of the paradoxes of and contrasts between the archaeological record in Ireland and Scotland in the subsequent Iron Age.

The Iron Age

The change from the Late Bronze Age to the Iron Age has been a problematic one for archaeologists. The Later Bronze Age was archaeologically rich, with multiple settlements, large hill forts an increasingly intensive arable agriculture and frequent finds of elaborate bronze work and gold. The Iron Age, by contrast, seems a bit of a paradox, with relatively few Iron Age settlements known, but lots of evidence for ritual Iron Age activity in Ireland and many Iron Age settlement sites known from Scotland, but perhaps fewer large ritual sites known there.

From bronze to iron

Some of the earliest indications of the beginning of the Iron Age in Ireland are iron artefacts, possibly dating to about 600 BC, or earlier, which are copies in iron of tools which 'in their form' would seem more typical of the Bronze Age, examples being socketed axes, morphologically the same as socketed axes made from cast bronze, but manufactured from sheet iron.[84] Much of this early evidence originates in County Antrim.[85] The implication of this is that iron is *not* brought to Ireland in a great invasion bringing an entirely new culture. Rather it shows new technology being expressed in old ways, showing continuity. This is a phenomenon which is found across Britain and Ireland at the onset of the Iron Age. Similar iron copies of bronze axes are known from Scotland, with one from the Traprain Law Hillfort in Lothian.[86]

After this initial evidence of adoption of iron technology there seems, in Ireland, to be a hiatus in the archaeological record between about 600 and 300 BC.[87] Ritual deposition begins again in about 300 BC, but the artefacts which are being deposited are very different from what went before. Many of the new ritual deposits are associated with horse use, such as horse bits and unusual 'Y' shaped pendants whose exact form of use appears to be obscure, but seems to be connected with horsemanship also. These horse accessories are all made of bronze, but in an artistic style which is more typically Iron Age and what could be described as 'Celtic'. The artistic style of the developed Iron Age in Ireland, post 300 BC, is called La Tène, and is found across Ireland, Britain and western Europe at this time also. Other La Tène decorated objects found in Ireland at this period include personal items like pins and fibulae (a fibula is a kind of Iron Age decorated safety pin), impressive display items like golden torcs, and weapons such as shields, swords and scabbards. Amongst the most famous, and most profusely decorated La Tène Items from Ireland or Britain, are the sword scabbards from a hoard at Lisnacrogher, County Antrim, apparently found at the site of a crannog (an island settlement in a lake, the island being usually artificial or at least an artificially enhanced, these date from the Late Bronze Age and are found in Ireland and Scotland). The scabbards are decorated in the most intricate La Tène designs. Non-metalwork La Tène items are known also, an excellent example being the stone beehive querns, a kind of rotary quern which improved the efficiency of grinding grain, compared to the older saddle quern, and which was typically decorated with La Tène style decoration on its upper surface.[88] Again, as with the metalwork, these querns have not, as might be expected, been found on settlement sites, but in lakes or rivers.[89] It has been suggested that although both La Tene metalwork and bee-hive querns have a predominantly northern distribution in Ireland they seem to be, to a large extent, mutually exclusive when their distribution is examined closely on a sub-regional basis.[90] It has also been noted that they seem to favour deposition in broadly different soil type areas, allowing the suggestion to have been made that the two artefacts represent mutually antagonistic, although culturally related, groups of ranchers and farmers.[91]

The Celts?

The appearance of La Tène artefacts in Ireland and Britain used to be thought to be the product of a movement of 'Celtic' invaders across the continent. Most archaeologists today see this somewhat differently. Anthropologists studying cultures without modern communications technology have been able to see how goods and ideas can be spread through wide areas without *necessarily* large movements of populations. Trade, networks of craftsmen, intermarriage can all rapidly spread ideas and ideology, techniques of manufacture and artistic styles through a region and archaeologists have moved away from the concept of a single great migration of 'Celts' through western Europe. What there was seems to have been more a group of similarly structured societies, with similar economies and technology, and a set of related languages. These societies were grouped together by antiquarians, who noticed the similarity in much of their material culture, and who used the theory of a migration and invasion of a group they named the Celts (a name used by the Greeks for barbarian tribes in northern Europe) as an explanatory mechanism for the similarities they saw across the continent. Of course in modern Europe there are similarities of social structure, technology and language, but we today see these as separate groups, regions or nations, as of course did the ancient peoples which later antiquarians and archaeologists called Celts. The term Celt and Celtic may still have use as convenient labels for categorising aspects of the culture of late prehistoric Europe, but we must be careful to remember that these peoples did not necessarily see themselves as part of an overarching group or culture, and there may have been no great migration or invasion spreading 'Celtic' culture through Europe, although there may have been wide-reaching contacts through trade, exchange, smaller migrations and aristocratic marriage.

Iron Age ritual sites in Ulster
There are a number of important surviving Iron Age ritual sites in Ireland. An excellent example is at Navan Fort, County Armagh. This is the famous Emain Macha of legend, capital of ancient Ulster. It began as a ritual monument of Late Bronze Age to Early Iron Age date with the construction of a 39m diameter circle of large wooden posts.[92] In the Early Iron Age, about 400 BC, a series of successive wooden, figure-of-eight-shaped structures was constructed within this post enclosure. These were replaced about 100 BC by a large circular post-built structure, using 269 oak tree trunks, with a diameter of 40m, which was enclosed by a ditch and bank. The post structure was then filled in with limestone boulders, and covered in earth of different types taken from many different parts of Ulster, to make a mound, possibly ritually signifying the unity of the territory. Other Iron Age ritual activity took place at a number of sites within a very short distance of Navan Fort. The ritual deposition of four bronze war horns, decorated in La Tène style, took place at nearby Loughnashade, and ritual deposits are also believed to have taken place at the artificial pool at the Kings Stables.[93]

It is harder to point to important Iron Age ritual structures in Scotland. This is at least partly because western Scotland largely shares with Ireland a body of Early Medieval mythology centring on Irish ritual centres like Navan Fort and Tara, possibly obscuring their equivalent centres in Argyll, although a likely contender for an important ritual centre must be Dunadd, which emerges as an important centre in the Early Medieval era, but which may have earlier origins.

The missing Irish Iron Age settlements?

In Ireland archaeologists have been puzzled by our inability to find Iron Age settlements. Hill fort and promontory fort sites where Iron Age occupation might have been hoped for, like Knockdhu, for instance, or Haughey's Fort, have shown evidence for Bronze Age or Early Medieval activity, but little in between. Raths or ringforts once thought to be a type of settlement which might have had its origins in the Iron Age, have consistently shown themselves, both from the artefacts found and radiocarbon dates obtained during excavation, to date to the Early Medieval period.[94]

Recently, Becker and others have attempted to address this problem by reviewing recent developer-funded excavations in Ireland, published or unpublished, in the hope of finding, amongst the very large numbers of recent digs carried out, evidence for this frustrating gap.[95] They have succeeded to some extent in that they have identified approximately six unenclosed occupation sites, with circular wooden post-framed houses, and some evidence for Iron Age occupation at hill fort sites, although not necessarily at the same level of intensity as earlier Bronze Age occupation. Nevertheless it is clear that, although there now do appear to be Irish Iron Age settlements, there are proportionally fewer than for the preceding Late Bronze Age or the succeeding Early Medieval period, something which must be connected with the decline in agriculture in the Early Iron Age noted above. The contrast between this paucity of settlement evidence and the profusion of ritual evidence remains a problem, however.

Recent work by Thomas McErlean has used literary evidence from the Ulster Cycle myths to identify a number of sites in north Antrim and north Londonderry which may date to the Iron Age. The Ulster Cycle myths are a series of early Irish stories, set at about the time of Christ (in other words in the Irish Iron Age), which tell of ancient Ulster under its king, Conor MacNessa, and its struggles with the other provinces, especially Connacht. The stories centre on the feats of the warriors of the Red Branch, particularly Cuchulain. One of the Ulster Cycle tales called *Tóchustol Ulad*, or 'The Mustering of the Men of Ulster', takes the form of a roll call of Ulster's greatest warriors and in some cases names their forts. Using this evidence, supplemented with other evidence from Early Medieval documents, McErlean has matched several of the forts in this story up with actual sites in north Ulster.[96] He summarises the literary references in the *Tóchustol Ulad* and other Early Medieval sources suggesting that the fort of Dunseverick is the fort of Dún Sobairche.

Dunseverick, County Antrim; the ruins are those of a Medieval castle

Dunseverick is a promontory defined by cliffs on three sides and linked to the mainland by a short strip of land. It has upon it a late sixteenth-century tower house built by O'Cahan tenants of the McDonnells and evidence for the footings of earlier Medieval buildings. McErlean also suggests that the hill fort of Dunmull, County Antrim, located a few miles north-east of Coleraine, is the fortress of the Ulster warrior Mulaig, mentioned in the *Tóchustol Ulad*. This hill fort encloses the entire summit of a hill on an otherwise quite flat plain, with views over north Ulster and Kintyre and the footings of circular and rectangular structures are visible from aerial photographs. An outer enclosure may also be fossilised in a field boundary around the site.

In north County Londonderry McErlean has suggested that the site known today as the Giant's Sconce may be the sites known as Dún da Bend and Dún Ceithrin in the Ulster Cycle. He links the Dún da Bend of *Tóchustol Ulad* to Dún Ceithrin using genealogical information preserved within Early Irish literature. Using locational information contained in Adomnan's 'Life of Colum Cille', in which Colum Cille visits Dún Ceithrin, McErlean suggests that the Giant's Sconce, a spectacular stone fort, with wonderful views, located roughly halfway between Coleraine and Limavady may be Dún da Bend/Dún Ceithrin. The Giant's Sconce is one of a number of sites which archaeologist Richard Warner suggests may have parallels with Iron Age Scottish settlements[97] and, interestingly, it was at the time of Colum Cille's visit occupied by the Cruithni, one of the peoples of early Ulster, who may have been connected in some way with the Picts of Scotland.

Iron Age settlement in Argyll

In Scotland there is no absence of Iron Age settlement, in fact the type of settlement we see in Iron Age Scotland looks very much like what we would *expect* to find in Ireland, but have had trouble identifying. Argyll is particularly rich in Iron Age settlement sites. Archaeologists divide them into several types, although whether the distinctions between some of these sites would have been obvious to the contemporary user of these sites is debatable. The most typical Iron Age settlement site in Argyll, and much of the rest of Scotland, is the dun, a relatively small dry stone enclosure usually erected on a rocky eminence with, according to the rather arbitrary Royal Commission on the Ancient and Historic Monuments of Scotland categorisation, an internal area of less than 375m², enough for a single family.[98] Duns are typically subdivided by archaeologists into two variants, the small dun houses, which were quite circular in plan and small enough to be roofed and dun enclosures which were larger, more oval or even irregular in shape and probably containing within them one or more free standing buildings.[99] Somewhat larger again are what Scottish archaeologists categorise as forts, which are larger than the RCAHMS threshold of 375m², and as such are considered to be potentially the dwelling places of a larger group than a single family.

Crannogs, settlements in lakes built upon artificial islands, also probably appear in Scotland at about this time, although whether they are really the developed large crannogs found in both Scotland and Ireland in the Early Medieval period is uncertain. It seems that early crannogs in Scotland may be more like a small dun house, but constructed on a platform in a lake. Radiocarbon dating of a crannog at Ederline Loch Awe, Argyll, has shown its construction in the Early Iron Age.[100]

An interesting, in fact iconic, settlement type of Iron Age insular Argyll, and more widely in western and especially northern Scotland is the broch. These structures have a similar ground floor area as a round house, but are often three storeys high, with walls built of dry stone construction. The best preserved of these sites have intramural passages and chambers, scarcements (recesses into the wall to support the timber floors of the upper storeys), guard cells at the doorways and bolt holes for the doors. Often the broch is set within an outer enclosure, in a manner typical also of several dun houses in the Hebrides and northern Scotland.[101] The dating of brochs rests on the excavation of a few sites, the most important of which is Dun Mor Vaul on Tiree, the exact dating and significance of which has been much debated, but which nevertheless seems to have been a functioning broch by about AD 200, built upon earlier occupation.[102] The site has provided the best dating evidence for two types of pottery, Vaul Ware, which the excavator believed to be a local type of pottery, and Everted Rim Ware (not to be confused with Irish Everted Rim Ware which is now renamed Medieval Ulster Coarse Pottery and which post-dates Scottish Everted Rim Ware by many centuries), which the excavator believed was introduced by refugees, possibly from southern Britain, retreating from the advancing Romans and making their contribution to Scottish vernacular architecture by building brochs. A broch site at Howe on Orkney is probably older, two earlier round houses having been demolished to make way for a broch by, at the latest, AD 100.[103] MacKie's view that brochs were the result of invaders from the south nowadays seems very old fashioned; there are no obvious prototype brochs in southern Britain, and yet there is an innovative ceramic style appearing in the Western Isles, which does bear some comparison to certain wares from southern Britain, although with a limited range of decorative possibilities on simple coarse pots non-existent parallels are possible to find.

Conclusions: *A* **longue durée** *view*

If one looks at the archaeology and history of Antrim and Argyll, and more widely Ireland and the west of Scotland with a *longue durée* view there seems to almost be an oscillation in the relative closeness of the two halves of our constructed region, with periods where contacts seem to be close, intense even, and where it is difficult not to see the history and archaeology of Antrim, Argyll and northern Ireland and western Scotland as completely intertwined, almost to the extent of eroding any concept of them having a separate identity. In other eras, however, Antrim and Argyll seem, if not quite to have turned their backs on each other, at least to have turned sideways, their gaze fixed on somewhere else. They may still have similarities, aeons of intercourse have ensured that, but they seem at these times to be running parallel to each other.

To look at the earliest era the Mesolithic hunter-gatherers of Antrim and Argyll may have had a common origin, but they seem to have developed independently. That there must have been cross channel movement of goods and people seems certain from the fact that much of the flint used in Mesolithic Scotland must have come from Antrim, but it seems as if this movement may not have been enough to encourage the kind of regular trading and intermarriage to create a single community. Occasional trips to the Antrim coast to obtain raw materials by the Argyll hunter-gatherers, or possibly, trading visits to Kintyre by the Irish hunter-gatherers, the only opportunities for close contact.

In the Neolithic there is evidence for much deeper and more sustained contact between Antrim and Argyll. The colonisation of Ireland and Scotland by Neolithic farmers seems to have happened just before 3700 BC. The evidence from the types of settlements, the new flint tool technologies and the pottery all suggests two societies in close contact. That these contacts were sustained for some time can be demonstrated by the emergence of stone tombs in both Antrim and Argyll, a few generations after initial Neolithic colonisation, which are very similar, both in the morphology of the tombs themselves and in the rituals of their use. The unity of this whole cross-channel cultural assemblage caused it to be named the Clyde-Carlingford Culture by Stuart Piggott.[104] This term withered as the New Archaeology took root in the 1960s and 1970s, a seemingly anachronistic survival of a less self-conscious age. It possibly suffered also from an archaeology of jurisdiction where archaeologists worked within the region in which they were employed and Clyde-Carlingford tombs were quietly split up into (Irish) court tombs and (Scottish) chambered tombs. Yet there is something about the concept of the Clyde-Carlingford Culture which seems to still have some utility.

The Middle and Later Neolithic give an impression of perhaps both Antrim and Argyll and their hinterlands having a relationship which was a little less intense, although we have perhaps a less rounded archaeological record in this era with little firm evidence for the nature of settlement, at this time, in either region. Passage tombs, henge monuments and Grooved Ware pottery are part of a milieu which seems to connect east Ulster as much to the northern isles and Orkneys as with Argyll in this era. Argyll has few passage tombs, while north Antrim has a cluster. Interestingly, the only Argyll passage tomb to be excavated, at Aghnacreebeg, displays material culture which seems to have more in common with a chambered tomb or court tomb, than what would typically be expected in an Orcadian or Boyne Valley Irish passage tomb. None of the Antrim passage tombs have been excavated to see if the Aghnacreebeg cultural variation is replicated there. If it was it would suggest a consistent cross-channel response to new ideas in this era also, possibly indicating closer ties than across the North Channel at this time than the apparent contrasts in the archaeological record, at present, suggest. The excavation of a north Antrim passage tomb could go a long way towards establishing if the regional pull of a long established North Channel culture was enough to cause a consistent adaptation of passage tomb funerary ritual on each side of the sea.

There can be no doubting the strong similarity in a number of areas between the Early Bronze Age archaeological remains in Antrim and Argyll and again in the surrounding areas. Many archaeologists believe that burial customs are one of the truest reflections of the nature and structure of a society. If that is the case Antrim and Argyll must have had a very similar culture and society in the Early Bronze Age. Early Bronze Age settlements have been hard to find in Ireland, although, as suggested by Macdonald's excavations at Knockdhu, County Antrim, a close examination of upland hut circles might be profitable. Although no Early Bronze Age settlements have, as yet, been found in Argyll, in other parts of south-west Scotland Early Bronze Age settlement *has* been found in upland locations raising the possibility that the settlement architecture and the settlement landscapes of both Antrim and Argyll and the surrounding regions was similar in the Early Bronze Age.

As the Bronze Age progressed there are common trends in Antrim and Argyll, with a movement towards cremation burial, sometimes in urns, and enclosed upland settlements being identified, again with similar developments in other parts of Ireland and Scotland. Metal technology becomes more complex, with new more sophisticated tools and weapons with distinctions so subtle that only an expert could easily identify a Middle or Late Bronze Age metal object as being from one region or another. There must have been considerable movement of goods and craftsmen around these islands at this time.

Something very unusual happens in the Irish Iron Age. There are a number of very large and impressive monumental structures associated with the collective functions of the society, but very little settlement evidence and, although some burials are known, there were not as many as for the preceding era. The contrast with Argyll and the rest of Scotland at this time could not be greater. There seems to be no evidence of a similar hiatus in the Scottish settlement record, rather there is continuity of settlement evidence through from the Late Bronze Age to the Early Medieval period. Many attempts have been made to explain the absence of Irish Iron Age settlements and recent work does seem to finally have identified some Irish Iron Age dwellings which can be compared with British analogues, yet they are still relatively few in number. Is there a population crash caused by some crisis in Ireland, an environmental catastrophe, famine, disease, or a combination of each? If there is such a crisis why does it not seem to affect Argyll? McErlean perhaps gives us a starting point for further investigation by suggesting there may be some north Ulster Irish Iron Age, high status, settlement sites, mentioned in Ulster Cycle tales which Dun Mor Vaul continued in use into the Early Medieval period and which may survive today to be further explored.[105] These sites may not actually date to the supposed time of the Ulster Cycle myths (about the time of Christ), but their presence in these tales lets us know that they were already considered to be ancient at the time these stories were written down. Warner's suggestion that some of those very sites, such as the Giant's Sconce in County Londonderry, have recognisable Scottish features is also fascinating. Taken together, if correct, their suggestions point to a period of renewed close contact across Ulster and western Scotland, possibly quite late in the Iron Age. This is a question which can only be answered by obtaining dating evidence from excavations of these sites and seeing if it is possible to identify late Iron Age occupation at them.

Notes

1 P. Woodman, 'Making yourself at home on an island: the first 1,000 years (+?) of the Irish Mesolithic', *PPS,* 78 (2012), pp 1–34.

2 D. G. Sutherland, 'The environment of Argyll' in G. Ritchie (ed.), *The Archaeology of Argyll* (Edinburgh, 1997), pp 10–24.

3 Woodman, 'Making yourself at home on an island'.

4 T. Ward and A. Saville, 'Howburn Farm: excavating Scotland's first people', *Current Archaeology*, 243 (2010).

5 Woodman, 'Making yourself at home on an island', p. 3.

6 Ibid., p. 10.

7 Ibid.

8 P. Woodman , *Excavations at Mount Sandel, 1973–77,* Northern Ireland Archaeological Monographs No. 2 (Belfast, 1985).

9 A. Bayliss and P. Woodman, 'A new Bayesian chronology for Mesolithic occupation at Mount Sandel, Northern Ireland', *PPS*, 75 (2009), pp 101–23.

10 P. Woodman, 'A review of the Scottish Mesolithic, a plea for normality!', *PSAS*, 119 (1989), pp 1–32.

11 H. Movius, 'An early post-glacial site at Cushendun, Co. Antrim', *PRIA*, 46C (1940), pp 1–84; H. Movius, 'Curran Point, Larne: the type site of the Irish Mesolithic', *PRIA*, 56C (1953), pp 1–195.

12 McSparron and Hurl *in prep.*

13 P. Woodman and G. Johnson, 'Excavations at Bay Farm 1, Carnlough, Co. Antrim, and the study of the "Larnian" technology', *PRIA*, 96C (1996), pp 137–235.

14 P. Woodman, 'Recent excavations at New Ferry, Co. Antrim', *PPS*, 43 (1977), pp 155–99.

15 H. Movius, *The Irish Stone Age. Its Chronology, Development and Relations* (Cambridge, 1942).

16 Woodman, 'A review of the Scottish Mesolithic'.

17 A. Morrison, 'The Mesolithic period in south-west Scotland: a review of the evidence', *Glasgow Archaeological Journal*, 9 (1982), pp 1–14.

18 A. Saville, 'A cache of flint axeheads and other flint artefacts from Auchenhoan, near Campbeltown, Kintyre, Scotland', *PPS*, 65 (1999), pp 83–123.

19 T. Collins and F. Coyne, 'Fire and water: Early Mesolithic cremations at Castleconnell, Co. Limerick', *Archaeology Ireland*, 17:2 (2003), pp 24–7.

20 P. Woodman, E. Anderson and N. Finlay, *Excavations at Ferriter's Cove, 1983–95* (Bray, 1999), p. 219.

21 M. O'Connell and K. Molloy, 'Farming and woodland dynamics in Ireland during the Neolithic', *PRIA*, 101B (2001), pp 99–128.

22 C. McSparron, 'Have you no homes to go to? Calling time on the early Irish Neolithic', *Archaeology Ireland*, 22:3 (Autumn 2008), pp 18–21; N. J. Whitehouse, R. J. Schulting, M. McClatchie, P. Barratt, T. R. McLaughlin, A. Bogaard, S. Colledge, R. Marchant, J. Gaffrey, M. J. Bunting, 'Neolithic agriculture on the European western frontier: the boom and bust of early farming in Ireland', *Journal of Archaeological Science*, 51 (2014), pp 181–205.

23 A. Whittle, F. Healy and A. Bayliss, *Gathering Time: Dating the Early Neolithic Enclosures of Southern Britain and Ireland* (Oxford, 2011).

24 D. Simpson, 'The Ballygalley houses, Co. Antrim' in I. Armit, E. Murphy, E. Nelis and D. Simpson (eds.), *Neolithic Settlement in Ireland and Western Britain* (Oxford, 2003), pp 123–32; N. Crothers, 'Ballyharry's Game', *Archaeology Ireland*, 10 (1996), pp 12–14.

25 D. O'Rourke 'Aghalislone', P. Bowen and W. Baillie, 'Ballinderry Road, Lisburn', and R. M. Chapple, 'Bush Road, Bush', all in *Excavations Bulletin 2008*.

26 Whitehouse et al., 'Neolithic agriculture on the European western frontier'.

27 McSparron, 'Have you no homes to go to'.

28 J. Thomas, 'Neolithic houses in mainland Britain and Ireland – a sceptical view' in T. Darvill and J. Thomas (eds), *Neolithic Houses in Northwest Europe and Beyond* (Oxford, 1996), pp 1–12.

29 Whittle et al., *Gathering Time*.

30 A. Sheridan, 'French Connections I: spreading the *marmites* thinly' in Armit et al., *Neolithic Settlement in Ireland and Western Britain*, pp 3–17.

31 E. B. Rennie, 'Excavations at Ardnadam, Cowall, 1964–82', *Glasgow Archaeological Journal*, 11 (1984).

32 G. Murdie and P. Richardson, 'Excavations of a possible Neolithic structure, Neolithic finds and later ditch features at Kingarth Quarry, Isle of Bute', *Scottish Archaeological Journal*, 28:2 (2006), pp 105–24.

33 S. O Nualláin, 'A Neolithic house at Ballyglass, near Ballycastle, Co. Mayo', *JRSAI*, 102 (1972), pp 49–57.

34 P. Ashmore, 'Radiocarbon dates from archaeological sites in Argyll and Arran' in Ritchie, *Archaeology of Argyll*, pp 254–7.

35 R. J. Schulting and M. P. Richards, 'The wet, the wild and the domesticated: the Mesolithic-Neolithic transition on the west coast of Scotland', *European Journal of Archaeology*, 5 (2002), p. 147.

36 Ibid., p. 174.

37 Ibid., p. 167.

38 S. Piggott, *The Neolithic Cultures of the British Isles: A Study of the Stone-using Agricultural Communities of Britain in the Second Millennium BC* (Cambridge, 1954).

39 V. G. Childe, 'Some sherds from Slieve na Callighe', *JRSAI*, 65 (1935), pp 230–34.

40 A. ApSimon, 'Chronological contexts for Irish megalithic tombs', *JIA*, 3 (1985), pp 5–15.

41 J. J. Tomb and O. Davies, 'Urns from Ballymacaldrack', *UJA*, third series, 1 (1938), pp 219–21; C. McSparron, P. Logue and B. Williams, 'Data Structure Report: Tirnony Portal Tomb, Maghera, Co. Derry/Londonderry', Centre for Archaeological Fieldwork, Queen's University Belfast (2011).

42 R. Schulting, E. Murphy, C. Jones and G. Warren, 'A proposed chronology for Irish court tombs based on new dates from the north of the island', *PRIA*, 112C (2012), pp 1–60.

43 Ashmore, 'Radiocarbon dates from archaeological sites in Argyll and Arran'.

44 T. B. Ballin, 'Re-examination of the Early Neolithic pitchstone-bearing assemblage from Auchategan, Argyll, Scotland', *Lithics*, 27 (2006), pp 12–32; A. Saville, 'A cache of flint axeheads and other flint artefacts from Auchenhoan, near Campbeltown, Kintyre, Scotland', *PPS*, 65 (1999), pp 83–123.

45 D. D. A. Simpson and I. Meighan, 'Pitchstone: a new trading material in Neolithic Ireland', *Archaeology Ireland*, 13:2 (1999).

46 Ibid.; Simpson, 'The Ballygalley houses'.

47 J. V. S. Megaw and D. D. A. Simpson, *An Introduction to British Prehistory* (Leicester, 1984), pp 136–7.

48 J. N. G. Ritchie, 'Excavations of a cairn at Strontoller, Lorn, Argyll', *Glasgow Archaeological Journal*, 2 (1971), pp 1–7.

49 Sheridan, 'French Connections I'; A. Tresset, 'French Connections II: of cows and men', in Armit et al., *Neolithic Settlement in Ireland and Western Britain*, pp 18–30.

50 ApSimon, 'Chronological contexts for Irish megalithic tombs'.

51 McSparron, 'Have you no homes to go to?'.

52 M. G. L. Baillie and D. M. Brown, 'Oak dendrochronology: some recent archaeological developments from an Irish perspective', *Antiquity* 76 (2002), pp 497–505.

53 Whitehouse et al., 'Neolithic agriculture on the European western frontier'.

54 Megaw and Simpson, *Introduction to British Prehistory*.

55 A. L. Brindley and J. N. Lanting, 'Radiocarbon dates from wedge tombs', *JIA*, 6 (1991/2), p. 23.

56 J. N. G. Ritchie, 'Monuments associated with burial and ritual' in Ritchie, *Archaeology of Argyll*, pp 81–2.

57 J. Waddell, *The Bronze Age Burials of Ireland* (Galway, 1990).

58 A. Brindley, *Dating of Food Vessels and Urns in Ireland*, Bronze Age Studies 7 (Galway, 2007).

59 R. M. Kavanagh, 'Collared and cordoned cinerary urns in Ireland', *PRIA*, 76C (1976), pp 293–403.

60 R. M. Kavanagh, 'The encrusted urn in Ireland', *PRIA*, 73C (1973), pp 507–617.

61 W. O'Brien, *Ross Island: Mining, Metal and Society in Early Ireland* (Galway, 2004).

62 J. Taylor, 'Lunulae reconsidered', *PPS*, 36 (1970), pp 38–81.

63 M. Cahill, '"Here comes the sun …": solar symbolism in Early Bronze Age Ireland', *Archaeology Ireland* (Spring 2015), pp 26–33.

64 J. Waddell, *The Prehistoric Archaeology of Ireland* (Bray, 1998).

65 A. E. P. Collins and W. R. M. Morton, 'A stone circle on Castle Mahon Mountain, Co. Down', *UJA*, third series, 19 (1956), pp 1–10.

66 Pers. comm. Philip Macdonald.

67 G. Ritchie and H. G. Welfare, 'Excavations at Ardnave, Islay', *PSAS*, 113 (1983), pp 302–06.

68 J. B. Stevenson, 'The excavation of a hut circle at Cul a'Bhaile, Jura', *PSAS,* 114 (1984), pp 127–60; J. W. Barber and M. M. Brown, 'An Sithean', *PSAS*, 114 (1984), pp 161–88.

69 J. Terry, 'Excavation at Lintshie Gutter unenclosed platform settlement, Crawford, Lanarkshire, 1991', *PSAS*, 125 (1995), pp 369–427.

70 Waddell, *Prehistoric Archaeology of Ireland*.

71 Ibid.

72 J. M. Coles, 'Scottish Late Bronze Age metalwork: technology, chronology and distribution', *PSAS*, 93 (1959–60), pp 16–134.

73 J. M. Coles, 'Scottish Early Bronze Age metalwork', *PSAS,* 101 (1968–9), pp 1–110.

74 Ritchie, 'Excavations of a Cairn at Strontoller'; E. J. Peltenberg, 'Excavation of Culcharron Cairn, Benderloch, Argyll', *PSAS*, 104 (1971–2), pp 63–70; J. N. G. Ritchie et al., 'Small cairns in Argyll: some recent work', *PSAS*, 106 (1975), pp 15–38.

75 V. Ginn and S. Rathbone, *Corrstown: A Coastal Community* (Oxford, 2012).

76 I. Suddaby, 'The excavation of two Late Bronze Age roundhouses at Ballyprior Beg, Island Magee, Co. Antrim', *UJA*, third series, 61 (2003), pp 45–91; B. Ballin-Smith, 'The excavation of two Bronze Age roundhouses at Townparks, Antrim town', *UJA*, third series, 62 (2003), pp 16–44.

77 Stevenson, 'The excavation of a hut circle at Cul a'Bhaile'; Barber and Brown, 'An Sithean'.

78 P. Macdonald, N. Carver and M. Yates, 'Excavations at McIlwhans Hill, Ballyutoag, County Antrim', *UJA*, third series, 64 (2005), pp 43–61.

79 J. P. Mallory, 'Excavations at Haughey's Fort', *Emania*, 8 (1991), pp 10–26.

80 Pers. comm. Philip Macdonald.

81 I. Armit, *Celtic Scotland* (Batsford, 1997), p. 51.

82 G. Plunkett, 'Land-use patterns and cultural change in the Middle to Late Bronze Age in Ireland: inferences from pollen records', *Vegetational History and Archaeobotany,* 18 (2009), p. 292.

83 Ibid., p. 293.

84 J. Raftery, *Prehistoric Ireland* (Batsford 1951); B. G. Scott, 'Some notes on the transition from bronze to iron in Ireland', *Irish Archaeological Research Forum*, 1 (1974), pp 9–24; Waddell, *Prehistoric Archaeology of Ireland*, p. 284.

85 Scott, 'Some notes on the transition from bronze to iron in Ireland'.

86 Ibid.

87 Waddell, *Prehistoric Archaeology of Ireland*, p. 287.

88 S. Caulfield, 'The beehive quern in Ireland', *JRSAI*, 107 (1977), pp 104–39.

89 Waddell, *Prehistoric Archaeology of Ireland*, p. 323.

90 R. B. Warner, 'Beehive querns and Irish "La Tène" artefacts: a statistical test of their cultural relatedness', *JIA*, 11 (2002), pp 125–30.

91 Ibid.

92 D. M. Waterman and C. J. Lynn, *Excavations at Navan Fort Co. Armagh, 1961–71* (Belfast, 1997).

93 C. J. Lynn, 'Trial excavations at the King's Stables, Tray Townland, Co. Armagh', *UJA*, third series, 40 (1977), pp 42–62.

94 A. O'Sullivan, F. McCormick, F. Harney, J. Kinsella, T. Kerr, *Early Medieval Dwellings and Settlements in Ireland, AD 400–1100* (Oxford, 2010).

95 K. Becker, J. Ó Néill and Laura O'Flynn, 'Iron Age Ireland: finding an invisible people', Report to the Heritage Council of Ireland (2008).

96 T. McErlean, 'The archaeology of the Ulster Cycle on the north coast' in G. Toner and S. Mac Mathuna (eds), *Ulidia 3: Proceedings of the Third International Conference on the Ulster Cycle of Tales, University of Ulster, Coleraine 22–25 June, 2009* (Berlin, 2013), pp 1–16.

97 R. B. Warner, 'Ireland Ulster and Scotland in the earlier Iron Age' in A. O'Connor and D. V. Clarke (eds), *From the Stone Age to the Forty Five* (Edinburgh, 1983).

98 *Argyll: An Inventory of the Ancient Monuments, Vol. 1, Kintyre*, Royal Commission on the Ancient and Historical Monuments of Scotland (Edinburgh, 1971), p. 18.

99 D. Harding, 'The function and classification of brochs and duns' in R. Micket and C. Burgess (eds), *Between and Beyond the Walls: Essays on the Prehistory and History of North Britain in Honour of George Jobey* (Edinburgh, 1984), pp 218–9.

100 D. Harding, 'Forts, duns, brochs and crannogs: Iron Age settlements in Argyll' in Ritchie, *Archaeology of Argyll*.

101 Ibid., p. 133.

102 E. W. MacKie, 'Dun Mor Vaul revisited: fact and theory in a reappraisal of the Scottish Atlantic Iron Age' in Ritchie, *Archaeology of Argyll*.

103 Armit, *Celtic Scotland*, p. 40.

104 Piggott, *Neolithic Cultures of the British Isles*.

105 McErlean, 'The archaeology of the Ulster Cycle on the north coast'.

3

Argyll and Antrim in the Early Medieval Period

Cormac McSparron

The arrival of Christianity changes our view of the past enormously. The most significant change is that archaeologists and historians are now studying a literate society, which writes about its own culture and keeps records. We are particularly fortunate that the early activities of what we now call the 'Celtic Church' have left us with an enormous legacy of written documentary records concerning Ireland and Scotland. Although it strengthens archaeological studies to not have to rely solely on sites, bones and artefacts to attempt to understand our past, the historical sources are frequently more than just a dry factual account. Each source is both an interpretation and a polemic, none of the historical sources can be considered completely impartial and reliable. The close interrelationship of Ireland and Scotland in the Early Medieval period (*c.* AD 400 to 1200) is a constant theme of many of these documents; in fact it was during the Early Medieval period that the narrative of a conquest of northern Britain (Alba) by an Irish dynasty and the subsequent creation of the kingdom of the Scots became a very durable national origin story for the Scots, which has only really begun to be re-examined in recent decades.

Kingship in Ireland in the Early Medieval period
There were no unitary kingdoms, as we might consider them today, in either Britain or Ireland in the Early Medieval period. In the earlier part of the Early Medieval period Ireland was composed of multiple small kingdoms, called *tuath*, each technically sovereign. This is the view of Early Medieval Ireland presented in early Irish legal documents such as the *Crith Gablach* and *Uraicecht Bec*, which were composed around AD 700. They detail a complex network of local kings, over-kings and provincial kings.[1]

The availability of a series of early legal descriptions of the organisation of power and sovereignty in Ireland has cast a long shadow, however, and it has not always been realised how much this was a feature of a very ancient style of Irish monarchical organisation, which was obsolete by the later years of the Early Medieval period. Kingship in Ireland was not static and it is clear that as the Early Medieval period progressed the nature of kingship changed significantly. By the time the Normans had come to Ireland Irish kingship was very different. The Norman poetic account of

57

Key
1 Aileach/Elagh Castle
2 Dún Ceithrin/Giant's Sconce
3 Candida Casa
4 Iona
5 Bangor
6 Camus
7 Applecross
8 Nendrum
9 Armoy
10 Drumadoon
11 Deer Park Farms
12 Big Glebe
13 'Parley Hill'
14 An Dún
15 Crew Hill
16 Dunmull
17 Grianan
18 Dunadd
19 Altagore Cashel
20 Doonmore
21 Dunshammer
22 Movilla
23 Rath Luraig (Maghera)
24 Doire Chalgaigh (Derry)
25 Curran
26 Demesne
27 Ballywillin
28 Kiloran Bay
29 Colonsay

Map of Early Medieval period

their early exploits in Ireland, sometimes called the 'Song of Dermot and the Earl', gives an account of contemporary views of Irish kingship at the end of the Early Medieval period. It states that the ordinary Irish king is simply the equivalent of a 'count' in the English or French system and that it is only the provincial kings who are actual kings.[2] It is likely that, in keeping with other areas of western Europe at that time, from the eleventh century Ireland was developing a feudal economy and modern royal administrations. Gaelic sources begin to refer to simple *tuath* kings as *dux*, meaning lord in Latin, the root of the modern English word duke, implying that they are losing their royal status. The few remaining important Irish kings are promulgating laws, granting land with charters and demanding dues and military service in return.[3] Irish royal administration was beginning to develop the types of offices that typified later European monarchies, such as the steward, bailiff, head of the king's household, marshal of the king's cavalry.[4] Perhaps most significant was the post of chancellor, which seems to have appeared as early as the beginning of the eleventh century with Mael Suthain, the chancellor of Brian Boru, a development which did not appear in England until William Rufus a century later. There was a further step beyond over-kingship, the oft discussed high kingship, which is not found in the earliest legal documents, but which does seem to have had an existence by the eighth century, although it does not seem to have implied sovereignty over the whole island,[5] seeming to have had a more honorific, first amongst equals, type of meaning.

Ulster and Scotland in the Early Medieval period

Ulster, Ulaid, emerges in this era as a shrunken version of the province of Ulster, which is referred to in the myths of the Ulster Cycle. Ulaid now occupied only a fraction of its supposed traditional territory, being confined to Antrim, Down, a portion of Louth and north County Londonderry. The reason for the contraction of Ulaid appears to be the expansion of a part of a group called the Uí Neill who pushed from Connacht into Ulster from about the fifth century AD and carved out a kingdom for themselves in the west of Ulster.[6] The former vassals of the Ulaid, a group collectively known as the Airgilla, who occupied much of mid Ulster, now gave their loyalty, officially at least, to the (Northern) Uí Neill. The remainder of the Uí Neill pushed into the midlands of Ireland and carved out a kingdom there, which effectively became recognised as one of the *coiceds* (province, literally a fifth) of Early Medieval Ireland, called *Midhe* (literally the middle).[7] They are known to historians as the Southern Uí Neill.

Above, Ulster before AD 900
Below: Ulster after AD 900
(modern county boundaries shown)

Within contracted Ulster at this time there were a number of dynasties divided into two broad groups with perceived different origins. The most dominant dynasty in Ulaid were the Dál Fiatach who held land in eastern Down and were usually the over-kings of Ulaid. The Dál nAraide of Antrim and the Uí Echach Cobo of western Down also shared the over-kingship on occasion. Also in north and north-east Antrim the Dál Riada were located, they never seemed to partake in the overlordship of Ulaid, but held land in Argyll, considered by Medieval and many later historians to be the core of what was to become the kingdom of Scotland. The Dál Fiatach and the Dál Riada were, at least theoretically, part of a wider ethnic group called the Erainn by Medieval historians and genealogists.[8] The Dál nAraide and the Uí Echach Cobo were part of the group called the Cruithni by early Irish annalists and genealogists, who seem to have had some kind of relationship with the Scottish Picts.[9]

As the Early Medieval era progressed, the branch of the Northern Uí Neill known as the Cenél nEógain pushed further east completely occupying north County Londonderry by the end of the eighth century,[10] and pushing the occupants of that region, the Uí Tuirtre and their subject tribe the Fir Li, across the Bann into north Antrim. The Uí Tuirtre, with their royal family, the O'Flynns, became one of the most important, and stable, kingdoms in Ulster, surviving there for approximately 500 years, and effectively resisting de Courcy's Anglo-Normans, even inflicting severe defeats upon them. The exact extent of their power in the later years of the Early Medieval period is uncertain; by the time of the Normans, in 1176, the kings of Uí Tuirtre are described by the Annals of Ulster as kings of Uí Tuirtre, Fir Li and Dál nAraide. This reference would suggest that the Uí Tuirtre controlled all of County Antrim, apart from Dál Riada. However, it is noticeable just how few references there are to Dál Riada in the Irish Annals in the later part of the Early Medieval period. It may be that the Uí Tuirtre had managed to establish themselves by the twelfth century as the dominant power in all of County Antrim apart from a small part of south Antrim probably dominated by the Dál Fiatach from the ninth century onwards.[11]

In general, there seems to be a coalescing of power in the hands of fewer and fewer kings in this period. In fact, the power of the provincial kings was so great by the end of this era that it is doubtful how much real independence groups like the Uí Tuirtre and Dál Fiatach actually had. The reach of provincial kings was very long. In the early decades of the twelfth centuries the Mac Lochlainn kings of Aileach (Aileach is a royal site outside Londonderry used initially as a capital of the northern Uí Neill and later used poetically to mean the north of Ireland) were effectively controlling all of the north of Ireland, placing their own appointees as kings of the main territories. An example of this is in 1113 when the Domnall Ua Lochlainn is recorded in the Annals of Ulster partitioning County Down between two lineages of his own liking and keeping some land for himself. In 1130, his successor Conchobar Ua Lochlainn did the same, invading Ulaid and defeating the various Ulster kings to impose his will upon them. By 1153 Muircertach Ua Lochlainn, described in the Annals of Ulster as 'King of Ireland', felt secure enough in his power to be able to make a grant of land in Newry, County Down, to the Cistercian order.[12]

Scottish kingship in the Early Medieval period

Scotland at the beginning of written history seems like Ireland to have been composed of a number of groups which probably considered themselves independent and sovereign. Ptolemy in the second century AD mentions 12 groups living within Scotland[13] which by the proper beginning of recorded history of these islands in the sixth century, seem to be being collectively referred to by writers in Latin as the Picts and in Irish as the Cruithni, both renderings of the ancient British word Pritani.

The Picts seem to have had a kingship structure similar to the Irish at this time, with differing grades of kings, including petty kings and over-kings. Within the Pictish territory there are a number of larger districts mentioned in historical sources, which might approximate to the Irish *coiced* or province. Two of the names of these 'provinces' have come down to us, Fortrenn and Atholl.[14]

The problems of the Picts?

The obscurity of the Picts has led generations of writers to view them as romantic, exotic almost. They have been believed to be matrilineal and speaking a non-Indo-European language, marking them apart from most of Europe's peoples except the Basques, Hungarians and Finns, their remoteness insulating them from developments elsewhere. Later writers like Jackson modified this somewhat, suggesting, from an analysis of tribal and place-names names mentioned on Ptolemy's map, two Pictish provinces, a northern and southern one; the northern speaking a non-Indo-European language, the southern one speaking some variant of 'P' Celtic ('P' Celtic is the name used by linguists for the dominant set of Celtic dialects in Britain of which Welsh and Cornish survive, as opposed to 'Q' Celtic, the dominant set of Celtic dialects in Ireland and Scotland).[15] This view has been strongly challenged, however, in recent years.

Firstly, the question has to be posed, what is Scotland, or for that matter Ireland, remote from? To a writer in London or a university in the south of England perhaps Scotland and Ireland do seem remote but that does not mean they were remote to ideas, technologies, languages and even population movements two thousand years ago.[16] The idea of Scotland or Ireland being remote is essentially a product of an Anglocentric world view.

Also Jackson's analysis of Celtic and pre-Indo-European Pictish place-names has been challenged. It is suggested that Jackson fails to take into account the tendency for place-names to conservatively retain elements from earlier languages. A good example of this can be shown by the way place-name elements meaning the same thing in different languages can all be added together to make the modern place-name, such as Pendle Hill in Lancashire which means 'Hill Hill Hill', Pen being hill in Brittonic, Del meaning hill in Anglo-Saxon and Hill the modern English suffix.[17] Jackson also seems to have made a number of mistakes; place-name elements which he believed were non-Indo-European can actually be shown to be 'P' Celtic by comparison with place-names in southern Britain and Continental Europe.[18]

The presence of a pre-Indo-European language in northern and north-east Scotland is further weakened by the presence of 31 ogham stones (pillar stones with a form of writing using incisions above and below a line, believed to have originated in Ireland in the early centuries AD, loosely based on the Latin alphabet), many of which can be shown to have writing on them which is some variant of a 'P' Celtic dialect or possibly Old Irish.[19] In fact, there seems to be little, if any, evidence for a non-Indo-European language being spoken in Scotland at any time in the first millennia after Christ. That is not to say that there may not be survival of earlier words and place-name elements; there is a for instance a suggestion of the survival of a pre-Indo-European substratum in Gaelic and other languages also,[20] but there seems little evidence to suggest that the Picts actually spoke a non-Indo European language.

Another exotic aspect of Pictish culture which was believed to have marked them off from the rest of the societies in these islands was their supposed matrilineality, or inheritance through the female line. In such a system a king's sons would not inherit his father's title but rather his maternal uncle's son, his cousin. The belief that the Picts were matrilineal was initially based upon a passage in Bede which recounts an ancient tale stating that that when the Picts first migrated from their supposed homeland in Scythia they landed first in the northern parts of Ireland, where they requested the right to settle, which was refused. It was suggested that they move from Ireland to Scotland, which they did. The Picts, however, had migrated to Ireland with no women and requested women from the men of Ireland who provided them with wives on condition that in future in the case of a questionable succession that succession would be through the female rather than male line.[21] Irish versions of Bede's tale, such as that of Mael Mura of Othain, were being composed from the ninth century.[22] This became the dominant and unchallenged narrative of Pictish succession that 'every schoolboy knows'. However, this lynchpin of Pictish separateness has been challenged in recent years also. Recent analyses of Pictish king lists suggest that direct father to son succession is rare, but then it is also rare amongst the Irish. Smyth believes that Pictish matrilineality is based on a misreading of Bede and an uncritical acceptance of later Irish texts which had a political agenda. He believes that the system was cognatic, as in Early Medieval Ireland, with several dynasties, within a prescribed royal family, no more than few generations descended from a previous king, competing for the kingship.[23]

Evans has suggested that the controversy about Pictish succession really refers to the Pictish over-kingship and that the succession rules for it were different than for other Pictish kingdoms.[24] He suggests that the over-kingship was effectively shared by several royal lineages with a set of loose rules and beliefs about appropriateness with a prohibition on direct father to son succession, and that succession to an appropriate candidate may be through a matrilineal or patrilineal route as appropriate. It was in effect a way of having an over-kingship without upsetting any dominant dynasty or allowing any dynasty to become too powerful. This succession was changing by the early eighth century with the dynasty of Oengus Mac Fergusso mostly dominating the over-kingship of the Picts for the next century. From the time of Cinead MacAlpin in the ninth century, who is traditionally viewed as a Dál Riadic king who 'conquered' Pictland (but who may in actuality have been of mixed Gaelic and Pictish background), succession seems to have followed Gaelic patterns, although there still seems to be a prohibition on direct father to son succession. This has been neatly explained by the historian Alex Woolf who suggests that the Cinead dynasty had two main lines which shared the kingship on a rotating basis, in the same manner as the kingship of Tara (the high kingship) was shared at the same time by the two branches, northern and southern, of the Uí Neill for several centuries until this arrangement broke down in the tenth century.[25]

'Semen est in Albania': the Dál Riada in Scotland

A new group had entered Scotland by the fifth century who have been a focus for historical study and debate ever since. The Dál Riada held land in north and north-east Antrim. Sometime during the early centuries AD they seem to have taken possession of land in Argyll also. There are two narrative traditions regarding the Dál Riada, which like all Early Medieval traditions of Ireland and Scotland, are to some extent contradictory.

The earliest tradition is called by historians the 'Reuda Tradition' and comes to us from Bede. Bede tells how,

> They came from Ireland under their leader Reuda and won lands among the Picts either by friendly treaty or by the sword. These they still possess. They are still called Dalreudini after this leader.[26]

Bede wrote these words in the 730s and it is likely that he was able to draw on Gaelic informants, Adomnan, the abbot of Iona and biographer of Colm Cille, being personally known to Bede.[27] This tradition accrued extra dimensions and detail in time but the core of a warlike migration by Reuda remained in all of them.

The second tradition is called by historians 'The Sons of Erc Tradition'. This version accepts the name of the eponymous ancestor Reuda but focuses on the role of the sons of Erc, a fifth-century king of Irish Dál Riada, and specifically his son Fergus, in the taking of part of Scotland by the Dál Riada. This is the account mentioned most commonly in the Annals of Ulster, the Tripartite Life of St Patrick and the Early Medieval history and census of Scottish Dál Riada, the *Senchus Fer nAlban* (History of the men of Alba (that is Scotland)).

This account has been criticised as being an invention by Scottish monarchs of the mid-tenth century who wanted to emphasise the importance of Dál Riada and the Scots because it suited their own dynastic purposes.[28] There seems little doubt that the Scottish kings from the tenth until at least the fourteenth century wanted to emphasise their Irish ancestry, and, at least until the reign of Alexander II in the early thirteenth century, downplay the significance of the Picts in the formation of the core of the emerging kingdom. By the mid-tenth century, and possibly from as early as the time of Cinead MacAlpin (Kenneth MacAlpine), the country that was becoming Scotland, was ruled by a dynasty (or two scions of a dynasty) which was culturally Gaelic, and possibly Gaelic by descent or of mixed Gaelic and Pictish descent, who wished to provide an impressive a Gaelic pedigree as any of the great dynasties of Ireland. Scottish rulers continued to do the same for several centuries, with the coronation ceremony of Alexander III emphasising his Irish ancestry in 1243 and even later, in his address to the 'Irish Princes' in 1314, Robert Bruce would state that, given the ties of history and culture 'stemming from one seed of birth', between the two lands, his envoy would be able to negotiate on his behalf with a view to 'permanently strengthening and maintaining inviolate the special friendship between us and you so that with God's will *our* nation may be able to recover her ancient liberty'. Bruce used the Latin phrase *nostra nacio*, indicating that he is talking collectively about Ireland and Scotland as 'our nation'.[29]

The first time Scotland actually conceived of itself, without reference to Ireland, probably came with the 1320 Declaration of Arbroath.[30] Some archaeologists have gone farther and suggested that the entire history of a Dál Riadic migration from Ireland is part of this post tenth-century historical revision,[31] citing also that there is lack of archaeological evidence for an Irish invasion of Scotland. However, Campbell seems unaware that there are several elements of both Dál Riada accounts, the Reuda account and the Sons of Erc account, which can be shown to exist in *much* earlier historical documents and it seems certain, from documentary evidence alone, that there is some sort of conquest or settlement in Argyll by the Dál Riada.[32] Also Campbell's analysis of the archaeological evidence for an Irish invasion/migration is simplistic. In recent decades anthropologists have studied the mechanisms of migrations and population movements and suggested that what archaeologists have traditionally expected in a migration, i.e. that the material culture of the home country appears in the destination country of the migrants, rarely happens in real life.[33] In fact in the real world migrants, whether peacefully settling or using the sword, are more likely to rapidly adopt the material culture of the society they migrate to rather than bring their pots, houses and metalwork with them. Furthermore, what material cultural evidence there is for migration is more likely to be found in the original homeland, where returning migrants may bring goods and artefacts from their new life back to the 'auld country'. In the case of the Dál Riada the migration was probably made by a group of highly motivated warriors. Did they bring their pots and pans, craftsmen and women and metalworkers with them, build houses and settlements anew? Or did they carve out a kingdom, seize the homes and forts of the vanquished and use the craftsmen of the indigenous population? The latter seems more likely. In fact, as will be discussed in more detail below, this is what we seem to be able to see in the archaeological record of County Antrim in the Early Medieval period.

The Cruithni

If it is the case that archaeologists have only referred to the areas of commonality between the Scottish and Irish archaeological records in passing then they have only addressed the Cruithni in the most fleeting of references. This is in part because the Cruithni are hard to discuss, the evidence relating to them sparse and contradictory. Some writers, from outside the ranks of professional historians or archaeologists, such as Dr Ian Adamson and Michael Hall have addressed them.[34] They researched their topic well and made interesting suggestions, but they have linked the question of the Cruithni, with the recent history of Northern Ireland, not of itself an unreasonable thing to do, but in a way which many archaeologists have felt uncomfortable engaging with. It is not so much that archaeologists and historians have either agreed or disagreed with their conclusions – some have vehemently disagreed, but others have been more supportive – it is more that archaeologists in general have since the Second World War era, taken the position that the ancient past 'is a foreign country' which, while interesting for academic reasons, and with lessons for humanity in how we manage the present and future, cannot, or should not, be directly related to contemporary political events. In the past archaeologists have watched and in some cases assisted political ideologies create self-serving narratives by a selective use of archaeological and historical information. In short, archaeologists have felt uncomfortable with the polemic nature of Adamson's and Hall's work, even though the actual works themselves have been moderate and, arguably, reasonable in some of their conclusions. The blind spot that archaeologists have had in this direction has with time become more apparent. A re-evaluation, by professional historians and archaeologists, of the Cruithni and their contribution to our shared archaeological and historical heritage is now due.

As discussed above, at the outset of the Early Medieval period the Irish population was split up into approximately 150 small kingdoms called *tuath*. These *tuath* were grouped together in a number of ways, both geographically and by supposed descent. They were grouped geographically into over kingdoms, like Ulaid, but they were also grouped collectively by presumed origin; the distribution of the groups collected in this way was not necessarily concentrated in one area of the island but could be spread much more widely. Cruithni was the collective name for one of these groups of supposed common origin.

In the geographical entity of Ulaid or Ulster (which for most of the Early Medieval period approximated to Antrim, Down and north Louth), there were a number of *tuath*, including the Dál Riada, the Dál nAraide, the Dál Fiatach, Uí Echach Cobo and the Conaille Muirthemne. Within Ulster these *tuath* were also divided into two broad groups. The Dál Riada and Dál Fiatach belonged to a group called the Érainn (who may have at one stage spoken their own language called by Medieval Irish writers *Iarnberle*).[35] The others belonged to the Cruithni, although in their attempts to retain and advance their political influence within Ulster some of these tuath, like the Dál nAraide and the Conaille Muirthemne, were keen to downplay this in later years. Other groups of Cruithni were known outside Early Medieval Ulaid, in particular in north Londonderry where it is known that the Cruithni held the fort at Dún Ceithrin,[36] and possibly also Aileach.[37] It is likely that Cruithni, probably the Dál nAraide, held most of north Londonderry until at least the middle decades of the seventh century AD. There are further references to groups of Cruithni, the Sogain and Lóigise, in Leinster.[38]

The Early Medieval Irish Annals refer to the Cruithni many times, frequently as a shorthand for the Dál nAraide, who on occasion were able to wrest the kingship of east Ulster from their non-Cruithni Dál Fiatach overlords. The name Cruithni has been shown by philologists to be derived from the same word as the term Pict, which was the collective name for a number of the peoples of Early Medieval Scotland. Interestingly, the Irish Annals on a number of instances refer to Scottish Picts as Cruithni, or similar, suggesting that at least to these Medieval annalists the two could be viewed as similar and related groups. In the early twentieth century a number of historians, like Eoin MacNeill for instance, held that the Cruithni and Picts must at some stage have been part of the same population group, a view which was partially challenged by O'Rahilly who emphasised that although the Irish annals sometimes referred to Scottish Picts as Cruithni, they never referred to any Irish groups as being Picts.[39]

Many of the objections which have traditionally been used by historians to differentiate the Picts from the Cruithni, have been shown to be rather less certain than once thought. The idea of the Picts as particularly remote, barbarous and backward has been shown to have been the deeply flawed product of Anglocentric scholarship. Even the supposed matrilineal succession of the Picts has been persuasively challenged. When all aspects of Pictish life are looked at there are few areas where they do not look similar to contemporary groups in Ireland.

One point which should be born in mind is that looking for an 'origin point' in archaeology or history is often futile. Trying to define such a time and place is impossible because of the ever changing and fluid nature of identity. Identity is not imposed from above; it is rather a manifestation of the collective consciousness of the group, informed, although not necessarily completely controlled, by an elite cadre of opinion makers. An example of how fluid concepts of identity may actually be, even within the Cruithni themselves, can be shown by how they sponsored professional genealogists in the later centuries of the Early Middle Ages to create for themselves fabricated genealogies, linking themselves to the origin characters of other dynasties and by default downplaying their Cruithni heritage. They seem to have done this both to bolster claims of the Dál nAraide to the kingship of Ulster and also to allow the Conaille Muirthemne to associate themselves with Conall Cernach, after Cú Chulainn the most famous of the heroes of the Ulster Cycle stories.[40] In other words they redefined how they viewed themselves to suit the political world in which they found themselves. Bearing this in mind it must be realised that in any attempt to pin down an aboriginal Cruithni (or for that matter any other grouping), the quarry may be equally a chimera invented for expedience or temporary advantage, part of a continual process of redefinition and reinvention. These points made, however, there is certainly something here worth investigating further.

One area of contrast between the Picts and the Cruithni appears to be language. We now know that that the Picts almost certainly spoke a 'P' Celtic language, similar to that of the ancient Britons. (Celtic languages are divided into two groups based on aspects of their pronunciation. One group are called the 'P' Celtic languages and include Pictish, ancient Gaulish, ancient British and modern Welsh and Cornish. The other group are called 'Q' Celtic languages as they render the P sound, as a Q or hard C sound, and include Irish and Scot's Gaelic and Manx.) The Cruithni in Ulster, however, appear to have spoken the 'Q' Celtic, Gaelic, from the time of the earliest records we have.

The question of how the Cruithni and the Picts appear to have spoken a different, albeit related, language is central to whether we can propose that at one stage they were part of a group or tribal confederacy which had a shared identity. One suggestion, originally proposed by O'Rahilly, is that Gaelic is a relatively late comer in Ireland and that other languages, including a 'P' Celtic language similar to Pictish, were spoken in Ireland prior to the arrival or emergence of Gaelic.[41] O'Rahilly evidences this with surviving Early Medieval Irish scholarly accounts of languages which were then in the process of dying out in Ireland, with in some cases the original monastic authors giving a few examples of their vocabulary. He also suggests that the evidence from Ptolemy's map, a second-century AD map of the world, shows 'P' Celtic place-names in Ireland. O'Rahilly believed that a 'P' Celtic language was the language spoken by a first wave of 'Celtic' invaders arriving in Iron Age Ireland. He sees the Cruithni as survivors of this first wave and the Gaelic language as the language of the last wave of Celtic invaders, coming from northern mainland Europe and effectively achieving dominance over the earlier waves of invaders. This process of Celtic invasions O'Rahilly sees as taking two or three centuries and being complete by between 150 and 50 BC.

As mentioned above, the idea of Celtic invasions, or even large-scale peaceful settlement, has fewer supporters amongst modern scholars than it once did. Many scholars doubt also O'Rahilly's time-frame for the appearance of Celtic languages in Ireland. Koch for instance proposes the concept of 'cumulative Celticity' for Ireland, where the island gradually absorbs little pieces of wider European culture through a mixture of trade, exchange, marriage, migration and war over many centuries, arriving at a culture which looks very 'Celtic' by the early centuries AD and speaks one, or more, Celtic languages, but which has never had a huge settlement or invasion of 'Celts', still less a succession of several waves of invasions and which has great continuity with earlier prehistoric population groups.[42] One could propose a similar series of events for Scotland.

The question of how languages spread and replace older languages is complex and there are many mechanisms by which it could happen. One mechanism is invasion, another large-scale peaceful settlement. Geographically close groups, in regular contact, but not necessarily speaking the same language, may form a kind of pidgin language and this has been suggested as a way in which Gaelic might have emerged in the North Channel area,[43] a lingua franca which eventually became the language of the entire population. However, if the North Channel area was the cockpit of this development why did Gaelic as a language make swifter progress in Ireland than in central and eastern Scotland? Also, where did the 'Q' Celtic nature of Gaelic come from if there were not 'Q' Celtic speakers on either side of the North Channel? It seems that there must have been some sort of group who entered Ireland in the late prehistoric period who used 'Q' Celtic. This group may not have changed Ireland culturally very much; it was likely to be a group operating in the same 'Celtic' cultural milieu as the indigenous groups, and it might be very difficult to identify archaeologically, but it does seem to have left a lasting legacy by contributing a 'Q' Celtic language to both Ireland and Scotland. This group, who become known as the Gaels (a term which originally referred to a small part of the Irish population, but which by the Later Middle Ages was the term being used for most of the population of Ireland and Scotland) may not have conquered Ireland but may have had sufficient cultural energy to make other groups want to emulate them. We can see the effects of this emulation by the way groups like the Erainn and the Cruithni are by the later centuries of the Early Middle Ages keen to see genealogies written which give them spurious links to one or other of the sons of the mythical ancestor of these early Gaels, Milesius or Mil, even though they had no real claim to descent from them.

The method utilised by these early Gaels to achieve cultural influence over other groups seems to have been, at least in part, good propaganda. They realised the value of controlling the output of the monastic scriptoria, the Annals of Ulster, for instance, are full of re-edits and later insertions into accounts of early events to suit the agenda and prestige of the Uí Neill, who claimed descent from Mil. It is also possible that the early Gaels were more hierarchical in their social structure than the other contemporary groups within Ireland. Concentration of power by elites and conspicuous consumption by unashamed warrior aristocrats may have caused considerable competition amongst different peoples of Ireland but in a cultural and linguistic climate constructed by the early Gaels. The practice of fostering, a common custom amongst the aristocrats of Medieval Ireland and Scotland, is likely to have rapidly accelerated this process. By the time of the earliest written scholarly accounts of Ireland and Irish life from the eighth century, Gaelic was the dominant language, the language of the aristocrats of all backgrounds not just the supposed descendants of Milesius, but earlier languages may have survived for a time in the lower echelons of society.

The Cruithni in Ireland may have found their language eroded by the cultural success of Gaelic without necessarily any conquest or subjugation, simply emulation, as they were still viewed as a free people by Early Medieval writers. In Scotland this may not have happened until the arrival of the Dál Riada, who were themselves Erainn, but who had adopted the

Gaelic cultural and linguistic package, and spread Gaelic into Scotland with an extra weapon in their arsenal, the Christian church. Within a few centuries, despite being outnumbered, and sometimes out-fought, by the Picts, the Dál Riada had planted the Gaelic language and culture, along with Christianity, as the core cultural values of Scotland, not to be challenged until the fourteenth century.

It is difficult to be certain about the true nature or the Cruithni or the Picts for the sources are too distant, too reworked and too edited, even in the Early Medieval period, but it seems most probable that the Cruithni and Picts may have at one stage believed themselves to have had a common ancestry and that the two names Cruithni and Pict are versions of a common collective term used to describe both. It is possible that at one stage they spoke the same 'P' Celtic language, and probably shared a similar social structure and customs. It is interesting that this original collective term, albeit altered by time, is found in both islands. It is especially interesting when we consider, as noted above, that some of the sites closely associated with the Cruithni, such as Dún Ceithrin in north Londonderry, the Giant's Sconce,[44] also seem to display attributes usually associated with Scottish Iron Age settlements.[45] This suggests that there may have been in the later prehistoric period a cultural continuum across Ulster and the west of Scotland which had some kind of name for itself, some sense of identity. It is unlikely that this group had any political unity and may have rubbed shoulders, even then, on both sides of the North Channel with groups which self-identified differently, such as the Erainn Dál Riada for instance. Ultimately it is probable that the distinction between the Cruithni/Picts and the other groups in the region was superficial. That they had differing identities at all may have been more the shifting expediencies of the ruling elite of these peoples rather than any deep-seated cultural differences.

The story of the Cruithni is illustrative of the deep connections between Antrim, Argyll and their surrounding regions. They are not an exception to be singled out as a period when Ulster, and for that matter Ireland, and Scotland were especially close, they are rather the default position, the way things seem to have been in most historical periods.

The Church in Ireland and Scotland in the Early Medieval period

The early church in Ireland

Settlement of the Dál Riada in Scotland was not the only route for cultural influence from Ireland in the Early Medieval period. The Church was also an important conduit for transmission of cultural ideas across the North Channel. The history of the Christianisation of Ireland and Scotland and the development of the Christian church there is different from that of much of Europe. In Europe the church found itself by the end of the fourth century the church of the empire. From southern Britain to Asia Minor and the Mediterranean a similar church structure, of diocese and bishops, was found in each Roman province. Ireland and northern Scotland never became part of this empire. It was, at the time of the appearance of Christianity, a society of small kings with a lesser number of greater over-kings who obtained loyalty from the lesser kings.

The conversion of Ireland was not as rapid as Patrick's biographers would have us believe. Patrick was probably not the earliest Christian in Ireland – there probably were Christian communities before he came to Ireland – but he did make an enormous impact, especially in the north where it is likely the fewest Christians were. However, by the end of his mission Ireland was still largely a pagan island, and it is likely that it was not a predominantly Christian country until the seventh century.[46] One of the ways in which Christianity advanced in Ireland was through monasticism. Initially Patrick had set up a standard secular church in Ireland upon the lines which would have been familiar to anyone in contemporary Christendom. Up until the middle of the sixth century it is likely that monasticism did not play a great part in Irish Christian life, the Irish annals note 25 bishops, but only one abbot in this era.[47] Between 549 and 600 this changes completely – 13 bishops and 17 abbots are mentioned in the Irish annals for these years. After 600 the number of bishops mentioned in the annals begins to be swamped by the number of abbots. This shows a major change in Irish Christianity. Early Irish monastic documents claim that both British monasticism and a monastic influence brought from the eastern Mediterranean via Gaul and Britain to Ireland were responsible for introducing monasticism to Ireland. There is no reason why both cannot have been important, with foundations like Candida Casa in Galloway and Welsh monasticism, which Bede suggests was growing rapidly in the sixth century AD, possible points of contact.

The reasons for the growth of monasticism in Ireland are partly spiritual – it obviously caught the zeitgeist of the place and the era – but also economic. Monasteries required land; in these the opening years of Early Medieval Ireland concepts of land holding made it difficult for an aristocrat or even a king to give away land to a monastery, for the king was the custodian of the kingdom's land not its absolute owner. To get around this, gifts of land to a monastery were normally made in such a way that the monastery was then tied to the kin group or dynasty which gave it away, usually through the abbot being a member of the family of the royal or aristocratic group giving them the land. In practice, the monastery was given a pre-existing estate, where the old tenants stayed on as (married) lay monks, where the abbot was frequently married (hereditary abbacies were common), and where a smaller number of deeply pious, celibate, aesthetics, lived a fuller monastic life. In undergoing this change the Christian church managed to accommodate itself to the different structures of Irish society and become, not just an important, but a completely integrated and vital part of it.

The spread of Irish monasticism to Scotland

Although there were Christian communities in southern Scotland, such as at Candida Casa, the main thrust of Christianity in Argyll and the rest of northern and western Scotland came from Ireland. Typically the great Irish monastic houses wanted to set up daughter houses, often in areas where there were few or no Christians at that time. These daughter houses became known as the monastic *paruchiae*. Two of the most important monastic *paruchiae* had their origins in Ulster: the *paruchiae* of the monasteries of Iona and Bangor, established by Colm Cille and Comgall respectively.

Iona was founded by Colm Cille, a senior aristocratic member of the Cenél Conaill, a branch of the northern Uí Neill. He left Ireland as an act of penance and went to Scottish Dál Riada where he founded a monastery on the unidentified island of Hinba, before setting up his more famous foundation on Iona, possibly around 563, although it has been suggested that an earlier ecclesiastical foundation had been founded by Oran there in 548 and that Gabrain, the king of Dál Riada, had been buried there in 560.[48] The *Vita Columbae* tells how from there Colum Cille travelled and preached to the Picts in the northern parts of Scotland along the Great Glen and the Moray Firth, meeting the Pictish king, Bridei. Bede credits Colum Cille with the conversion of the northern Picts, saying the Picts received them from Iona; it is likely that Bede had Pictish informants.[49] One of his most important acts was his active sponsorship of the kingdom of Dál Riada; he may have presided at the coronation of Aedan macGabrain, the king of Dál Riada, in 574, and may have picked Eochaid Buide, his successor while Aedan was still alive.[50] It is also possible that he played an active role in the politics of later sixth-century Ireland.

St Comgall was Ulster's other great monastic founder, who established the monastery at Bangor, a monastery which, every bit as much as Iona, was one of the great seats of European monasticism, and in particular was responsible for much of the learning with which we associate what has become known by later historians and archaeologists as the Celtic Church. Unfortunately, there is not a single biographical source for Comgall and Bangor in the way that we have for Colum Cille and Iona. There are, however, numerous documents and entries in annals which tell us much about the monastery and its famous founder. One set of important documents concerning Bangor and St Comgall is the Bangor Antiphonary;

it has survived because at some stage in the Early Medieval period it was brought to a daughter house of Bangor at Bobbio in Italy, founded by that other great monastic founder Columbanus, who was trained at Bangor and who left to found monasteries in continental Europe. The Bangor Antiphonary, along with a number of hymns and prayers used at Bangor, lists the names of all the first 15 abbots of Bangor from Comgall to Cronan, with a brief note regarding the character and works of each one. Most of these abbots have corresponding obituaries in the Irish annals.[51]

The Irish annals mention Bangor on numerous occasions. In most cases the mention is a simple reference to the death of an abbot or other senior monastic figure. On a few occasions more detail is given. The first noticeable point is that there are more annalistic references to the first few centuries of Bangor, from its foundation by Comgall around 555/6. A significant early event was the burning of the monastery in 616/7 which is mentioned in all the main annals. No group or culprit is identified making this likely to have been an accident, not an unlikely event in a monastery presumably constructed from wood. The later church buildings appear to have been stone, however, with the murder of a king of Ulster there in 1065 in the 'stone church at Beannchair' being recorded in the Annals of Ulster. Violence seems to have come to Bangor on several occasions during its history. The first occasion may have been its plundering 'by the heathens', meaning the Vikings, in 822, according to the Annals of the Four Masters, or 824 according to the Annals of Ulster and the Annals of Inishfallen, and again in 958 when the Vikings killed the abbot. The Annals of Ulster does not make further reference to Bangor after this event, save the 1065 murder. It also makes no reference to any of Bangor's daughter houses and generally seems to downplay Bangor's importance. This is probably a reflection of the Armagh-based Annals' support for the Cenél nEógain branch of the Uí Neill, the emerging force in central Ulster which was to dominate Ulster from this point until the seventeenth century. The Annals of the Four Masters, a late compilation of Gaelic learning and annalistic sources compiled in the early seventeenth century had a different political bias and it regularly recounts the deaths of abbots of Bangor through the tenth century, with the death of one abbot, Colman, noted for 1058, and a final record of the death of Sitric, abbot of Bangor recorded in the Annals of the Four Masters for 1211.

The general impression from the annals collectively, is that Bangor's best days were in the pre-Viking era, perhaps not surprising for a foundation with a largely maritime *paruchia*, and that it does not seem to have been as noteworthy in the later part of the Early Medieval period. The Annals of the Four Masters also give hints at the spread of Bangor's influence, mentioning the Bangor daughter houses of Camus (Macosquin, County Londonderry) and Applecross in the west of Ross, Scotland, founded by the Bangor monk St Mael Ruba. He left Ireland in 671, possibly forming the monastery in 673 and a number of other churches on the way.[52] From there he headed out to preach the gospel in the Hebrides, about which much folklore still survives, and then east into Moray, founding churches as far as Keith.[53] He died in 721, allegedly the victim of Vikings, although they did not become active until many decades later.

The archaeology of the Early Medieval church in Antrim and Argyll
The physical form of church sites in Early Medieval Antrim and Argyll is similar, as it is for Ireland and Scotland more widely. As discussed above, the earliest churches were probably of diocesan character but in the sixth century the parish structure of the earliest Irish Christianity became replaced by a largely monastic church better fitted to the structure of society. It is at this time that this church of distinctive character is exported to Scotland.

It has been suggested that the earliest Irish monastic centres were unenclosed, but by the seventh century all monastic centres seem to have been surrounded by one or more banks, frequently with ditches and stone walls, separating the monastery from the world beyond.[54] Edwards has argued that the desire to protect relics and graves lay behind this enclosure, but that a biblically-based ideology and concepts of differing levels of sacredness were being reflected in the multiple zones and enclosures around some larger monasteries.[55] Inside the innermost enclosure there seems to have been a church, the monastic cemetery and, in some cases at least, a round tower, as can be seen in the layout of the inner enclosure at Nendrum, County Down.[56] Outer enclosures, if present, may have contained cells of individual monks and areas of craft-working. Although hard to substantiate archaeologically, there may be a division of space based on the status of the monks in each zone; celibate anchorites, bishops, abbots, married or unmarried, lay brothers, married Christian tenants, may have had right of access to some parts of the monastery and had their access to other areas restricted or not permitted, according to their status. The structure of wider Gaelic society may have been, almost unconsciously, reflected in the organisation of space within these foundations. Excavations of monastic sites in Ireland and Scotland have been limited. Some of the excavations, like Lawlor's excavation at Nendrum in the early 1900s, were carried out in a very unscientific manner and vast amounts of vital data were lost to archaeology. Two sites that have had modern scientific excavations carried out at them are both within what was Dál Riada: the monasteries at Armoy and Iona.

Excavation at Armoy, County Antrim

A small portion of the Early Medieval monastery at St Patrick's Church Armoy, County Antrim, was excavated by the Centre for Archaeological Fieldwork at Queen's in 2005.[57] A church was, according to the Tripartite Life of St Patrick, founded by St Olcan, a fifth-century disciple of Patrick, at Armoy. The location of the church is significant, being sited both along the great north road called the *Sli Mid Luachra*, which ran from Tara, County Meath, to Dunseverick County Antrim, and at the traditional border of Dál Riada with Dál nAraide. Despite enormous disturbance from tree roots to the north of the site, the excavations uncovered evidence for an ancient enclosing ditch around the modern church and its accompanying eleventh- or twelfth-century round tower. The ditch had been recut on at least one occasion and when it silted up was replaced by a stone wall. Inside the ditch the remains of a stone hearth, probably at the centre of an otherwise destroyed building was found. Close to this hearth was a souterrain, which may have attached to the now demolished building. Also inside the enclosure were a number of gullies, pits, footings of a probable Later Medieval stone building and a number of Post-Medieval burials. Radiocarbon dating suggests that the earliest activity at the site dated to between AD 420 to 550, compatible with the monastery's origin story of a Patrician-era foundation, with the ditch surrounding the site first dug between AD 605 and 665. The ditch was re-dug and remodelled between AD 710 and 890. The hearth was dated to between AD 890 and 990. There was evidence for Early Medieval craft working at the edge of the monastery in the form of iron furnaces located in the partly silted enclosure ditch and a workshop for the manufacture of lignite bracelets where hundreds of partially made bracelets and waste lignite chips were found. The site may have become abandoned for a time at the end of Medieval period when an iron furnace seems to have taken advantage of the draft provided by the disused souterrain, before being used as a parish church from the seventeenth century onwards.

At Iona there are no surviving above ground early monastic structures, with most of the upstanding remains being much later, but there have been a number of excavations there which have shed some light on the early monastery. There is a large, sub-rectangular enclosure visible from aerial photographs at Iona, surrounding the centre of the monastery, occupied by later buildings. In addition, there are multiple other banks and enclosures. Barber's excavations of the ditch around the monastery[58] indicate that, like Armoy, the ditch was probably built in the early seventh century and that it rapidly filled up, becoming in time a shallow depression. Environmental evidence from Barber's dig shows that it was probably supplemented by a hedge of elder, hawthorn and holly. The replacement of the ditch at Armoy with a low stone wall may also suggest a dry stone wall surmounted by a hedge also. A large circular post-built building was also uncovered and waterlogged wood from the ditch showed worked oak timbers typical of the type used in Irish-style Early Medieval constructions. The likely presence of an Irish-style watermill has been uncovered during excavations by O'Sullivan in Iona with the finding of gullies, depressions and evidence for timber buildings in the appropriately named *Sruth a' Mhuilinn* area within the monastery.[59] Evidence for craft-working of metal and glass, of approximately seventh-century date, has also been found during a number of excavations in the 1970s.[60]

There are also a number of well-preserved small monasteries or hermitages in the Inner Isles. These, presumably because of the lack of wood for building on these islands, used stone construction, with stone walls, stone monks cells and small stone churches; examples are Sgor nam Ban-Naomha, on the more northerly island of Canna, where a number of rectangular and circular structures and small cells are enclosed within a stone enclosure wall, and Eileach an Naoimh on the Garvellach Isles where well preserved stone monks cells are found along with monastic terraced fields and a circular stone-walled graveyard. In general, these small hermitages are more reminiscent of the types of small monastic sites found in and off the coast of Kerry. Similar sites are not known from Antrim or east Ulster, although this may have more to do with the greater availability of wood in this area, and the subsequent difficulty for archaeologists in detecting them, than anything else.

Early Medieval settlement in Ulster and Scotland
The predominant settlement type of Early Medieval Ireland is the ringfort. These are the defended farmsteads of wealthy farmers and aristocrats of the era. They are approximately circular enclosed settlements, not especially large, typically with an internal diameter of around 30m, although there are many larger and smaller examples. They come in two main types, the *rath,* an earthen ringfort, composed of a ditch and a bank cast up from it, and the *cashel*, a stone-walled ringfort. Ringforts are found across the whole of the Irish landscape with only very upland or low-lying areas entirely excluded from ringfort distribution. There are some areas of relatively higher or lower density which may be partly accounted for by different landholding systems – for instance, ringforts may be less common on land owned by the church – but which was probably influenced by a range of other factors also.[61] They are also *very* numerous: there are at least 45,000 ringforts known from Ireland which are either still extant or which have had their presence recorded, prior to their destruction, by early map makers, the Ordnance Survey or similar.[62] There seems to be no evidence for rath construction in the Iron Age in Ireland, that is, before about AD 400, and the evidence from the now significant body of radiocarbon-dating evidence is that most ringforts were constructed between AD 600 and 1000.[63]

The interior of the typical ringfort has been revealed by quite a large number of excavations. Although not all raths show evidence for complex internal structures – in fact it is possible that some may never have functioned as more than cattle kraals[64] – most do seem to have been settlements in which there was one or more houses and a number of outhouses and ancillary buildings. The houses within the ringforts were circular in the earlier period, up to approximately AD 800, but rectangular after that date.[65] Within ringforts aristocratic houses were significantly larger than those of the middle class.[66] The poor probably lived in yet smaller houses in unenclosed settlements.[67]

Souterrains are frequently found within ringforts and sometimes on their own, not within a ringfort. These are stone-lined and stone-roofed tunnels. They are typically 20–30m in length, sometimes with more than one passage and chamber. Communication between the parts of the souterrain is generally restricted by one or more constrictions, sometimes called creeps, where the user has to crawl or even slide on his or her belly through the opening. Souterrains are generally believed to have been used for defence, and it seems, especially given the presence of creeps within them, that they were used as such. However, it has been noted at sites like Drumadoon, County Antrim,[68] where a souterrain was found on an elevated Early Medieval settlement, that the entrance passage, leading into the souterrain, before passing through the creep, was constructed of very finely dressed dry stone walls, with very flat schist lintels picked for the roof. However, beyond the creep, in the portion of the souterrain designed as a refuge chamber, the stone work was much coarser, with large boulders used for the side walls and huge basaltic blocks utilised to make the roof. It was also noted that the base of the entrance passage was strewn with large fragments of wide but shallow pottery vessels, whereas only a few small pieces of pottery were found within the refuge chamber. The conclusion of the excavators was that the entrance passage had been used as a cold store, it was large, stone-lined and underground, and as such was cool and perfect for the storage of food. As somewhere which was going to be accessed frequently, it was designed to be functional but pleasant, which is why it had much finer stonework than the more utilitarian refuge chamber beyond the creep.

Within the *rath* class there are two further major sub-divisions related to status. There are raths which have more than one surrounding bank and ditch, which are called *multi-vallate raths*; these were the traditional settlements of the higher classes of Early Medieval Irish farmers. *Raised raths* are raths constructed on an earthen platform, which either accrues gradually over centuries leading to the final phase of occupation being constructed on an already elevated mound, such as that found at Deer Park Farms, County Antrim,[69] or a platform deliberately built to accommodate an elevated settlement, such as Big Glebe, County Londonderry.[70] Thom Kerr has argued persuasively that raised raths were the possessions of successful farmers who farmed good quality land with the emphasis on cereal production rather than the more traditional livestock farming of Early Medieval Ireland.[71] He has noted that the radiocarbon evidence suggests that the raised rath is somewhat later than the multi-vallate rath, with most multi-vallate raths dating to before AD 750 and most raised raths dating to after that date, and that the raised rath replaces the multi-vallate rath as the settlement site of choice for the upper classes.

These settlement sites formed the centres of farms which carried out both pastoral and arable farming. The prevalence of cereal growing seems to have been underestimated by historians and archaeologists of Early Modern Ireland until recent years. The finding of large numbers of water-powered mills from recent developer-led excavations archaeological excavations in the Republic of Ireland now gives an indication that cereal crops must have been grown on a much larger scale than previously realised.[72] These water-powered mills were usually located in low-lying waterlogged areas and consequently are frequently well preserved allowing archaeologists to realise the complexity of their construction and the sophistication of the bearings and turbines used within them. The presence of preserved oak beams has allowed many of the mills to be dated using the technique of tree ring dating or dendrochronology. The earliest mill so far encountered is from Nendrum, on the Ards peninsula, County Down, the timbers of which have been shown to have been cut in AD 619.[73] Mill building continued through the eighth and ninth centuries with a peak in mill construction in the middle of the ninth century.[74] The scale of cereal production at this time is shown by the excavations of an Early Medieval enclosure at Raytown, County Meath, where eight watermills were found, indicating industrial production and milling of grains.[75] Although no similar sites on quite this scale have yet been discovered in Ulster, it seems likely that they will be found here too. The accumulated evidence of the emergence of raised raths from the mid eighth century and a building boom in watermills in the eighth and ninth centuries is leading archaeologists towards a consensus that in Ireland there is a move about AD 750 away from a primarily cattle economy towards one based on the production of cereal crops.[76] As noted earlier about the changing political structures of Early Medieval Ireland, archaeologists and historians have been perhaps too slow to realise that the Irish law tracts surviving for study are really just a snapshot of a society at quite an early stage of its development, which undergoes a great deal of change in successive centuries. It has been the contribution of archaeology, through the analysis of settlement types, the finding of mills and the ability of archaeology to date these structures precisely, which has more than anything else led to this realisation.

Settlement in Early Medieval Argyll, and more widely Scotland, shows, unlike in Ireland, great continuity with the previous Iron Age. The dun houses, dun enclosures and nuclear forts described above for the Iron Age all continue to be constructed and used through this period.

Evidence is beginning to emerge of the importance of more large-scale cereal production in Scotland also. Until recently there has been little evidence of Early Medieval water mills in Scotland but in recent years a mill, very similar to the type you might find in Ireland, has been uncovered at the Early Medieval monastery of Portamahomack, Tarbert Ness, in north-east Scotland.[77] This monastery was founded in the sixth century, probably by Colum Cille himself, and flourished in the eighth century. Given that this was, initially at least, a Columban foundation, it seems very likely that monasteries on the west coast and secular sites also were adopting Irish watermill technology – in fact it may be that the large numbers of rotary quern stones sometimes found at dun sites, such as the large collection from Dunadd,[78] may indicate traditional family scale milling becoming obsolete, or even being supressed, by the emergence of new large scale milling facilities, owned by the church or by the local lord, and charging the peasantry a tithe of their corn for the use of the mill. There are hints of a possible mill at Iona, where there is a small stream, *Sruth a' Mhuilinn* (the mill stream), which appears to indicate the location of a possible monastic mill. Although excavations there found structural elements close to the stream and a possible mill pool, they were difficult to date and the tradition of milling cereal using water-powered mills, not dissimilar to Early Medieval Irish ones, continued in the Highlands and Islands until comparatively recent times.[79]

Links in the material culture of Antrim and Argyll in the Early Medieval period

There are a number of artefact types which seem to have been common to Ireland and Scotland in the Early Medieval period which have been, in recent years, the subject of discussions regarding the interrelationship between the two regions. There were similar traditions of exquisite metalworking such as zoomorphic penannular brooches and gold-working. Also linking Antrim and Argyll is a much more numerous, but geographically limited, type of artefact; Souterrain Ware pottery. Early Medieval Ireland used almost no pottery, although ceramic technology was widely used in metalworking for moulds and crucibles. This is especially surprising given the fact that pottery was in widespread use for several thousand years of Ireland's prehistory, before apparently being eschewed in favour of wooden cups and bowls during the Iron Age. At the outset of the Early Medieval period Scotland is largely free of domestic pottery also – only the north-western mainland and Outer Hebrides using pottery in domestic contexts. In the middle of the eighth century, however, a type of utilitarian coarse pottery begins to be used in east Ulster. It has been called Souterrain Ware by archaeologists, because a number of early discoveries were found within souterrains, although it is found frequently in all kinds of sites after that date. The possibility that Souterrain Ware begins to be made in Argyll in imitation of the ceramics of the north-west Scottish coastal area and isles has been raised by Armit.[80]

Early Medieval, non-church, ritual sites in Ireland and Scotland

Early Medieval Ireland was a society which was converted to Christianity from a polytheistic pagan faith. The structure of society and the nature of kingship had grown from this pagan society and while Christianity became grafted on to it many of the rituals of this society were influenced by the older beliefs. In both Ireland and Scotland a number of sites were known as royal centres. Often these were not royal residences but simply inauguration centres intimately linked to the sacred landscape. There were also assembly sites called *oenachs,* which seem to have been a multifunctional place of assembly, fairs, where tribute was collected by kings, and royal lineages read out, marriages arranged, craftwork sold and games and festivities held.[81] They may have played a part in inauguration rituals also, although they were not necessarily the inauguration site itself. These *oenach* sites typically took the form of a ritual landscape within which there were several elements including large enclosures, an example perhaps being the large enclosed site 'Parley Hill', situated on the boundary of the aptly named townlands of Slievenagh (perhaps the hill of the oenach) and Ballynafie (the townland of the green, most oenachs included 'green' for mass assembly), near Portglenone, County Antrim which may have been an assembly site of the Dál nAraide.

In east Ulster a number of sites are known or thought to be royal inauguration sites. The kings of Ulster may have used Emain Macha or Navan Fort as their inauguration centre, in the early centuries AD before they were pushed back east of the Bann and created a new royal centre at An Dun, the Mound of Down, where the kings of the Dál Fiatach continued to reside until the arrival of de Courcy. Craebh Tulacha, or Crew Hill, near Glenavy, County Antrim, may have originally been an inauguration site of the Dál nAride before it fell into the possession of the Dál Fiatach as they expanded into the former's territory in the ninth century.[82] In north-west Antrim the flat topped rocky outcrop of Dunmull dominates the local landscape. There are local traditions that it was used by the O'Floinn kings of the Uí Tuitre, the dynasty which dominated much of mid and north Antrim from the ninth century to the fourteenth or fifteenth century;[83] it is possible that the branch of the Dál nAride, called the Eilne, who resided in north-west Antrim may have utilised it for similar purposes before them. Another possible place of coronation is at Elagh Castle, County Londonderry. Here there is a rocky outcrop, located on excellent arable land, with wide views across the landscape, which has a fragment of a Medieval stone castle, located upon it. Elagh Castle, located within the townland of Elaghmore, may be the site of Aileach, the capital of the Cenél nEógain, the important branch of the northern Uí Neill, one of the most important royal dynasties of ancient Ireland. Aileach is sometimes assumed to be the impressive cashel called Grianan, a few miles away in County Donegal but the evidence fits Elagh Castle better in a number of ways.[84] Aileach is suggested from Late Medieval Gaelic praise poetry not just to have been a capital and a residence but also to have been an inauguration site. In a collection of Early Medieval place-name lore, compiled by twelfth century monastic scholars, called the Metrical Dindshenchas, Aileach is also suggested to have had its origins as a site of a megalithic tomb and to later have been made into a fortress which was subsequently owned by Frigriu, a Pict.[85] Recent excavations have uncovered a large Early Medieval ditch and stone-faced bank surrounding the site with a diameter of around 100m, much larger than even the largest rath, and evidence of high status Early Medieval glass-working.

Later Medieval tower from Elagh, County Londonderry
(photograph by Betina Linke)

Aileach is reminiscent in many ways of one of the most important inauguration and/or royal centres in Medieval Scotland, the probable inauguration site of the Dál Riada at Dunadd, near Kilmartin, in Argyll. Dunadd is a small rocky hill, 53m in height, dominating the plain upon which it sits. At its top, excavations have revealed the remains of a dun, typical of those found throughout the west of Scotland, with additional outworkings making further enclosures around it.[86] This puts it firmly into the 'Fort' category as described by the Royal Commission on the Ancient and Historic Monuments of Scotland. It is also typical of what Stevenson has called a *nuclear fort*, where additions are made over time to a smaller dun nucleus.[87] Amongst the finds uncovered during the excavation were remnants of jewellery production and exotic imported 'E' ware pottery from France,[88] which appears to concur with Adomnan, the abbot of Iona and Colum Cille's biographer, referring to Colum Cille's trip to the '*caput regionis*' where he met with traders from Gaul.[89] Just below the summit there is a flat smooth stone with the impression of a footprint within it, which folklore suggests is Colum Cille's footprint and which, like similar stones in Ireland, appears to have been used in the inauguration of the Dál Riadic kings. The date for the beginnings of construction at Dunadd is unsure, and it may predate the Dál Riada by many centuries, but it is mentioned twice in the Annals of Ulster as a possession of the Dál Riada in the seventh and eighth centuries.

The question of the date of the construction of Dunadd highlights one of the problems we have with studying the Early Medieval settlement archaeology in Argyll, compared with that in east Ulster or other parts of Ireland. There seems to be similarity in the settlement archaeology in the two areas, but the Scottish settlement pattern shows continuity with the earlier Iron Age settlement, whereas the Irish settlement pattern does not seem to show the same continuity. The Scottish duns and smaller forts can be seen as analogous to Irish ringforts. The larger Scottish forts, which are too large for the use of a single family group and, therefore, must have some wider function, may have more in common with Irish ritual and assembly sites, like the inauguration sites and assembly sites or possibly the *oenach* sites. The Scottish sites can be shown, in some cases at least, to originate in the Iron Age where as in Ireland, as discussed above, it has proved more difficult to find evidence for Iron Age settlement. An interesting suggestion put forward a number of years ago by Richard Warner speculated that certain architectural features which occur on some Scottish duns and brochs, and which may therefore date to the Iron Age, also occur on a number of Irish sites, specifically cashels. The architectural features which he suggests are intra mural passages, stone passages constructed within the stone walls of duns, brochs and cashels and some other features such as guard rooms and bolt holes, which he suggests have similarity also. Warner notes that there is evidence of Scottish influence on Ulster architectural styles which could be as early as the third century AD. Sites like the Grianan in County Donegal, the Giant's Sconce, near Limavady, County Londonderry, and Altagore Cashel, near Cushendun in County Antrim, Warner notes for their similarity to Scottish duns. He also notes a number of artefacts of similar type in Ulster and Scotland at the same time period and postulates that Scottish settlement and artefact types are influencing Irish types through the 'reflux' of a migration from Ireland to Scotland.[90] Warner raises some interesting possibilities and he may be correct in suggesting an Iron Age movement from Ireland to Scotland bringing influences back home. However, the span of use of Scottish duns and brochs, which continues right through the Early Medieval period, and into the Later Medieval period, and possibly beyond in the case of some duns, could suggest that Early Medieval Ulster/Scottish activities, such as the activities of the Dál Riada in Argyll, or possibly even contacts between the Irish Cruithni and the Scottish Picts, or some other combination of the above, may be responsible. Ultimately, excavation of some of these Ulster sites which display parallels with Scottish ones to obtain dating evidence for their construction and use is the only way to shed light on this problem.

In Scotland Ian Armit has suggested a hierarchy of Early Medieval settlement with nuclear forts at the pinnacle, the residences of the elite, with simple duns beneath them, and that aspects of the settlement structure might be similar in Antrim, specifically suggesting Doonmore in County Antrim as an Irish example of a nuclear fort,[91] a suggestion previously made by Professor Leslie Alcock at a seminar in Queen's in 1987.[92] The idea of the settlement pattern in Argyll being reflected in parts of north-east Antrim has been developed by McSparron and Williams who have suggested that in the barony of Cary, on the north-east Antrim coast, there are a number of settlement sites which in terms of their siting, on top of natural eminences, like rock stacks, and in their morphology, they are typically small and enclosed by a stone wall, more resemble Scottish duns than the Irish raths with which they are usually classified.[93] The term 'fortified outcrop' has been proposed to distinguish them from more traditional Irish rath types. This initial survey of sites identified eight sites which could be classified as fortified outcrops and a further six which probably could be so classified. It is likely that a further detailed examination of a number of other sites classified as simply enclosures or similar in the Northern Ireland Sites and Monuments Record could add to this number. Three of these fortified outcrops have been excavated. At Doonmore Gordon Childe dug a fortified outcrop near Fair Head, County Antrim.[94] It was a small oval enclosure constructed upon a rocky outcrop, with a stone enclosure wall and evidence of hearths and paved areas. An outer enclosure was detected also. Finds included Early Medieval

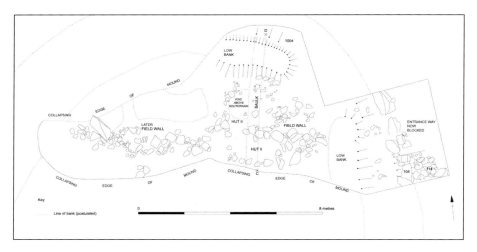

Above: Phase 2 occupation at Drumadoon, County Antrim
Below: Doonmore, County Antrim

Souterrain Ware and Later Medieval Ulster Coarse Pottery and Later Medieval glazed pots. Childe believed the structure to be an Anglo-Norman fortification.

Excavations by McSparron and Williams at Drumadoon, Ballyvoy, County Antrim, located only a short distance from Doonmore have revealed a very similar structure.[95] The site at Drumadoon was constructed on a gravel mound, with excellent views over the Cary River valley. Although partially collapsed, the shape, oval, and approximate size, not greatly in excess of 14m diameter, could be estimated. The enclosure wall was of earth, but clad in stone. Internally hearths and paved areas were found also. In addition, a souterrain was discovered; no souterrain was found at Doonmore but the tough bedrock may have dissuaded the builders from constructing one. Finds, as at Doonmore, consisted of Early Medieval Souterrain Ware and Later Medieval pottery including glazed pots. At Drumadoon the earthen-cored wall had collapsed and been repaired several times, the earth and stones of the wall spreading across the site, allowing the Drumadoon excavation to be split into three phases of use, two Early Medieval phases, a period of abandonment and then reoccupation, probably in the thirteenth century. Radiocarbon dates show that main Early Medieval use of the site was from the late eighth to the early tenth centuries AD.[96]

The likelihood is that Doonmore has a similar date range to Drumadoon – Early Medieval construction and use, but with *reuse* during the Norman era; Childe did not have radiocarbon-dating to assist him. A third fortified outcrop at Dunshammer, Ballintoy, County Antrim was excavated by W. Jackson in the 1930s but unfortunately the excavation was not published and his notes, photographs and drawings were lost. However, the artefacts from the excavation have survived and are in the Ulster Museum. They are very similar to the artefacts found at Doonmore and Drumadoon.

So on current evidence, based as it is on only a few radiocarbon dates and two published excavations, it seems that the Fortified Outcrops of east Antrim may be the result of ideas being transferred to Ulster from Scotland because of the activities of Dál Riadic colonists in Scotland. It is not impossible, however, that Drumadoon and Doonmore are at the tail end of a process of settlement architecture in Ireland being influenced by Scotland and more, possibly quite small scale, targeted research excavation, with the primary aim of finding dating evidence to build comparative chronologies, is needed to address this question.

The impact of the Vikings

In 794, the Annals of Ulster record, 'Devastation of all the islands of Britain by heathens' and in 795 the Annals of Ulster record the 'burning of Recru (Rathlin) by the heathens'. For the year 795 the Annals of Inishfallen note 'The plundering of Í Coluim Chille (Iona), and of Inis Muiredaig, and of Inis Bó Finne'. The relative stability of the previous three hundred years was shattered. The Vikings who came to Ulster and western Scotland were mainly from western Scandinavia, not Danes as was the case for much of Britain, and they made an impact especially upon the church, the wealth and relative defencelessness of monasteries, especially on isolated islands, made them tempting targets. Throughout the early years of the ninth century there were numerous attacks noted on monasteries, but also on secular sites as well, with records as early as 798 from the Annals of Ulster of 'incursions both in Ireland and in Alba'. These seem to have provoked an early native response in Ulster with as early as 811 the Annals of Ulster telling of a 'slaughter of the heathens by the Ulaid', with the succeeding several years witnessing slaughters inflicted on and by the Norse recorded in Ireland. In 821, the Annals of Ulster report the carrying off of women by the Vikings, presumably to be slaves or wives. In the early 820s much Norse activity was centred on north Down with both Bangor and Movilla abbeys being sacked with a counter attack by the Ulaid in 826 when they 'inflicted a rout on the heathens in Mag Inis, in which very many fell' (Annals of Ulster). In the same year Iona was also sacked, for the fourth time, on this occasion the abbot, Blathmac, an Irish prince and former warrior, evacuated all but the strongest of his monks from the monastery and carried out a spirited defence of the monastery, but resisted, to death, revealing the hidden shrine of St Columba. The attack was recorded not just in the Irish annals, since many details were also recounted in a poem written by a German monk, Walafrid of Strabo, abbot of Reichenau from 838–849.[97]

The attacks at Iona were so intense during these years that the monastery began to relocate to a new, safer, site at Kells, County Meath, from as early as 807, the abbot of Kells continuing to use the title of abbot of Iona, although, as Strabo of Reichenau tells us, Christian worship continued at Iona.[98] The intensity of Viking attacks on Ulster increased in the 830s and in 831 Armagh itself was plundered three times in one month with Rath Luraig (Maghera, County Londonderry) and Connor, County Antrim, plundered that year also.

Further battles were won over the Norse in Ulster and in 832 the Annals of the Four Masters note 'battle was gained by Niall Caille and Murchadh over the foreigners, at Doire Chalgaigh (Derry), where a slaughter was made of them'. In Leinster and Munster there were numerous Viking attacks in the mid 830s with, according to the Annals of the Four Masters, 'A fleet of sixty ships of Norsemen on the Boyne. Another fleet of sixty ships on the Abhainn Liphthe (Liffey)'. In 836, the Annals of Ulster and the Annals of the Four Masters record that the Norse were active on Lough Erne and Devenish was burnt. They were active on Lough Neagh in 839, raiding the area around the Lough.

There was almost certainly at least as much, if not in fact much more, Viking activity and attacks on Argyll during this period. The Irish annals, with communication lines stretched with Scotland, record only occasional references to the activities of the Vikings there. It has been suggested that the Dál Riada and the Picts were jointly slow to react to the Norse threat; a reference in the Annals of the Four Masters for 835 states 'Gofraidh, son of Fearghus, chief of Oirghialla, went to Alba, to strengthen the Dal Riada, at the request of Cinaeth, son of Ailpin', this must be a response to the threat of the Norse, although it seems not to have been successful as the in 839 the Annals of Ulster note that 'heathens' won a battle against the men of Foirtriu (Pictland). The success of the Norse in coastal Argyll has been suggested as one possible reason why the kings of Dál Riada pursued their interests in mainland Scotland, leading in time to a unification of Dál Riada with Pictland.[99]

Viking raiding continued in Ulster, Argyll and the rest of Ireland and Scotland, but it was changing. During the middle years of the ninth century the Norse began to establish fortresses and towns, such as Dublin. This led to a change in the Norse who now involved themselves increasingly in Irish life and politics. For instance, the Annals of Ulster entry for 850 (849) states that 'Cinaed son of Conaing, king of Cianacht, rebelled against Mael Sechnaill with the support of the foreigners, and plundered the Uí Néill from the Sinann to the sea'. This is the Norse joining in the internal politics of north-west Ulster. The activities of Gofraidh, son of Fearghus in Argyll, in reinforcing the Dál Riada, may also give a clue to the fact that the Norse are integrating. His Christian name is Norse, Gofraidh, his patronymic, 'son of Fearghus' is Gaelic. His mother may have been Norse and when he died he was described in the Annals of the Four Masters for 851 as the chief of the Innsi Gall, the Islands of the Foreigners, in this case foreigners meaning Vikings.[100]

In the middle years of the ninth century there were further raids, such as the sacking of Armagh in 852; these were yet larger armies, often led by important Norse kings from Scandinavia, sometimes in alliance with Irish groups. This new burst of even more intense warfare affected Scotland too, as the Annals of Ulster note for 866: 'Amlaíb and Auisle (two Norwegian kings) went with the foreigners of Ireland and Scotland to Fortriu, plundered the entire Pictish country and took away hostages from them'. However, this heightened activity seems to have led to a swift response later the same year, for the Annals of Ulster report that, 'Aed son of Niall plundered all the strongholds of the foreigners, i.e. in the territory of the North, both in Cenél Eógain and Dál nAraide, and took away their heads, their flocks, and their herds from camp by battle.'

Two years later, in 871, the Annals of Ulster recount the storming of Dunseverick, County Antrim, 'which had never been achieved before' by a combined force of Cenél Eógain and Norse, showing the continuing integration of the Norse into an increasingly violent Irish series of dynastic conflicts. After this Norse activity in Ulster seems to have subsided somewhat, although there was a Norse raid on Armagh in 895, noted in the Annals of Ulster, in which 710 persons were taken into captivity. In 896, the Annals of the Four Masters record 'a slaughter was made of the foreigners by the Ulidians'. In 897, the Leinstermen attacked Dublin and expelled the Norse leading to an island-wide lull in Norse attacks.

The next activity by the Norse in Ulster seems to have been an invasion of Armagh in 921, which the Annals of Ulster relate, followed by Norse activity on Lough Erne and Lough Cuan (Strangford Lough) in 924, followed up the next year by another attack on Dunseverick when many men were killed or captured. The Strangford Lough Norse were then active on Lough Neagh, according to the Annals of Ulster, in 930 harrying the land about building some kind of camp or fortress at a place called Ruib Mena, which is probably on the north-east shore of Lough Neagh close to the place where the River Maine flows into the lough. The Norse fortress at Strangford Lough may have been destroyed by the men of Lecale about the year 943; the Annals of Ulster record how 'The Leth Cathail inflicted a rout on the foreigners of Loch Cuan, in which nearly all were destroyed'. In 945, the Lough Neagh Norse suffered a rout: 'The foreigners of Loch nEchach were killed by Domnall son of Muirchertach and by his kinsman, Flaithbertach, and their fleet was destroyed'. This battle seems to mark the end of large-scale Norse harrying in Ulster. During the century and a half of Norse raids only Strangford Lough and Lough Neagh seem to have had any lasting settlements, and even these seem only to have lasted for a relatively short time, in the case of Strangford, possibly the most durable, as little as 20 years.

Viking archaeology in Antrim and Argyll

The nature of the Viking activities in Antrim and Argyll and the surrounding areas has left a very different archaeological record of their activities. In Ulster generally there are few remains which can convincingly be shown to be Norse and all can be summarised briefly. A Viking burial appears to have been uncovered by workmen at Curran near Larne in 1840. The skeleton of a man with a double-edged Viking sword, spearhead, ring pin and bone comb was found in a grave about 70 yards from the shore, with no evidence of a covering mound or cist.[101] It has been suggested by Richard Warner that a burial at Demesne, Rathlin, County Antrim, close to a standing stone and accompanied by a pen-annular brooch, is probably Viking, based on the brooch being a Norse variant of an Irish design.[102] Also in Demesne, Rathlin, reports were made to NIEA archaeologists by local informants of a Viking boat burial discovered there in 1920, close to the shore. A possible ship burial encased in a mound of diameter approximately 40 feet was found at Ballywillin, near Portrush, County Antrim, in 1813.[103] At Ballyholme, County Down, an apparently Viking burial was found in 1906 accompanied by two Viking tortoise shell brooches.[104]

In Argyll there is a much greater wealth of Norse archaeology: 13 certain and 13 probable Viking graves have been found in Argyll on the islands of Coll and Tiree, Mull, Colonsay, Oransay, Islay and Gigha.[105] Some of the graves were wealthy, displaying weapons, jewellery and in some cases evidence of trade as well as piracy; a grave at Kiloran Bay on Colonsay having, as well as the more usual weapons and jewellery, a set of scales and weights. There are fewer indications of Viking burials on the mainland, just a few antiquarian references to doubtful boat burials at Cul na Croise, Goirten Bay, Ardnamurchan and Oban.[106] All of the burials on the islands are ninth or tenth century, Christianisation robbing archaeologists of the means to identify Norse burials in this region after that.

Further evidence of the Norse in Argyll is given by place-name evidence where the influence of the Norse language is preserved. In some of the more northerly isles in Argyll, such as Coll and Tiree, up to half of the place-names are Norse or Norse influenced, the remainder mainly Gaelic. In Islay, to the south, this proportion drops to 30 per cent and in Mull and Lismore, the proportion is 15 per cent, whereas on Gigha, Colonsay, Oransay and mainland Argyll Norse influenced place-names are only occasionally found.[107]

The influence of the Vikings on mainland Ulster and Argyll was significant but limited. The Norse raided and burned, but probably at a rate somewhat less than rebuilding could take place. They seem to have focused on regions for a time and then moved on. In Ulster, in particular north Ulster, they seem to have faced firm resistance, which possibly led to a lessening of attacks upon Ulster in the tenth century and beyond. The greatest effects were felt on the islands (including Rathlin), here the evidence of relatively common Viking burial shows that there were deeper, more long lasting effects. Perhaps the most significant date for the future history of both Antrim and Argyll in the entire Viking adventure in these islands is the death of Gofraidh Mac Fearghus in 851, a man with Gaelic and Scandinavian elements in his name, and his description as the chief of the Innsi Gall, the Islands of the Foreigners (meaning Vikings). It was the first step in establishing an important sea kingdom which was to become the Lordship of the Isles, and it may well have contributed to the formation of the kingdom of Scotland, by pushing the Dál Riada and the Picts into each other's arms (possibly quite literally) and led, in time, to the expansion of the Lordship of the Isles into County Antrim.

Antrim and Argyll in the Early Historic era

The oscillation between periods of intense contact between Ulster and the west of Scotland was matched by periods where they seem to have developed separately continues in the historic era. With Early Medieval Antrim and Argyll, traditional narrative history explicitly states an origin for the emerging Scottish nation amongst the Irish of Dál Riada. Recent Scottish scholarship has rightly queried this narrative, laden as it is with the dynastic concerns of Scotland at a later date, but has sometimes gone too far in rejecting cross-channel contacts and the Dál Riadic influence on the early development of Scotland. Once again the sea unified, not separated.

The sea became an obstacle, however, at the very end of the eighth century when the control of the seas, if not actually lost, became contested with the arrival of the Vikings. The difficulty in communications is apparent in the decreasing frequency of entries regarding Scottish affairs in the Irish annals as a North Channel world, for a time, becomes a memory. At the same time, the power of the most important over-kings in both Scotland and Ireland was increasing. East Ulster found itself increasingly falling under the influence of the MacLoughlain over-kings, aspirant kings of the whole of Ireland in the eleventh and twelfth century, who appoint under-kings and make grants of land all over the north of Ireland at will. In Scotland the same process is happening with new forms of monarchy emerging, more powerful over-kings beginning to look like what we might think of as king in the sense of Europe in the High Middle Ages with monarchs like David I keen to take on all trappings of modernity, influenced by his Irish councillor, St Malachy.

Ireland and Scotland jointly were looking inward, consolidating their monarchical institutions, powerful dynasties striving to emerge as the sole royal family. Yet they were developing in parallel and, for the Scottish in particular, the narrative of the emergence of the leading Scottish dynasties from an Irish aristocracy with long roots, and a highly developed supporting body of genealogy and literature, was of vital importance. The closeness of their peoples and institutions was about to be interrupted by a new event, however, which would bring the Early Middle Ages to an end and shatter the co-development of the emerging kingdoms, the influence of the Anglo-Normans on Scottish institutions and their rather more warlike arrival in Ireland.

Notes

1 F. J. Byrne, *Irish Kings and High Kings* (Dublin, 1973).
2 Ibid.; G. H. Orpen, *The Song of Dermot and the Earl* (Oxford, 1892).
3 D. Ó Cróinín, *Early Irish History and Chronology* (Dublin, 2003), p. 292.
4 Ibid.
5 Byrne, *Irish Kings and High Kings*, p. 42.
6 Ibid., p. 107.
7 J. V. Kelleher, 'Early Irish history and pseudo-history', *Studia Hibernica*, 3 (1963), pp 113–27.
8 Byrne, *Irish Kings and High Kings*, p. 128.
9 Ibid.

10 Ibid.

11 Ibid.

12 M. T. Flanagan, *Irish Royal Charters: Texts and Contexts* (Oxford, 2004).

13 A. P. Smyth, *Warlords and Holy Men: Scotland AD 80–1000* (London, 1984), p. 41.

14 L. Alcock, *Kings and Warriors, Craftsmen and Priests in Northern Britain, AD 550–850* (Edinburgh, 2003), p. 39.

15 J. H. Jackson, 'The Pictish language' in F. T. Wainwright (ed.), *The Problem of the Picts* (Edinburgh, 1955).

16 K. Forsyth, *Language in Pictland: The Case Against 'Non-Indo-European Pictish'* (Utrecht, 1997).

17 M. Williams, 'Folklore and placenames', *Folklore,* 74 (1963), pp 351–76.

18 Forsyth, *Language in Pictland*.

19 Ibid.

20 Ibid.

21 B. Colgrave and R. A. B. Mynors, *Bede's Ecclesiastical History of the English People* (Oxford, 1967).

22 T. F. O'Rahilly, *Early Irish History and Mythology* (Dublin, 1964), p. 343.

23 Smyth, *Warlords and Holy Men*.

24 N. Evans, 'Royal succession and kingship among the Picts', *Innes Review,* 51 (2008), pp 1–48.

25 A. Woolf, 'The "Moray Question" and the kingship of Alba in the tenth and eleventh centuries', *SHR*, 79:208 (2000), pp 145–64; A. Woolf, *From Pictland to Alba: 789–1070* (Edinburgh, 2007).

26 Colgrave and Mynors, *Bede's Ecclesiastical History*, p. 19.

27 Ibid., p. 255 n.

28 D. Broun, 'The birth of Scottish history', *SHR*, 76:201 (1997), pp 4–23.

29 S. Duffy, 'Medieval Scotland and Ireland: overcoming the amnesia', *History Ireland*, 7:3 (1999), pp 17–21.

30 Broun, 'Birth of Scottish History', p. 13.

31 E. Campbell, 'Were the Scots Irish?', *Antiquity*, 75 (2001), pp 285–92.

32 C. McSparron and B. Williams, '"… and they won land among the Picts by friendly treaty or the sword": how a re-examination of early historical sources and an analysis of early Medieval settlement in north Co. Antrim confirms the validity of traditional accounts of Dál Riadic migration to Scotland from Ulster', *PSAS*, 141 (2011), pp 145–58.

33 D. W. Anthony, 'Migration in archaeology: the baby and the bathwater', *American Anthropologist*, 92:4 (1990), pp 895–914.

34 I. Adamson, *The Ulster People: Ancient, Medieval and Modern* (Bangor, 1991); M. Hall, *Ulster, the Hidden History* (Bangor, 1986); M. Hall, *Is there a Shared Ulster Heritage?* (Belfast, 2007).

35 O'Rahilly *Early Irish History and Mythology*, p. 85.

36 T. McErlean, 'The archaeology of the Ulster Cycle on the north coast' in G. Toner and S. Mac Mathuna (eds), *Ulidia 3: Proceedings of the Third International Conference on the Ulster Cycle of Tales, University of Ulster, Coleraine 22–25 June, 2009* (Berlin, 2013), pp 1–16.

37 C. McSparron, 'Data Structure Report: Elagh Castle', Centre for Archaeological Fieldwork, Queen's University Belfast, DSR 99 (2013).

38 J. MacNeill, 'Early Irish population-groups: their nomenclature, classification, and chronology', *PRIA*, 29C (1911/12), p. 98.

39 Ibid.; O'Rahilly *Early Irish History and Mythology*.

40 O'Rahilly *Early Irish History and Mythology*, pp 348–52.

41 Ibid.

42 J. T. Koch, 'New Thoughts on Albion, Ierne, and the Pretanic Isles (Part One)', *Proceedings of the Harvard Celtic Colloquium*, 6 (1986), pp 1–28.

43 Campbell, 'Were the Scots Irish?'

44 McErlean, 'The archaeology of the Ulster Cycle'.

45 R. B. Warner, 'Ireland, Ulster and Scotland in the earlier Iron Age' in A. O'Connor and D. V. Clarke (eds), *From the Stone Age to the Forty Five* (Edinburgh, 1983).

46 K. Hughes and A. Hamlin, *The Modern Traveller to the Early Irish Church* (Dublin, 1977), p. 45.

47 Ibid., p. 65.

48 W. D. Simpson, *The Celtic Church in Scotland* (Aberdeen, 1935), p. 11.

49 Adomnan of Iona, *Life of St Columba*, trans. R. Sharpe (Harmondsworth, 1995).

50 Ibid.

51 W. Reeves, 'The Antiphonary of Bangor', *UJA,* first series, 1 (1853), pp 168–79.

52 A. B. Scott, 'Saint Maelrubha', *SHR*, 6:23 (1909), p. 264.

53 Ibid., p. 269

54 N. Edwards, *The Archaeology of Early Medieval Ireland* (London, 1994), p. 107.

55 Ibid.

56 Ibid., p. 108.

57 E. Nelis, S. Gormley, C. McSparron, A. Kyle, 'Excavations at Armoy, Co. Antrim', Centre for Archaeological Fieldwork, Queen's University Belfast, DSR 44 (2007).

58 J. W. Barber, 'Excavations on Iona 1979', *PSAS*, 111 (1981), pp 282–380.

59 J. O'Sullivan, 'Excavations beside Sruth a' Mhuilinn ("the Mill Stream"), Iona', *PSAS*, 124 (1994), pp 491–508.

60 I. Fisher, 'Early Medieval archaeology in Argyll' in G. Ritchie (ed.), *The Archaeology of Argyll* (Edinburgh, 1997), p. 187.

61 M. Stout, *The Irish Ringfort* (Dublin, 1997), p. 108.

62 Ibid., p. 53.

63 T. R. Kerr, 'The height of fashion: raised raths in the landscape of north-west Ulster', *JIA*, 18 (2009), p. 64.

64 F. McCormick, 'The decline of the cow: agricultural and settlement change in Early Medieval Ireland', *Peritia*, 20 (2008), pp 209–24.

65 C. J. Lynn, 'Houses in rural Ireland, AD 500–1000', *UJA*, third series, 57 (1994), pp 81–94.

66 A. O'Sullivan, F. McCormick, F. Harney, J. Kinsella, T. Kerr, *Early Medieval Dwellings and Settlements in Ireland, AD 400–1100* (Oxford, 2010) pp 48–9.

67 Ibid.

68 C. McSparron and B. Williams, 'The excavation of an Early Christian rath with later Medieval occupation at Drumadoon, Co. Antrim', *PRIA*, 109C (2009), pp 105–64.

69 C. J. Lynn and J. A. McDowell, *Deer Park Farms: The Excavation of a Raised Rath in the Glenarm Valley, Co. Antrim* (Belfast, 2011).

70 C. J. Lynn, 'Civil engineering in the Early Christian period: Big Glebe, Co. Londonderry' in A. Hamlin and C. J. Lynn (eds), *Pieces of the Past: Archaeological Excavations by the Department of the Environment for Northern Ireland, 1970–1986* (Belfast, 1988).

71 Kerr, 'The height of fashion'.

72 O'Sullivan et al., *Early Medieval Dwellings and Settlements in Ireland*, p. 95.

73 T. McErlean and N. Crothers, *Harnessing the Tides: The Early Medieval Tide Mills at Nendrum Monastery, Strangford Lough* (Norwich, 2007).

74 O'Sullivan et al., *Early Medieval Dwellings and Settlements in Ireland*, p. 98.

75 M. Seaver, 'Through the mill – excavation of an Early Medieval settlement at Raystown, County Meath, in J. O'Sullivan and M. Stanley (eds), *Settlement, Industry and Ritual*, National Roads Authority Monograph Series, No. 3 (Dublin, 2006).

76 O'Sullivan et al., *Early Medieval Dwellings and Settlements in Ireland*.

77 M. Carver, 'An Iona of the East: the Early Medieval monastery at Portamahomack, Tarbert Ness', *Medieval Archaeology*, 84 (2004), pp 1–30.

78 E. Campbell, 'A cross-marked quern from Dunadd and other evidence for relations between Dunadd and Iona', *PSAS*, 117 (1987), pp 105–17.

79 J. O'Sullivan, 'Excavations beside Sruth a' Mhuilinn'.

80 I. Armit, 'Irish-Scottish connections in the first millennium AD: an evaluation of the link between Souterrain Ware and Hebridean ceramics', *PRIA*, 108C (2008), pp 1–15.

81 P. McCotter 'Drong and Dál as synonyms for Óenach', Peritia, 22/23 (2012), pp 1–6;
P. Macdonald, N. Carver, M. Yates, 'Excavations at Macilwhans Hill, Ballyutoag, County
Antrim', UJA, third series, 64 (2005), pp 43–61.

82 E. Fitzpatrick, Royal Inauguration in Gaelic Ireland, 1100–1600 (Woodbridge, 2004);
P. Macdonald, 'An archaeological evaluation of the inaugural landscape of Crew Hill
(Craeb Telcha), Co. Antrim', UJA, third series 67 (2008), pp 84–106.

83 Fitzpatrick, Royal Inauguration in Gaelic Ireland, p. 139.

84 McSparron, 'Data Structure Report: Elagh Castle'.

85 E. Gwynn (ed.), The Metrical Dindshenchas (5 vols, Dublin, 1903–35), vol. 4, p. 93.

86 A. Lane and E. Campbell, Dunadd: An Early Dalriadic Capital (Oxford, 2000).

87 R. B. K. Stevenson, 'The nuclear fort at Dalmahoy, Midlothian, and other Dark Age
capitals', PSAS, 83 (1948–9), pp 186–98.

88 Lane and Campbell, Dunadd.

89 Campbell, 'A cross-marked quern from Dunadd', p. 113.

90 Warner, 'Ireland, Ulster and Scotland in the earlier Iron Age'.

91 Armit, 'Irish-Scottish connections in the first millennium AD', p. 3.

92 Pers. comm. Dr Colm Donnelly.

93 McSparron and Williams, '"… and they won land among the Picts by friendly
treaty or the sword"'.

94 V. G. Childe, 'Doonmore, a castle mound near Fair Head, Co. Antrim',
UJA, third series, 1 (1938), pp 122–35.

95 McSparron and Williams, 'The excavation of an Early Christian rath … at Drumadoon'.

96 Ibid, p. 113.

97 M. M. Brown, 'The Norse in Argyll' in Ritchie, Archaeology of Argyll.

98 Ibid.

99 Ibid., p. 208.

100 Ibid.

101 T. Fanning, 'The Viking grave goods discovered near Larne, Co. Antrim, in 1870',
JRSAI, 100 (1970), pp 71–8.

102 R. Warner, The re-provenancing of two important penannular brooches of the Viking
period', UJA, third series, 36–37 (1974), p. 53.

103 C. J. Donnelly, Living Places: Archaeology, Continuity and Change at Historic Monuments
in Northern Ireland.

104 'Proceedings', JRSAI, 36 (1906), p. 451.

105 Brown, 'Norse in Argyll', p. 209.

106 Ibid., p. 229.

107 W. F. H. Nicholaisen, 'The Viking settlement of Scotland: evidence of the place-names'
in R. T. Farrell (ed.), The Vikings (London, 1982); Brown, 'Norse in Argyll'.

Excerpt from Kitchen's
map of Scotland, 1773

4

Sounds Across the Moyle: Musical Resonances Between Argyll and Antrim

Stuart Eydmann

Introduction

> It is important to remember that the traffic has always been in both directions; if the most important single event in early Scottish history can be said to have been the foundation of the kingdom of Dalriada by *Scoti* (Irish Gaels) who had crossed that same strip of water, it is also true that Ulster history has often been influenced by visitors from across the Moyle. It was not for mere literary effect that Camden (in his *Britannia*) described the peninsula of Kintyre as thrusting itself 'greedily towards Ireland'. Another historical fact which has to be borne in mind, when one scrutinises the cultural mix, is that both Ulster and Kintyre were successfully colonised, in the seventeenth century, by Lowlanders from Renfrewshire and Ayrshire, and that in both areas the Gaelic language has co-existed with Lowland Scots right up to the present century.[1]

With Antrim and Argyll closely separated, or rather joined, by the Straits of Moyle or North Channel, logic would suggest that there must have been, and might still be, musics that resonate across those waters. Indeed, it is generally accepted that music and song has been carried and passed between Scotland and Ireland for centuries and traditional musicians know that even the gentlest of scraping beneath the surface of many songs or tunes will reveal or suggest equivalents in each country. It is possible, therefore, to find material heard in Antrim that can be traced back to or from, or shared with Scotland, or music in Argyll that links to greater Ireland. It is more of a challenge, however, to identify concrete musical connections and resonances between the two areas and to understand the processes involved. In this we are not helped by the fact that, although acknowledged, the history of musical transmission between Scotland and Ireland remains under researched and poorly understood and that, to date, there have been no detailed and comprehensive musical studies of either area to allow comparison and exploration of linkages.

Both locations are peripheral to their parent countries in geographical and cultural terms and each has been passed over by those who have chosen to privilege the more 'authentic' and less compromised cultural survivals of other places thought to better represent national musical repertory and style. Furthermore, from the eighteenth century onwards, writers, collectors and promoters of the music have tended to work to agendas seeking to celebrate the uniqueness of their countries' music rather than any shared heritage, dismissing concurrence and raising boundaries where they may have been non-existent or minor.[2]

Fortunately, there are numerous references to musical connections in national musical histories, collections and genre-specific works as well as much material scattered across local histories, manuscripts, journals, archives and public records. Approaching the subject, therefore, requires the herding of a wide range of sources and fragments of evidence. Of crucial importance too, of course, are the lived experiences, output and testimony the musicians themselves, those of the past and those who are making music today.

This essay comprises a preliminary and selective survey of such sources that, hopefully, will suggest lines for further inquiry. However, it is offered with the recommendation that the interpretation and drawing of conclusions from the evidence should be tempered by a degree of caution on a number of counts.

While cultural links between Scotland and Ireland have been under-appreciated, the significance of proximity can be overestimated, the Moyle having acted as a barrier as well as a bridge.[3] Ideas of a Medieval Gaelic kingdom spanning the North Channel or of a homogenous Gaeldom with a 'seamless web' of shared culture can be helpful in drawing attention to the rich heritage, as in Delargy's view of oral culture that 'no distinction can be made by the student of Gaelic oral tradition between the folk-tales of Munster and Connacht and the tales of the Highland and Hebridean shanachies.'[4] However, such ideas been have challenged by more recent scholarship that recognises that while Scottish Gaels historically attached great significance to the Irish connection, Ireland was always culturally dominant and perceived Scotland as somewhat distant and peripheral.[5] It also acknowledges that there has been a 'substantial divergence' of folk culture between Scotland and Ireland and even within each country.[6]

Although interaction between the two areas has occurred over millennia, the music as heard today, or read from scores and manuscripts, is a modern phenomenon, largely the product of the last three centuries at most, a period that has seen considerable change and development in every way. Therefore, the idea of an ongoing musical Dál Riada, while a neat label, has little practical relevance in explaining current sounds and musical practices.

Given the colourful history of the Medieval period, it is tempting to privilege the musical implications of its ancient and elite dynasties, aristocratic patronage and political relationships and events. In reality, however, most musical activity was actually quite routine, low-key and occurred at the local and interpersonal levels. Centuries of soldiering, from the days of the mercenary redshanks and galloglasses onwards, is one area that would certainly have facilitated musical interaction and transmission. There was also considerable business and commercial contact, through fishing, trade like the annual exchange of seed-potatoes,[7] migration for seasonal and domestic employment and the movement of skilled workers such as stone masons or thatchers.

Later, there was emigration from the Glens of Antrim to Scotland where work was found as quarrymen, farm servants, bleachers, linen weavers and labourers.[8] Recreation and leisure had their roles too, as in the regular visits of Argyll islanders to Ballycastle Lammas Fair.[9] The education of Irish professionals, in medicine and divinity was often undertaken in Scotland, and links between landed families would have seen the easy, early and influential adoption of modern music and dance fashions from across the water.[10]

Although peripheral, neither area was ever as isolated as might we might assume, there being long established links with the principal urban centres and influence from across the British Isles and Europe. Both areas experienced tensions and underwent realignments of political allegiance and faith and both were subject to outward migration and inward plantation with populations from elsewhere. Old settlement patterns, such as the close-knit *baile* township of the Highlands, were destroyed and new towns and villages created.[11] Neither escaped the modernising processes of commercialisation, commodification and regularisation of music and, as accessibility by land and sea routes were improved and regularised, the cities of Belfast and Glasgow exercised their pull on the rural populations, affecting language, traditional customs, practices and social relations in all but the most isolated and conservative communities.

Contact and interaction would, of course, have been strongest in those parts closest to each other. In 1654, it could be written:

> Today in the Irish language, which is in use over this whole area, it is called Kintyre, that is Head of Land. It is inhabited by the family of Mac-Conell, which has lordship here but at the pleasure of the Earl of Argyll; they regularly go off to Ireland for booty in their light ships, and have occupied the small provinces called Glens and An Rata/The Route.[12]

Of the island of Rathlin, Nils Holmer observed in 1942:

> ... the population used to be fishermen and sailors, [and] a considerable intermarriage with (Mainland) Irish and Scots may be

expected. Thus, of the nineteen persons listed as Irish speakers, three have mentioned Scottish parents or grandparents, three have supposed that their ancestors came from Scotland, while the rest know of no other than their Irish. As for those who believe their ancestors were Scots, it must be remembered that there is a common theory in the island that every single family of those living there now are descended from Scots settlers who came to the island after the complete massacres in the sixteenth or seventeenth century ... Leaving the truth value of the historical evidence of a transplantation of the inhabitants aside, it still remains a fact that the connections with Scotland are important.[13]

And we read of the Scottish island that:

> Islay is very near Ireland, and there is a safe passage from Lochindall to Loch Foyle and poets travelling on their circuits from the home of one chief to that of another, doctors and other men of skills travelling on their professional affairs, using the Islay route, all helped keep the people of Islay in touch with the greater world beyond the sea.[14]

However, the geographical proximity of two locations does not in itself guarantee or explain a shared musical inheritance. Proximate places can also be points of transit, sites of embarkation or landing before moving on or passed through on the way to some other destination.

Then there is the music itself. Many factors are at play in music change and transmission and it is necessary to accept that the processes involved are rarely straightforward, complexity and contradiction being the norm. Music is not a single object or artefact to be passed around and there has been no one, linear mechanism of change, but rather layers, some concurrent some not, moving at different rates across groups, genres, classes and communities.

We can only speculate on how transmission of music actually occurred, but the concept of the tradition as a 'carrying stream,' while helpful in some situations, is far too simplistic for here. Similarly, talk of music surviving unadulterated from a distant past, introduced forcibly through colonialism, or carried in the blood, DNA or via other pseudo-genetic concepts have no serious use. Such seductive explanations can be detected in popular histories that promote the music of Ulster as the key building block of the North American white folk song and dance music traditions, but invariably without concrete historical evidence, musicological demonstration or rich explanation. The extrapolation of the Ulster traditions back to sixteenth-century Scotland stretches things even further. The development of fiddle music in both Scotland and Ireland, and the relationship between the two are still not adequately understood,[15] never mind the centuries of change and influence that occurred on the other side of the Atlantic.[16]

Music, as organised sound, does not exist in isolation, but is always conditioned by the wider cultural context in which it is created, developed and maintained. It is continually in a state of flux, being moulded and shaped by historical, political, economic and social factors. A melody can at different times, and in different places and situations, be made to serve any one of a variety of functions, such as in a military march, as an anthem, as part of a dance set or orchestrated for close listening in a concert programme. It might be made to sound whimsical or tragic, sacred or martial, played to a large public gathering or be heard in the intimate experience of a house *ceilidh*. Music is highly portable and moves easily from person to person and from place to place and it is both pliable and resilient. Metre, rhythm and tempo can be varied and components (tunes, motifs, figures etc.) disaggregated, the fragments selectively recycled or rearticulated as new pieces and reused to suit different functions. Printed scores or manuscripts can be relied upon for only a small part of a story more concerned with aural and oral exchange.

Similarly, a new air can become attached to and sustain an older text just or an old tune can carry fresh words. Then there are the moulding factors of the fashion, collective taste and selection of a community as well as the musician's personal artistic judgement and creativity to consider. Fresh material is continually being added to the store of tradition and, over time, existing music can become more closely associated with new groups or classes or be set aside and left to fade until rediscovered or revived.

Our modern sensibilities do not equip us for easy understanding of the context of the old music without the guidance of scholarship. The current view of music as a discrete commodity of entertainment leads us to miss its previous close integration into everyday life and rituals and associations with myth and legend, poetry and literature. A piece of instrumental music heard today on CD or in the concert hall might once have carried words linked to specific places, landscapes, groups and individuals that are now long forgotten. Similarly, the words or theme of a song may include an archaic fragment of a very much earlier classical bardic verse long detached from its original context and floating freely in oral tradition and recycled, say, in the new context of a labour song. In the past there were closer links with language and music and song were often mutually supporting, although words and meanings can become separated from their original functions or changed in transmission and through translation. When we encounter a Gaelic chant or lullaby from Scotland that praises the men of Ulster, for example, we cannot assume that the song-maker or singer had first-hand knowledge or direct association or affinity with those people:

Were strains or stress to trouble thee, A host from Ireland would rise with thee; Antrim's earl of pacing steeds would join thee; and MacFelim's noble race, should they hear it said thou wert in need, their mighty force would come to aid thee.

Assuredly would rise with thee the host of Iain Mor and Iain Cathnach, And the race of Maclean, And the men of Kintyre and Lorne; And woe to the lowlanders that should aim at thee when these nobles are in pursuit of them![17]

Bidh clann Ulaidh luaidh 's a lurain, Bidh clann Ulaidh air do bhanais, Bidh clann Ulaidh luaidh 's a lurain, Dèanamh an danns air do bhanais.

My love, my darling child, The Clan of Ulster will be at your wedding, My love, my darling child, The Clan of Ulster will dance at your wedding.[18]

Music is constantly employed in the recording and telling of histories and in the support and promotion of ideology. Moreover, primitive musical survivals can be conveniently privileged as 'ancient' and dressed in cultural significance and endearing melodies used to support legend and shroud the historical landscape in mystifying mist and twilight. Antrim and Argyll were both affected by processes of cultural, linguistic and music revivals. The eighteenth-century obsession with Gaelic antiquity, the nineteenth-century concern for the folk, the Celtic revival with its linguistic and nationalistic focus and the folk song revival of late twentieth century, each brought their own interpretations of history and significance of the music. Music is currently implicated in initiatives such as the Iomairt Chaluim Chille, which fosters links between the Gaelic speaking communities of Scotland and Ireland, and in the Ulster-Scots movement as a means of reinforcing and reimagining identity.

Descriptive evidence is often ideologically coloured. Tune and song titles, both orally transmitted or written down, are also unreliable guides to the origin and history of a tune or song and can lead us to false assumptions. The same is true of places mentioned in song texts.

For convenience, the topic is addressed through the examination, in turn, of different genres (song, piping, fiddle etc.) although this can be misleading as there was considerable cross-fertilisation across their boundaries and change was always uneven across genres, time and place. Aspects of classical and sacred and popular music are unfortunately outwith the scope of this work and await similar surveys by others.

If the results lack balance in terms of quality and quantity, this is partly as a consequence of the evidence available. It is also a reflection of the inadequacies of the author's knowledge and abilities as researcher and scholar. However, it is hoped, that this will be just the first step in a worthy exploration of two shining, if underappreciated, facets of a much larger musical gem that has endured because of its inherent beauty and the fact that it retains a capacity for continuing creative development and enjoyment.

Ancient airs and lays

> Central to the Gaelic culture of early and medieval Scotland and Ireland was the shared legacy of heroic narratives and the cycles of legends and ballad literature disseminated orally and in manuscripts by highly-literate, professional poets and bards. In time, their themes and texts entered popular currency and were passed down in vernacular tales and songs by local singers and story tellers.[19] These continued to be heard among the Gaelic speakers of the Glens of Antrim until the late nineteenth century[20] and even later in pockets of Argyll.[21]

Many of the events, places and characters of the very old Irish narratives became linked to specific sites through place-names and mentioned real locations in Antrim and Argyll in the texts. In this way, the relationship between place and lore, tangible and intangible heritage, became cemented. The Medieval verse '*Oidheadh Chloinne hUisneach*' preserved in the *Glenmasan Manuscript*,[22] for instance, uses places in Scotland as the setting for its story including Glen Masain, Glen Orchy, Glen Etive and Glendaruel. The story also embraces Antrim, including Rathlin and Carraig Uisneach, where Deirdre sang her farewell to Scotland and to her happiness.

Loch Etive from William Beattie, *Scotland Illustrated* (1838), vol. 2

In both countries we find many other examples of Neolithic monuments and landscape features associated, at some time, with the lives and deeds of legendary heroes[23] such as Ossian's Grave at Lubitavish, County Antrim.

Texts often survived only as fragments of a verse or in song, re-articulated with other material or redeployed away from their original contexts, such as in a work song. But it was the fact that they were sung that kept them alive: 'The popularity of the ballads was due in no small measure to the fact that they were sung to ancient airs' and that 'the singing of the ballads has helped to preserve their actual words'.[24]

From the eighteenth century onwards, partly inspired by the interest in things 'Ossianic', this inheritance attracted the attention of collectors, editors and translators (often local scholar-clergymen) and Argyll was a particularly fertile ground.[25]

A number of local airs 'most common in that part of the country' were taken down by Rev. Patrick McDonald, minister of Kilmore, south of Oban, and perhaps also by his brother Joseph. These included tunes to ballads from the Finn Cycle[26] and other songs as well as instrumental music. The resulting collection is perhaps the earliest published source of music for Gaelic heroic ballads or *laoidh*,[27] although these scores 'are unfortunately without their texts, and are moreover forced into regular modern rhythms between bar-lines'.[28] The collection contains the 'ancient' '*Dan Fhraoich*'[29] among its 'Argyllshire airs'. '*Laoidh Fhraoich*' ('The Lay of Fraoch'), one of the great Irish heroic ballads that tells of handsome Fraoch and Meadhbh, survived in Ireland 'in Rathlin Island only',[30] but remained popular in Scotland associated with specific places. In one version it is linked to the site of Fraoch Eilean, a small island in Loch Awe, Argyll, with a fort linked to the MacNaughtan chieftains. A version was subsequently collected by Frances Tolmie[31] and field recordings of sung versions can be auditioned on the *Tobair and Dualchais* website[32] along with reinterpretations by Rev. William Matheson.[33] John Purser has transcribed and discussed Matheson's 'unmetered approach of singing' the ballad.[34]

Interest in the musical heritage of Antrim was encouraged by the physician James McDonnell (1763–1845), who had family roots in Cushendall. He had trained in Scotland where he may have encountered the early efforts of the Highland Society of London to record and present old Scottish music.[35] McDonnell and his brothers were taught the harp by the blind harper Art O'Neill and he was to become a key player in the revival of interest in the Irish harp tradition in the 1790s by engaging the young Edward Bunting (1773–1843) to note down the music heard at the Belfast Harp Festival of 1792 and to progress his collecting and publishing work.

Bunting subsequently issued 'Long is the day without the Sons of Uisneach',[36] (also recorded as 'The Lamentation of Deirdre for Sons of Usneach' and 'Song of Clan Uisneach in the Poem of Deirdre') which he

The gravestone of Art O'Neill (d. 1816),
Eglish, County Tyrone, erected in 2016

said was 'still sung in various parts of the country to words corresponding
with those of the old national romance of the "Death of the Sons of
Usnach"'.[37] Bunting had taken down the notes 'from the singing, or rather
recitation, of a native of Murloch, in the county of Antrim' and remarked
that 'the same air and words are sung by natives of Scotland. A blind
woman from Cantyre [Kintyre] gave the identical notes in singing the
piece at Belfast about forty years ago'.[38] That version had come from the
'old Marchioness of Londonderry' who had learned it from the 'Blind
Highland Woman'.[39]

He published 'The Battle of Argan Mór – In the time of Ossian',
'written down from a Cushendall man in 1809, tenant to Dr
McDonnell'[40] and promoted the idea of a direct cultural link to Argyll:

> From the neighbouring ports of Cushendun and Cushendall was
> the principal line of communication with Scotland, and doubtless
> it was by this very route that the Ossianic poems themselves
> originally travelled into the country of Macpherson.[41]

In addition he issued an 'Ossianic Air, sung in the Highlands of
Scotland' as supplied by Sir John Sinclair of Edinburgh in 1808 who had
it from the Rev. Mr. Cameron, Minister of Halkirk in Caithness 'who
learned it many years ago from a very old man, a farmer on my estate, who
was accustomed to sing some of Ossian's poems to that air with infinite

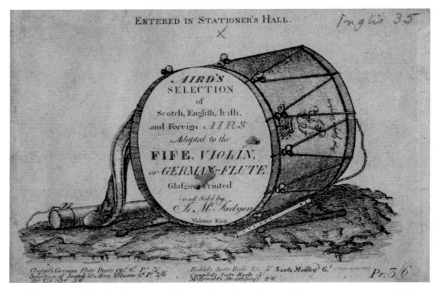

Title page of *Aird's Selection of Scotch, English, Irish and Foreign Airs …* (*c.* 1782)
(National Library of Scotland, Ing.35)

delight and enthusiasm'.[42] This air was also supplied by Sinclair to others who published it in their collections.

In 1815, the Gaelic-speaking musician Alexander Campbell travelled through the Highlands, including parts of Argyll, for the Royal Highland Society of Scotland with the purpose of collecting material for a 'great National Repository of Original and Vocal Poetry'. He returned with almost 200 items, including Ossianic material, a selection of which appeared in *Albyn's Anthology* where he wrote of the many Irish tunes that bear a 'striking resemblance to our Highland and Hebridean Airs' and 'the well-known fact, that there exists characteristic shades of difference only in the Music peculiar to both sides of the water'.[43]

Scotland also saw the collecting and publishing activities of Simon Fraser (1773–1852) and his son Angus (*c.* 1800–70).[44] Simon's *Airs and Melodies Peculiar to the Highlands of Scotland and the Isles* (1816) included 'Dan Ossian – Fingalian Air', the same as the 'Ossianic Air, sung in the Highlands of Scotland',[45] that had also been supplied by Sir John Sinclair to Bunting, '*Fonn lionarachd do bhriarabh Ossian* – Another air to which Ossian is recited'[46] and 'Dan Feinne – Fingalian Air'.[47] The last two had come via Simon's father from Alastar Mac H'uistan who was known in the eighteenth century as a 'sterling reciter of Ossian, and a bard'.[48] The first was 'a favourite Ossianic measure, to which the Editor has heard a great many fragments of the original recited.'[49] In his notes to the tune '*Caistal Inn 'rara*' ('Inveraray Castle') (perhaps his own composition) he stated that he was not particularly familiar with Argyll.[50]

Fraser was familiar with Ireland through military service and, like Campbell, stressed the similarities between Scottish and Irish music:

> ... it may become matter of very interesting research, to trace the Analogy and Similitude betwixt the ancient Music of the Highlands of Scotland, now first brought forward, and that of Ireland, or if they bear the affinity which their languages do; when their Languages appear to have been the same at one period, it will not seem surprising that a few of the melodies sung in the language are common to both Countries, with little variation.[51]

There are other sources of apparently old music that might link Ireland and Scotland, Antrim and Argyll, although Francis Collinson has cautioned against trusting their authenticity[52] on account of the composition of new Ossianic verse, and the fashionable re-branding and modernisation of tunes under the influence of the eighteenth-century international cult stimulated by the works of James Macpherson (1736–96). Such sources include Bowie's 1789 collection which contains three 'Airs by Fingal'[53] and other music possibly from the harp tradition, the collections of Niel Gow and his sons have 'Fingall's Lamentation', 'a very Old Gaelic Air',[54] and yet another occurrence of 'An original tune to which the poems of Ossian were originally sung' as provided by Sir John Sinclair in an arrangement with an 'under bass by an eminent organist of London' to be played 'very slow and pathetick' as well as a setting in Strathspey time.[55] The little-known Alexander Mackay collection[56] of 1775 has a strong Islay connection and is interesting on account of the simplicity of its settings while, possibly from the same island, is the two-volume *A Collection of Celtic Melodies*[57] (*c.* 1830) issued anonymously by 'a Highlander', which contain many 'original' airs 'never before published'. Most items have Gaelic titles.

Ossianic tunes in the early bagpipe collections such as 'Ossian's Hall', 'Fingal's Weeping', 'Oscar's Jig' are likely to have come from popular late eighteenth-century stage productions from London.[58]

It is thought that some of the airs included in the *Maclean-Clephane Manuscript* (1808) may be of the ancient Fenian lay type[59] and *The Elizabeth Ross Manuscript* of 1812, compiled in Raasay rather than Argyll, has three three ballad airs linked to the early Gaelic tales '*Bàs Dhiarmaid*' ('The Death of Diarmaid'),[60] '*Duan Fhraoich*'[61] and '*Cath Mhànuis*' ('Mànus' Battle').[62] Its modern editors also refer to the use of the 'air of an Ossianic hymn' as the tune to the well-known love song '*Feasgar Luain is mi air chuairt*' ('On a Monday evening, out for a stroll') by the poet William Ross (1762–91).[63]

In the Irish collections there is 'Deirdre's Lamentation for the Sons of Usnoth' in *O'Farrell's Pocket Companion*[64] and in Petrie's collection we find

'The Dirge of Ossian – as sung in the glens of Derry' and 'The Lamentation of Deirdre for the Sons of Usnach – set in Mayo',[65] 'Ossian's Lament' in Capt. Francis O'Neill's *Music of Ireland* (1903) and 'The Fingalian's Dance' is printed in O'Neill's *Waifs and Strays of Gaelic Melody*[66] and said to be taken from Thomson's *Hibernian Muse* of c. 1790.[67] They are undoubtedly others.

Ossianic titles also appear in the late nineteenth century as the Celtic Revival takes hold as in several pieces in Jane Fraser Morison's collection[68] and in published compositions of the fiddler James Scott Skinner.

Francis Collinson mentions the 'interesting' chants in the volumes of Marjorie Kennedy–Fraser and Kenneth Macleod's *Songs of the Hebrides*,[69] some of which were collected from singers in the early years of the twentieth century. There is suspicion that MacLeod (1871–1955), a native of Eigg who spend a part of his life on the Island of Gigha, had reworked or even composed some of the material, but it is invariably attractive. He certainly 'restored' the song 'Deirdre's Farewell to Scotland' from an Ossianic fragment and an ancient air he claimed to have collected.

Despite issues of authenticity and interpretation, the very old tunes and texts should be regarded as a precious resource with great cultural and artistic potential and enjoyed as effective and pleasing music. Fortunately, 'such songs are fast becoming recognised as the jewels that they are'[70] and there has been some sensitive reconstruction of verse and music[71] and scholarly and practical work around the most appropriate means of their performance.[72]

Modern folk-song collecting and study has recorded other heroic ballads collected in the field in the Scottish Gáidhealtachd outwith Argyll, including its diaspora[73] some of which can be auditioned at the *Tobair an Dualchais* website (A search using 'Ossianic' or 'Fingalian' is a good starting point). Also in the mid-twentieth century, the Gaelic scholar and lecturer Rev. William Mathieson (1910–95) of Edinburgh University worked diligently to identify and reconnect written texts with viable airs such as those in the Patrick McDonald and Simon Fraser collections.[74]

The Scottish musicologist, composer, writer and broadcaster John Purser has, in recent years, combined the Deirdre text from the Scottish *Glenmasan Manuscript* with the Irish music from Bunting's 1840 collection for public performance.[75]

The 'ancient' airs are attracting contemporary instrumentalists as well as singers, particularly harp players, who recognise their usefulness in an appropriate, historically-informed repertory.[76] One player of the Highland bagpipes has successfully adopted the air 'The Lamentation of Deirdre for Sons of Usneach', suggesting that as one of the oldest known pieces of Irish music it could easily have served, or might still serve, as the ground to a *piobaireachd*.[77]

Image showing a harpist performing at a Gaelic lord's feast
from John Derricke's *Image of Irlande* (1581)

Harp

The wire-strung harp or clarsach had a central role in both Scotland and
Ireland from Medieval times when it was integral to classical Gaelic bardic
culture. Verse was sung or declaimed to harp accompaniment and the
harpers were composers of songs and airs.[78] There is material evidence of
the harp in Argyll, including the carved detail of a fifteenth-century grave
slab preserved at Keills in Knapdale, and archaeological finds.[79]
Professional harpers were itinerant, staying for extended periods under the
patronage of different big houses across wide geographical areas, and some,
such as Duncan Dewar or Mac In Deor, harper to Campbell of
Auchinbreck, were able to make a comfortable living.[80] Patronage
extended across Gaelic Scotland and Ireland. Irish harpers, travelled
frequently to Scotland, such as Ruairi Dall Ó Catháin who almost
certainly passed through Argyll and the training of Scottish players, as with
Ruaidhri Dall Morison (*c.* 1656–*c.* 1714), may have been undertaken in
Ireland.[81] There were two principal families of harpers associated with
Kintyre; the MacIlschenochs, (later MacShannons), who were patronised
by the Lords of the Isles and held lands at the south of the peninsula, and
the Mac an Bhreatnaigh (or Galbraith) family that had lands from the
MacNeills on Gigha. In the sixteenth century the Campbells of Argyll were
served by the MacVicar family.[82]

The harp tradition went into decline as the social and political
infrastructure supporting the bardic schools waned.[83] While some Irish
players adapted to new conditions, those in Scotland may have been slower
to change with the result that harp playing in the Highlands faded rapidly
in the eighteenth century.[84] The aftermath of the Jacobite Risings

accelerated the demise of the tradition as old patterns of aristocratic patronage disappeared. Nevertheless, the instrument survived in the hands of amateurs and more versatile professionals, such as Patrick McErnace of Campbeltown[85] and the Kintyre musician and bard William McMurdy (d. *c.* 1780).

Irish professional harpers continued to visit Scotland, perhaps seeking the patronage being lost to them at home. Among these was Echlin O'Cathain (1729–*c.* 1790), a pupil of Cornelius Lyons (*c.* 1670–1740), harper to the earl of Antrim.[86] O'Cathain was admitted as a Burgess of the Burgh of Inveraray in 1751 and at Inveraray Castle he would have had contact with local musicians. The Maclean-Clephane Manuscripts contain old Gaelic harp tunes or *ports* and arrangements that may have been taken down from him in Scotland.

There were subsequent attempts to revive the harp in both Scotland and Ireland including initiatives in Antrim and Argyll. Dr McDonnell of Antrim, who had encouraged the work of Edward Bunting, worked with others in 1808 to establish an Irish Harp Society in Belfast.[87] A school was established for a while, with some pupils from Ballymena and the Glens of Antrim, and after it was re-launched in 1819 one of the tutors was the harper Valentine Rennie (*c.* 1796–1837) a native of Cushendall, County Antrim, and the second cousin of Robert Burns. Another musician associated with the school was Patrick Byrne (*c.* 1794–1863) 'the last of the great Irish harpers' who visited Edinburgh on a number of occasions. There was renewed revival activity in the early twentieth century associated with the Celtic revival and a harp festival was held in Belfast in 1903.

In Scotland, the first Gaelic Mód festival was held at Oban, Argyll, in the 1890s, and included competitions for harp. A subsequent revival in harp playing in Scotland was driven, in part, by a number of individuals with Argyll associations, including Lady Elspeth Campbell of Inveraray, Hilda Campbell of Airds, and Heloise Russell-Fergusson. There was an active Argyllshire branch of the Clarsach Society and summer schools were held in Oban and elsewhere from the early 1930s. These revivals consciously set out to identify and promote the separate 'national' music of each country, although there was exchange such as an invitation to the Mód competition winner to perform in Belfast.

Bagpipes

The special place of the Highland bagpipe within the culture of Argyll has been explained, somewhat simplistically, by its culturally strategic position between Ireland and the Hebrides:

> The pipers in Kintyre, on the whole, belonged to the group of Irish/Hebridean extraction, and they included MacAlisters,

MacCallums, MacMurchies, MacNeills, MacDonals, Macleans, Mackays, MacMichalls, McGeachies, MacKerrals, MacIntyres, MacQuilkans and Wilsons, all of whom probably moved from Antrim to Kintyre, sometimes by way of Islay or Gigha, over a considerable period of time.[88]

There is an early reference from around 1585, rare in classical Gaelic verse, to bagpipe music in the work of a poet associated with the McDonnells of Antrim.[89] The instrument was then an essential element of military activity, but came to assume by the seventeenth century an eminent role in elite Gaelic society, with its own musical forms and repertory.[90] A number of *piobaireachd*, or pibroch, the classical music of the Highland bagpipe, are associated in tradition with leading Irish personages. 'The Lament for the Earl of Antrim' may have been made following the death in 1636 of Randal McDonnell, the first earl of Antrim and son of Somhairle Buidhe. Somhairle, who died in 1590, is said to be the subject of 'The Lament for Samuel'. Furthermore, 'The Lament for Hugh' might have been made for either of the two Irish earls, Hugh O'Donnell or Hugh O'Neill, most likely the latter on account of his links with the Hebrides.[91] There are likely to be other examples[92] and old pipe music may survive in surviving examples of the Irish 'clan march'. There is also a traditional belief that the piper Donald Mor MacCrimmon (*c.* 1570–*c.* 1640) studied at a bardic school in Antrim in early 1590s, thus laying the foundation for the development of Scotland's most esteemed piping dynasty.[93]

Other examples of piping in the lore of Argyll and Antrim includes the tale of a raid cattle from Scotland. One of the pipers on the expedition was related to the people of the Antrim Glens, and to warn them he played the tune '*A mhnathan nan gline gur mithe dhuibh eirigh*' ('Ye wives of the glens, it's time you would rise') that enabled the women to protect their livestock.[94] A coded message also features in the story of Colla Chiotaich's piper, who, being held captive by Campbells in an Argyll castle (variously given as Duntroon, Dunyveg, or Dunaverty), was able to warn his master of the danger of capture as he approached by sea from Antrim by playing the pibroch '*A Cholla, a rùin, a seachain an dùn*' ('Coll, O, my dear, dinna come near').[95]

Aristocratic patronage of pipers was commonplace in the eighteenth century. MacDonald of Largie, at Killean, on the west of the Kintyre peninsula, for instance, had a piper named Maclellan and a multi-instrumentalist bard of Irish extraction, William McMurchy.[96] The MacAlisters of Loup, in north Kintyre, who claimed to able to trace their line back to the Clan Donald in Antrim,[97] are said to have maintained pipers drawn from their own clan[98] and there were also pipers in private service of the duke of Argyll, Campbell of Kilberry and others. As a boy on Islay in the 1820s, the folklorist John Francis Campbell had, as his first nurse and instructor in all things Highland, the piper John Campbell.

In common with the Lowland burghs, there were professional town pipers in Campbeltown, and Inveraray. The last Campbeltown incumbent, John MacAlister, a son of the piper to the laird of Loup, served until 1777.[99] The Inveraray piper in the 1760s was John McIlchonnel, who also had the trade of boat carpenter.[100]

Piping existed at the folk level too and was central in social dance, weddings, funerals and private entertainment. McIntosh tells of one piper of the late eighteenth century, called John Graham, 'who was simple but inoffensive, could play some tunes on the bagpipes and sing and talk wittily at times'[101] and, writing in 1796 of the large herring fleet on Loch Fyne, Thomas Pennant noted how 'on the week-days, the cheerful noise of the bagpipe and dance echoes from on board'.[102]

Highland pipers fulfilled important roles in clan campaigns, in the activities of various European armies of the 1600s and ultimately in the British army, where they were generally provided and maintained by the officers. Military piping in Argyll would have been strengthened by the presence of Dugald Campbell of Kintarbert. Dugald, an original officers of the Black Watch, who took charge of the Argyll Militia after 1746. The 42nd regiment had extended periods of service in different parts of Ireland in the years 1749–56 and 1767–72 and were present at various times in Antrim. The regiment went once more to Ireland in 1817, remaining there until 1825, and returned yet again in 1839–40. Also, during the peninsular War many young Irishmen joined the Highland regiments.[103] Piping also had a central place in the routines of the local Militia, Fencible and Volunteer Corps that were raised for internal defence.[104] One such outfit raised at Campbeltown participated in the Battle of Ballinahinch in 1798, after they were sent to Ireland to counter rebellion and French invasion.[105]

There are traditional fiddle tunes with titles suggesting military service by Scottish regiments in Ireland. The bagpipe-influenced strathspey 'The Highland Watch' or 'The Highlander's Farewell to Ireland' was published in Edinburgh in 1761.[106] The tune remains popular in Ireland as the reel 'Farewell to Ireland' or 'Farewell to Erin' and a setting, with words, was collected in Cape Breton in the 1970s.[107] A version, 'The Highlander's Farewell,' was collected in 1941 from fiddler Emmett Lundy of Grayson County, Virginia (1864–1953), along with the suggestion that its two contrasting represent a narrative between two parting lovers.[108] Simon Fraser published a tune 'An t-aiseadh do dh'Eireann' ('Crossing to Ireland').[109] This is clearly not a bagpipe tune and may have been originally devised for a military band of other instrumentation.[110] It is associated with the 78th Fraser Highlanders regiment that crossed to northern Ireland in 1757, probably at Carrickfergus, on route to Cork and embarkation for service in North America[111] and that no doubt returned via Ireland also. Today, the tune is commonly played a slow waltz rather than a march and has attracted a popular and romantic 'history' that it was written by an Irish emigrant returning to his native home from North America.

Standardised military pipe bands were introduced around the time of the Crimean War in the mid-nineteenth century.[112] Civilian pipe bands were established throughout Scotland and beyond in the late nineteenth century and among the first in the Highlands was the Inveraray Pipe Band. Both types of ensemble helped change and develop the bagpipe repertory and styles of playing. They also stimulated interest in piping among the general population through learning and performance opportunities and competitions, and still do so today.

A number of Argyll personnel were highly influential in the development and promotion of modern bagpiping, both light music and *piobaireachd*. John Campbell of Kilberry was a founder of the Pibroch Society in 1902, as was Lady Elspeth Campbell, piper and niece of the duke of Argyll. Argyll has also produced many of the 'heroes' of modern bagpiping including Duncan MacLean, Archie Kenneth, and John MacColl and there have been several family 'dynasties' of outstanding players.

Argyll has long been the site of major piping events such as the Dunoon Highland Gathering, the Argyllshire Gathering at Oban and other local highland games and competitions. There is a considerable body of bagpipe music composed by Argyll-related pipers with much named after local people, places and events.[113] The large number of tunes associated with the Campbells of Argyll has also been itemised.[114]

While the history of the Highland bagpipe in Ireland is still to be written, references extracted from the Ordnance Survey Memoirs for various parishes of Antrim in the 1830s confirm that the instrument was popular there, along with the fiddle.[115] Just as there is evidence of Scottish Gaelic song on Rathlin it is not surprising to note piping on the island.[116] The Celtic Revival in Ireland saw the promotion of bagpiping, including the use of a two-drone 'war pipe' version of the Highland instrument, and in 1909 it was reported that the pipes were being put to 'more characteristically Irish use than the ordinary fife and drum, or brass band'.[117]

Despite efforts to establish a distinctly Irish form of bagpipe playing, the influence of the Highland bagpipe and its repertory, reinforced by military, police and civilian bands, came to exercise a dominating influence in Ireland. This would have happened relatively easily in Antrim where there were already survivals of Scottish music, ongoing culture contact and an identification with Scotland. It is not surprising, therefore, to find pipers from Antrim achieving outstanding status within the world-wide network and infrastructure of Highland piping.

Music from Scotland and Ireland, Argyll and Antrim continue to cross over, as part of a larger complex interchange of bagpipe repertory within the modern piping world. Away from the band and competition circuit, it is difficult to determine the extent of more informal interaction and exchange.

Gaelic song

Argyll supported a lively culture of song in Gaelic well into the modern period. The history of the heritage is diverse and complex with different traditions and interacting over centuries. Some songs had origins in the classical bardic verse of the thirteenth century onwards associated with the clans and their chiefs that became diluted and spread into the vernacular practice. New styles emerged after the sixteenth century involving a variety of types of song maker, with different levels of literacy, including highly-accomplished women.[118] Donald Meek talks of the 'almost inexhaustible' number of poets and songsters 'particularly of the local 'township bard' type, commemorating events and personalities within their own districts'[119] while John Shaw has written that:

> Throughout the twentieth century many hundreds of songs were recorded from singers in Argyll, embracing the well-known Gaelic genres: love songs, panegyrics, songs of exile, waulking songs for shrinking the tweed, humorous and satirical songs, sea songs, and religious songs. Many are attributed to specific bards such as Duncan Ban MacIntyre and the earlier Maclean bards of Mull, but a good number, as is universally characteristic of Gaelic song, are anonymous. Modern fieldwork bears witness to the survival of a lively and vigorous community song tradition. The wealth of older songs recorded in Tiree since the 1950s is complemented by a dynamic tradition of song-making from local bards; locally-composed songs have played a central part in the social life of the community at all levels and have survived in great numbers. Of these, the older compositions go back to the middle of the eighteenth century … Often they are associated with the numerous families of song composers, some of whom have been active for two centuries … Like other songs, these have been passed down primarily by oral transmission, often set to well-known airs, and dealing with favourite topics such as love, religion, politics, and satirical commentary.[120]

Furthermore, Anne Lorne Gillies has noted that 'In the glut of nostalgic Gaelic songs which appeared from the mid-nineteenth century onwards, a large number originated in Argyll.'[121] Argyll was, of course, just one part of Gaelic Scotland and its singers would rarely restrict their repertories to only local material.

Vernacular Gaelic song was sustained, along with the language, within the more remote pockets of both communities where old ways of communal entertainment survived:

> In the rural districts of Kintyre, which were numerously inhabited – a number of families residing in each town – the people were in the habit of going 'a ceilidhing' of visiting during the long winter nights, amusing themselves with pastimes – chiefly with singing Gaelic songs and the poems of Ossian, and occasionally a tune on the fiddle or bagpipes.[122]

The singer Joy Dunlop has recently explored Argyll-related songs held in the sound archive of the School of Scottish Studies at the University of Edinburgh and has made a commercial recording featuring her own singing of a selection of these.[123] Although only a small sample, this illustrates the breadth of the heritage outlined above and demonstrates its artistic potential.

Listeners can audition the archival versions of the items she used via the *Tobair an Dualchais* website. Among other relevant recordings that can be auditioned at the site is Angus MacFadyen's singing of '*Birlinn Cholla Chiotaich*',[124] the words of which were composed by Duncan Johnston of Islay (1881–1947). This describes the galley of Colla Chiotaich (Colkitto), praises his bravery and tells of his descent from the noble MacDonalds of Islay and Antrim. An arrangement of the song can also be heard on *Sruth air a' Charraig*, a compact disc of local songs sung by Islay Gaelic Choir.[125] Choral singing became an important part of Gaelic culture in Scotland from the late nineteenth century, introduced through the efforts of a number of Argyll-based aristocrats and enthusiasts anxious to preserve, promote and 'improve' the song tradition.

The Argyll song '*A Dhòmhnaill nan Dòmhnall*' ('Donald of the Donalds') is said to celebrate the historic connections between the two localities[126] and there is an intriguing record from Rathlin in 1837, that describes communal occupational singing similar to that employed in the Highlands of Scotland in waulking cloth:

> ... being musically inclined a song was commenced. The peculiarity of the tune attracted my notice, and one of the men having kindly requested my presence, if I wished to hear a Raghery song, I gladly joined the party. A new song was now begun – it was a duet, to which a chorus was attached, sung by the whole party.

The two principal performers took hold of each other by the right hand, and kept time with the tune by striking their hands, thus entwined, on the table. The song lasted at least fifteen minutes and was sung in their native language, with greater spirit and warmth of feeling than is usually displayed by more fashionable vocalists.[127]

McIntosh mentions waulkings, to both female and male singing, in Kintyre.[128]

While it might be expected that the corpus of Gaelic songs sung in Argyll included material with Antrim origins, connections or counterparts, there remains a need for extensive and expert research to identify more than these few examples, bearing in mind the proviso that:

> There is very little overlap between the folk-song traditions of Gaelic Scotland and Ireland – very few shared songs, or even lines of songs – and several important styles and subjects are found in one country's tradition that are entirely unattested in the other.[129]

Although there are references to Gaelic songs from Antrim,[130] Nils Homer observed in 1942 that 'It is a pity that there are very few songs in Irish from the Glens.'[131] One such song that still lives is '*Àird a' Chumhaing*'. According to tradition this is the lament of a Glensman living in exile in Scotland (Kintyre or Ayrshire are variously given) from where he can see the mountains of home. Some attribute the words to one Cormac Ó Néill, a native of Glendun, but living in Glenariffe, while others suggest it was taken down in the early nineteenth century from John McCambridge, a native of Mullarts born about 1793, whose descent can be traced back to settlers from Kintyre in the early 1600s. The song and its air became a favourite in the twentieth century folk song revival when it was recorded by some of its leading performers.[132] More recently, in 2012, it was featured in a BBC Northern Ireland documentary *Amhráin Aduaidh*[133] where it was sung by Ciaira McCrickard and is included in the repertory of Scottish Gaelic singer and piper Griogair Labhruidh, who is from a well-known musical family from north Argyll.[134]

Given the flourishing of song in Argyll at a time when Irish was still spoken in pockets of Antrim, we would expect to find that a few of the more fashionable Scots Gaelic folksongs were taken up by Irish singers. One such example might be the popular Scottish song '*Fear a'Bhata*'[135] that was known on Rathlin where it was associated with Katie Glass (1859–1954) who had family links back to Tarbert in Kintyre. There was an informative TG4 television documentary *Ceol nan Oileán: Oileán Reachrainne*[136] concerning the song in Ireland that also featured '*Each ceanann dubh*', a naturalised version of a Scots Gaelic song of the seventeenth century sung by Michaél Mac Uigín in 1972. Other songs, since popular in Donegal, ('*Donal agus Morag*' and '*Mo Choill*') are said to have been brought there via Rathlin by singer and piper Niall McCurdy who had worked as a stonemason in Scotland and on lighthouses.[137]

Song in English and Scots

> There is not any ancient music in the parish. Their airs and ballads are merely those commonly known in the county, and are strictly Scottish. There is much taste for music, but their voices are not generally good, nor is their taste by any means correct.[138]

> Their ears are generally much better than their voices, which are by no means soft or sweet. There is much taste for music, but they have not any other than the common airs of the county.[139]

The fruits of the collecting of Sam Henry, and others before and after him, confirm Antrim as a repository of vernacular song in both English and, to a limited degree, in Scots.[140] Despite the strong Scottish poetic strain in the song of Antrim, 'even with the most strongly Scottish-influenced areas, less than 10 per cent of the present repertory was originally Scottish. Nevertheless, Scottish words pervade Irish song and Scottish accents dominate the singing style of some areas.'[141] The music of Joe Holmes (1906–78), County Antrim singer, fiddle player and bearer of verse and stories, exhibited clear links to Scottish tradition[142] as did that of the singer and musician John Kennedy whose songs 'immediately confirm a musical affinity with the Lowland Scots song tradition in both repertory and delivery'.[143]

Cooper[144] has discussed ballad survivals in Northern Ireland and he, Moulden,[145] Hewitt[146] and others[147] have drawn particular attention to the wealth of song and verse making among Antrim's rural and weaver community in the nineteenth century. In terms of the Scottishness of the output of these songsmiths, Moulden has suggested that:

> It would be easy to suppose that the poets of Down and Antrim wrote in imitation of Burns and other Scottish poets but the reality is much more complex. In fact there was an independent Ulster-Scots poetic tradition the roots of which travelled with Scottish immigrants to Ulster in the sixteenth and seventeenth centuries. Hugh McWilliams' poetry was a branch of the same trunk as supported Burn's works. The dual centres of this Ulster-Scots tradition were North Down and Mid Antrim, in both of which McWilliams lived. They were the most thoroughly colonised parts of Ulster where the language was Scots modified by Irish at the peripheries. A variety of Scots was the natural language of much of North Ulster and when it took poetic form it did not copy Scots: it

was Scots. It did not copy Burns: it was influenced and encouraged by Burns and in some ways it was his superior.

This poetic tradition in Ulster had its greatest flowering during the early to mid- nineteenth century when about 40 poets achieved publication.[148]

As in Scotland, the audience for their songs included, not just the families of farmers and handloom weavers, but also those engaged in the secure specialist trades such as farriers and smiths, joiners, saddlers, millwrights, masons, slaters and thatchers, tailors and shoemakers. These were 'the people who crowded the fireside in "Tam o' Shanter"' who "came to form a distinct subculture, neither entirely urban nor rural.'[149] The cultural environment that nurtured this song culture was highly literate, musical, participatory and oral. There was close integration of traditional music into many aspects of everyday life and rituals, favoured dance and march tunes invariably carried words and instrumental music drew heavily on the song repertory.

There was a Scottish Lowland strand in song in Argyll also and attention was drawn to a rich seam of Scots song there by Hamish Henderson in the middle decades of the twentieth century. A speculative song-hunting foray into southern Kintyre in the summer of 1940 brought him into contact with the singing shepherd Jimmy McShannon of Kylepole near Machrihanish who was a bearer of agricultural 'bothy songs'. His informant was proud of his Irish and bardic forebears:

> I asked Jimmy to tell me about his surname, which I had never come across before, and he explained that the original form of the name had been MacShennack; he believed his family was descended from the *seanchaidh* (historian/storyteller) who had come over from Ireland with General Alexander MacDonald – this being the famous Alasdair Mac Colla Chiotaich, alias Young Colkitto, who played such a dramatic part in Montrose's campaign of 1644.[150]

On a return visit in 1956, he located Willie Mitchell, a butcher in Campbeltown who collected and wrote songs and poetry. Mitchell had painstakingly documented material from local oral tradition, copied songs from newspapers and other printed sources and gathered items from local writers. Subsequently, valuable contributions came from Jimmy McShannon and other members of his family including Alec McShannon who gave a localised version of the Irish song 'The Blazing Star o' Drum' in which:

> … a man from Londonderry working in Kintyre falls in love with a young maid, but is unable to court her because of her parents'

anger. The song closes with the singer wishing her a good life, mentioning that she is aboard a ship.[151]

Accordion to Hugh Shields, Drum may refer to a number of locations in Ulster and that:

> The song is at any rate a local one, commonplace in its description of courtship, love and parting, broad enough in its appeal to have taken root on the margin of Scotland.[152]

Adoption into Argyll was, no doubt, aided by the fact that '*Druim*' (Sc. Gaelic: 'ridge'), anglicised as 'Drum', is commonly found in place names in Scotland and the presence, west of Kilchenzie near Machrihanish, of a farm named 'Drum' from at least the 1860s.[153] Alec also gave 'Machrihanish Bay' a local version of the Irish ballad 'The Wreck of the Enterprise' which related to the loss of a ship called the 'Enterprise of Lynn' on the reef at Ringfad, one mile north of Carnlough, County Antrim, in 1827.

Another local song collector, Archibald McEachran, a farmer at Kilblaan, provided Mitchell with the Irish version of 'The Blazing Star o' Drum' that he had got from Sam Henry. McEachran also supplied the song 'The Thatchers of Glenrea' that he had also given to the Irish collector. This had come originally from a Hugh McMillan of Kilbride who had it from the singing of its author, Hector McIlfatrick (d. *c.* 1900) a thatcher of Ballycastle. Henderson identifies this as a clear illustration of music and song crossing the Moyle drawing attention to the mixture of Scots and Irish dialects in one of the verses as further evidence of interaction:

> 'I can theek wi' ould rashes, wi' heather or ling,
> Bent, bracken, or dockens or any wan thing.'
> 'Oh, you're just the man 'il get plenty tae dae,
> And I'll get you a ladder,' says McNeill o' Glenrea.[154]

Willie had a number of other popular Irish songs and used Irish song airs for his own, some no doubt gathered some while on his cycling holidays in Ireland. This material he propagated in the community through the weekly ceilidhs that always ended with 'The Parting Glass', an Irish equivalent of the old Scots song of departure 'Good Night and Joy be wi ye a'. His repertory was maintained by his family and other local singers, but during the Troubles much of the more overtly Irish material was set aside. It is also interesting to note that in his later years Willie Mitchell took a great interest in Irish poetry, including the work of contemporary writers from Antrim. Only later was it realised that his great-grandparents had come from Ireland.[155]

Transmission, adoption and localisation of songs in English and Scots was therefore relatively straightforward and 'The songs of Scotland came easily across the seas of Moyle to the northern part of this island. In the Glens of Antrim, for instance, there were songs like the Glenshesk version of "The Mountain Streams".'156 This song was associated with the singer Denis Cassley:

> … a traditional singer with a beautiful voice … [who] lived here and had a fine store of Glen songs. His version of 'The Mountain Streams' is different … but the melody is one that haunts for many moons and deserves to be better known:
>
> > Then I'll bid adieu to Scotch and valleys
> > To yon mountain stream and the plains below
> > And in your arms, love, I will embrace you
> > Near yon mountain streams where the moorcocks crow.157

Another example of the easy relationship between Argyll and Ulster through song is found in an Irish text that mentions the Scottish location as if it were just another familiar part of the singer's home area:

> Farewell to Londonderry town likewise Lough Swilly shore
> It was there I spent some happy days I never might see them more
> Farewell a while to sweet Argyll where oftimes I have been
> And twice farewell to my own dear girl she dwells near Ardmore Green.158

There is also the transfer and adaptation of the well-known Scottish song 'The road and the miles tae Dundee', sung in Antrim as 'Sweet Carnlough Bay'.159

The Scots and English material sung in both Antrim and Argyll was subject to Gaelic influence. On this, Moulden has singled out the output of Hugh McWilliams (fl. 1816–31) for its '… features which throw doubt on the existence of any clear separation of cultural concerns in the mid Antrim valleys and glens during a part of the nineteenth century'160 while others suggest it is possible to identify Gaelic influence in the language, meter and structure.161 Angus MacVicar wrote on the Kintyre song 'Flory Loynachan':

> … sung at the concerts in the old days was 'Flory Loynachan', a kind of ballad. It was composed by John Brollachan or Brodie, a native of Campbeltown. … a valuable specimen of the dialect of the people of Campbeltown and Southend 100 years ago [i.e. *c.* 1865], the words and phrases deriving from Gaelic, Irish and broad Scots.

The subject was said to have been born at Shenachie, Glenhervie, but latterly lived at Eden Farm before leaving for Canada where she married.

> Dear Flory Loynachan, if thou
> Thro Sanna's soun wert tossed,
> And rouchled like a shougie-shoo
> In a veshal with ane mast;
> Though the nicht was makin for a roil,
> Though rallaich were the sea,
> Though scorlins warpled my thowl pins,
> My shallop wad reach thee.

Anne Lorne Gilles mentions the interplay between Highland Gaelic and Scots texts and airs:

> … the Gaelic musical tradition has had a considerable effect on so-called 'Lowland' Scots music and vice versa: despite their apparent divergence over the centuries, Scots and Gaelic song have much in common … In fact the two cultures have lived side by side to a much larger extent than is often realised by people who think of Gaelic as being confined to the far north-west hinterland …. And it is clear that Burns and his contemporaries were quite familiar with Gaelic music.[162]

Similarly, Irish influence on traditional song texts and tunes in Scotland, including the song-rich North East, is widely accepted. Post-famine immigration, seasonal labour are obvious routes for this while Gavin Greig attributed much to contact between Scots and Irish soldiers serving together in British armed forces in the nineteenth century.[163]

No discussion of links in traditional song can ignore the role of the traveller community that has been passing between Scotland and Ireland for centuries, as marked in Jimmy MacBeath's signature song 'Come a' ye Tramps and Hawkers':

> I think I'll go to Paddy's land, I'm making up my mind
> For Scotland's getting' gammy noo,
> I can hardly raise the wind.
> But I will trust in Providence, if Providence will prove true,
> And I will sing of Erin's Isle when I come back to you.

The travelling people have a long association with Argyll, many being regarded as tradition bearers[164] and surely it is members of this community that nineteenth-century historian of Kintyre, Peter McIntosh, describes here:

A number of vagrants went round regularly among the people, who were cheerfully welcomed, and in no instance were any of them refused admittance. Some of these beggars amused the people with stories and songs, and could repeat many of Ossian's poems, many of them having extraordinary memories. The people were very glad when any of them came that way, and made every effort at being successful in getting them to their houses, and the neighbours would assemble at night to hear their stories. Some of them could play the bagpipes and fiddle.[165]

The singer and story-teller Duncan Williamson (1928–2007), who was born by Loch Fyne, has been recognised as a modern bard. Williamson was:

> ... arguably the finest storyteller from Argyll [he described] storytelling scenes from his childhood. On winter nights in a tent with a paraffin lamp and a fire in the middle of the floor, he would listen to tales told by his grandmother and grandfather.[166]

He also learned songs while working the turf in the mountains of Argyll as a youth with 'an old Irishman', Patrick O'Donnell, and while engaged in dry-stone dyke building at Auchindrain. He recalled travelling to Ireland and how, in Ulster and elsewhere, he would surprise the company he was in by singing the old Irish songs he learned as a boy.[167] From him was recorded a fragment of the classical ballad 'Hind Horn' (Child 17) and a set of verses of 'Lady Margaret', a ballad which was later developed into a version of 'Tam Lin'. The latter underlines the importance of both Argyll and Antrim as a repository of the old ballads as Sam Henry also collected a substantial version of the song from Alexander Crawford of Leck, Ballymoney.[168]

Some of the Kintyre repertory found new life during the modern folk song revival in Scotland and in Ireland. The Borders shepherd and singer Willie Scott (1897–1989) adopted the emigrant song 'Callieburn' ('Machrihanish Bright and Bonnie')[169] and Dick Gaughan recorded 'The Thatchers of Glenrae' in 1972.[170] Greenock-born folksinger Tony Cuffe (1954–2001) took a version of the song 'The Road to Drumlemble' around the world with his band Ossian and the song was also taken up by others. Another revival favourite, found in Scotland on broadsides in the nineteenth century and recorded in Kintyre and elsewhere,[171] is 'Erin-Go-Bragh'. This details the treatment of a man from Argyll who, on a visit to Edinburgh, is persecuted when he is mistaken for an Irish immigrant.

My name's Duncan Campbell, from the shire of Argyle,
I've travelled this country for many a mile—

I've travelled through England. And Ireland and a';
And the name I go under 's bold Erin-go-Bragh.[172]

Many other songs live on and interaction and exchange clearly continues, as observed recently by the traditional singer Len Graham:

> The North Channel being just 12 miles from Fair Head to Argyll and Kintyre, I used to be able to look over to Kintyre, to Campbeltown, to Islay, from where I grew up ... We have some migrant versions of Scottish songs in Ulster, usually they have been matched up with a different melody and words altered, but that is the tradition. It's a living tradition and that is what makes it so fascinating that you have all these variations of songs. It's been a lifelong fascination of mine and I can't imagine life without having that interest.[173]

Fife, flute and drum

Antrim is noted for its tradition of fife and drum playing and for marching flute bands, both of which are principally associated with the Protestant community. The lambeg drum and fife combination is a unique Ulster phenomenon without direct links to Scottish musical practice although flute bands have been known elsewhere in the British Isles.

Fife and drum playing in British military service had been inspired by the musicians of the *Landsknechten*, the Swiss and German mercenaries of the fifteenth and sixteenth centuries,[174] but was abandoned by the 1690s.[175] However, it was reintroduced after the Battle of Culloden:

> It is said that a contingent of Hessians hired to augment the government forces during the suppression of the '45 Rebellion brought with them a band of fifers and drummers, and that their music so impressed the Duke of Cumberland that he ordered the fife to be reintroduced into the British Army.[176]

After its founding in 1795, the Orange Order adopted the established military marching format of fife and drum to accompany its rituals. A wider band tradition developed that, by the 1870s, was 'more broadly based, borrowing material, some from the British Army, but including classical and popular material, a basic corpus of 'Party tunes' and some traditional material as well.'[177] The army repertory already included Irish and Scottish song and dance music:

> ... think of the good old tunes, 'Larry O'Gaff', 'Old Rosin the Beau', 'Hills of Glenorchy', 'Molly MacIntyre', 'Kinegad Slashers', 'Timour the Tartar', 'Paddy Whack', 'Devil among the Tailors', 'Roaring Jerry', 'Johnnie Cope', and the rest.[178]

Title page of Fraser's *Airs and Melodies Peculiar
to the Highlands of Scotland and the Isles* (1816)

Military tunes also passed into popular usage as in the Aberdeenshire folk
song 'Where Gaudie Rins' which is sung to the tune formerly known as
'The Hessian's March'.[179]

Of potential interest here, is the small collection of music manuscripts
used by the 42nd Regiment (The Black Watch) that survives in the

National Library of Scotland.[180] These date from 1813 although it is known that the outfit had fifes from the 1760s. Inscriptions in the books indicate that their players were from or based in the Oban area and that some were Gaelic speakers. They contain mainly Scottish tunes, but also English marches, Continental waltzes and Irish jigs. Their content might be taken as the official tunes of the regiment although there are personal selections too that may be taken from published collections for the fife[181] and the fiddle.[182] While there is no obvious influence from piping nor any musical or title links to Argyll there are tunes with Irish origins or connections ('Money in Both Pockets', 'The Monaghan Jig', 'Crop the Croppies' and 'St Patrick's Day in the Morning'). This could simply reflect popular taste or the fact that the 42nd had seen extensive service in Ireland. Fife manuscripts also survive in Ireland (including material collected by Bunting[183] and those considered by Cooper[184] and Hastings[185]) that offer opportunities for comparative study.

Of the Militia, Fencible and Volunteer regiments active in Argyll, it is noted that a regiment based at Inveraray that had seen service in Limerick area in 1798 marched to fife and drums.[186] Those volunteer outfits that continued after the signing of the Treaty of Paris in 1815 continued to employ fife or flute and drums. Such bands also arose among the civilian population as an accessible and inexpensive means of communal 'rational recreation' when other instruments were not affordable or appropriate. These were associated with towns and burghs, trade guilds and craft associations, educational institutions and temperance groups that participated in annual processions, demonstrations and civic rituals. Over time, they gave way to more high-status brass, reed and bagpipe ensembles, although there are survivals in the temperance bands of north-east Scotland,[187] the flute and drum heard at the annual burgh celebrations in Linlithgow, West Lothian, and at the Common Riding at Langholm in the Scottish Borders. There is a record of fife or flute accompaniment of the annual Masons' Walk at Rosehearty in Aberdeenshire,[188] including the repertory involved, and it is noted that such rituals were a feature of life in parts of Antrim also.[189]

Marching bands also continue in Scotland in association with the Grand Orange Order and other groups. While there is a County Grand Lodge of Ayrshire, Renfrewshire and Argyll with several lodges in Argyll, it is not known if there is any associated musical activity.

The concert flute enjoyed popularity in both Scotland and Ireland during the eighteenth and nineteenth centuries, but this declined with changes in musical fashion and the rise of the more 'national' instruments such as the fiddle and bagpipes. One interesting source is the 1835 flute manuscript of Andrew Small of Carrickfergus.[190] Comprising mainly Scottish dance tunes from the fiddle repertory, song airs and military pieces there are also tunes of Irish interest including 'Paddy O'Carroll' (pasted in), 'Paddy Whack', 'Sprig of Shillela', 'Humours of Glen', 'Irish Jig', 'Paddy Carey', 'Kitty Tyrrel' and 'Boys of Killkenny'. Preliminary research indicates that Small was a Scottish draper (born in Angus) who married at Carrickfergus where he worked. By 1851, he and his wife Margaret and a child were living at Blairgowrie, Scotland, close to Andrew's place of birth. He may have subsequently relocated to the Carolinas, perhaps after experiencing business difficulties. There may also be an Argyll connection on account of a faint pencil note in the manuscript: 'Richard … Campbeltown 1835'.[191] Irish music occurs in other Scottish flute collections and manuscripts including a duet setting of the air 'Carrickfergus'[192] with variations put down in the period between 1790 and 1820.

Scotland and Ulster both have a number of flute choirs that specialise in arranged music of all types, but there is no known activity of this type in Argyll.

Fiddle and accordion

> The violin is the favourite instrument with the men and several perform on it.[193]

Evidence such as this, found in the Ordnance Survey Memoirs, suggests that fiddle playing, and social dance, was closely integrated into social life in parts of Antrim during the first decades of the nineteenth century.[194] Analysis of the styles and repertories of Antrim fiddlers Joe Holmes, James Perry (1906–85) and other players indicates that, in the first part of the twentieth century, mid and north Antrim still supported a fiddle culture, with distinct regional stylistic characteristics that included strong Scottish elements.[195]

There are references too to fiddle playing in Argyll from the eighteenth century onwards. In the 1790s it was recorded that the parish of Gigha and Cara included, in its population of 614 persons, 100 farmers, crofters and cottagers and, by handcraft, 5 weavers, 4 tailors, 2 boat carpenters, 2 inn keepers, 1 mason, 1 distiller, 1 blacksmith, 1 fiddler and 2 pipers. Gaelic was spoken, but was 'not reckoned the purest' due to the 'vicinity to Ireland' and 'intercourse with the low country.'[196] Passing through north Argyll on his music collecting foray in 1815, Alexander Campbell encountered and described a number of fiddlers, most notably Angus MacDonald of Clachy near Aros in Mull, a cabinet maker and jack-of-all-trades who, 'draws a bold, rough fiddle stick, and is no mean dab at a dancing measure of any sort'.[197] The Swiss traveller Necker de Saussure's 1822 record of a tour of Highland Scotland describes a dance in Iona with fiddlers[198] and there are references[199] to the Ayrshire fiddler Matthew Hall and Highland fiddler James MacLachlan (or McLauchlan) as resident musicians at Inveraray under the patronage of the duke of Argyll around 1790. Hall is recorded as a cellist and dance band-leader to the aristocracy[200] while MacLachlan, who had previously been footman to Lord John Campbell at Inveraray, was known to Robert Burns.[201] On Islay, the folklorist John Francis Campbell (1822–85) had 'made early acquaintance with a blind fiddler who could recite stories'[202] and in 1859 he engaged Hector MacLean schoolmaster at Ballygrant, to gather ancient Gaelic folk tales from him that were subsequently published in his *Popular Tales of the West Highlands*. The blind fiddler/storyteller was James Wilson who had had got his tales directly from one Angus MacQueen of Ballochroy, near Portaskaig, 'who could recite Ossian's poems.'[203]

The fiddle was used to accompany dancing at all levels of society at popular 'winter balls' and at wedding dances, or dancing weddings, which were open affairs attracting people from a wide distance.[204] In a letter from G. Brandon, governess to Mary Campbell, wife of Alexander Campbell, advocate, in November 1805 we read of a Halloween event at Barcaldine:

> … we drank Tea and had a splendid Ball, we had not the coarse Music of a Bagpipe but a very capital Fiddler … we stayed to Supper and returned about 2 o'clock, your Maids were still more fashionable for they did not return till near 5 o'clock for they had the tricks of Halloween to perform after we left them.[205]

A description of the annual estate ball at Kilberry in the period 1887–1914 indicates a local preference for the music of the pipes over that of the fiddle:

> There was no M. C., the principle being that the piper was in control of the proceedings, and whatever he chose to play the company had to dance. Sometimes there was a tune by a fiddler, but reels, polkas, and schottisches were always played on the pipes, for in those days pipers were tolerably numerous in the locality.[206]

Other Argyll fiddlers active in the eighteenth and nineteenth centuries included 'one of the MacKerrals at Gar, who gave his occupation as 'musician' in the parish register.[207] Garvachy was a weaving community close to Campbeltown that was originally populated with people from Antrim and noted for its poets and musicians. Peter McIntosh, historian of Kintyre, stated that musicians were much celebrated and appreciated in that peninsula:

> The chief instruments in use half a century ago [i.e. *c.* 1810] were the bagpipes and fiddle, or violin, which were used at marriages, and other occasions. McPhee in Carradale was an extraordinary performer on the violin. Donald Macandoire, or Dewar, a blind man, father of the celebrated Dr. Dewar, Principal of Aberdeen [Marischal] College, was a sweet player on the fiddle, was much respected, frequently employed and well remunerated.[208]

The fiddler McPhee of Carradale may have been the same 'Town fiddler called MacPhee' at Inveraray in the 1760s.[209] This and the other Scottish references point towards a pattern of a relatively small number of local professional or semi-professional fiddlers, perhaps enjoying a degree of patronage, scattered across Argyll[210] rather than any wider participation which did not occur throughout Scotland as a whole until after the middle of the nineteenth century. There were also professional dancing masters were working in Kintyre from at least the 1750s[211] and the people 'were well trained, having dancing schools in the neighbourhood, generally for a month in the year'.[212] Such teachers were also active in Ulster from the end of the century, including Antrim,[213] offering instruction in the fashionable 'Scotch Dances'.[214] It is most likely that the circuits of at least some of these individuals took in both Antrim and Argyll and that, as fiddlers, they would have supplemented their income by giving music tuition, thus helping to spread the music further.

It was not unusual for pipers to play fiddle also. Mackenzie notes that 'MacDonald of Largie, at Killean, on the west side of Kintyre, opposite the island of Gigha, was a patron of music and had his own pipers. In 1745 these included a piper called Maclellan, and another, William MacMurchy, whose family was probably of Irish origin. William was also his bard, a most talented man who played the pipes, the fiddle and the harp, as well as being an accomplished Gaelic poet'.[215] Others included Sandy MacBeill, coachman and chauffeur at Kilberry, 'a good orthodox player of MSR [march, strathspey and reel] and a competent fiddler'[216] and champion piper John MacColl (1860–1943) who was 'a more than competent violinist'[217] having followed in the footsteps of his father Dugald, who was a tailor at Kentallen and an enthusiastic piper and fiddler.[218]

We know nothing about how or what these early Argyll fiddlers played, but we might assume that the repertory and style was closely related to that of the Highland bagpipe. Clues to a possible local style might be found in the playing of twentieth-century West Highland fiddlers. Aonghas Grant of Lochaber[219] and Farquar MacRae of Roshven (neither in Argyll) are perhaps the most notable players in this context. Given the strong affinity for bagpipe music, Argyll may have heard playing of slow airs with extended variations in the bagpipe manner known as the 'fiddle pibroch'. Rev. Patrick McDonald, who was a competent violinist, published a setting of '*Cumha Mhic a h-Arasaig*' (McIntosh's Lament) as 'communicated by Mr Campbell of Ardchattan'[220] while the McFarlane Manuscript contains '*Cumha Easbuig Earraghàidheal*' (Lament for the Bishop of Argyll) which may be dedicated to Donald Carswell, the sixteenth-century bishop of Argyll.[221] Further evidence linking to piping is Angus Martin's reference to fiddler Rob Campbell's 'cantering' by which 'his richly timbered voice would charm to dancing many a guest'.[222]

There is little to suggest a strong Argyll fiddle tradition in the names of tunes in published collections of fiddle music, other than pieces dedicated to the pre-eminent Campbell family found in high-status publications (e.g. 'Islay House', 'Iveraray Castle', 'Duchess of Argyle', 'Duke of Argyle's Strathspey', 'Lady Charlotte Campbell', 'Lady Elinor Campbell', etc.). This contrasts greatly with the piping repertory that contains many tunes named after local places, events and individuals of every status in Argyll, including the aristocracy.[223] An examination of the subscriber lists attached to eighteenth- and nineteenth-century collections of Scottish fiddle and bagpipe music might offer additional local references.

Given the traffic between the two communities in the eighteenth and nineteenth centuries and the existence of musical families of Antrim origin in Kintyre, we should expect to find some Irish elements in Argyll. One promising source is the collection of tunes copied by Anna-Jane Maclean-Clephane in December 1816 from a manuscript of a Mr MacDonald, (possibly Patrick McDonald) with 'a section of fiddle music, apparently collected by Mr MacDonald from fiddlers including one called O'Docharty, and one called Murphy, at Campbeltown.'[224] As with the Clephane family, the amateur musicians of the landed gentry were important in undertaking and supporting the gathering, performance and passing on of such material and their social networks, which often extended across the British Isles, may offer an explanation for the transmission of music during the boom in fiddle playing and composition of late eighteenth-century Scotland. Given its proximity and strong family links, it is possible that upper-class domestic Antrim may have been early factor in the absorption of Scottish instrumental music into that part of Ireland. The extent to which this might account for the wider dissemination of Scottish fiddle playing across Ireland as a whole remains unclear.[225]

A preliminary examination of the names of the fiddle tunes included in Scottish eighteenth- and nineteenth-century collections[226] indicates few with titles suggesting an Antrim origin or connection, although there are many names of other places in Ireland. Exceptions are 'Carrick Gergues' in the *Gillespie Manuscript* of 1768 and 'Ballemonny Races' in Islay fiddler/composer Alexander MacKay's collection of *c.* 1802.[227]

Cooper's studies of Antrim fiddlers found their repertories were largely Irish, but included a number of common Scottish tunes. Such a mix has also been found in manuscript sources and through fieldwork in east and central Down,[228] Louth[229] and Donegal.[230] Clearly absent in the Antrim cases are tunes and styles that are obviously Gaelic or 'Highland' in character or origin. This suggests little direct influence from Argyll in the relatively recent past, although Cooper does discuss possible bagpipe elements in the playing of Antrim fiddler Paddy McClusky.[231]

Fiddle players are adept at building networks and opportunities for interaction through festivals, clubs and societies and modern media encourages the sharing of repertory. There are records of fruitful musical exchanges from in the 1950s through the Derry and Antrim Fiddle Society and others[232] and despite interruption by the Troubles and a degree of polarisation of music along national lines, informal contact continues, assisted by fiddle and accordion clubs, fiddlers' rallies, public house sessions and a myriad other informal arrangements. As fiddle playing currently flourishes in both Scotland and Ireland it is not surprising to find a renewed healthy interest in each other's music among the leading players of Antrim and Argyll.

Maurice Duncan, described as 'one of Scotland's finest exponents of Scots fiddle music and a talented piper',[233] is from a musical family that includes links to the McShannon pipers and singers of Kintyre. He has been associated with the Oban and Lorne Strathspey and Reel Society[234] and is known as a prolific composer[235] and a competition adjudicator. Images and music relating to a visit he made to Antrim have been posted on the internet.[236] Archie McAllister, also of Campbeltown, featured in an edition of the 2011 BBC television programme *Mark Wilson's Scottish Musical Journey* that considered links between his part of Scotland and Ulster.[237] The idea of a distinct Argyll style and repertory is reinforced by the fact that this fiddler was engaged to give a recital and to such material at the Scots Fiddle Festival in Edinburgh in November 2015. Dominic McNabb, an Antrim fiddler with Scottish ancestors, has maintained relationships with musicians throughout Ireland and Scotland (including Islay) through his solo playing, his band The Cuckoo's Nest Trio, Maine Valley Fiddle and Accordion Club and Ballycastle Comhaltas Ceoltóirí Éireann.[238]

The instruments of the accordion family were adopted into Scottish traditional music as early as the second half of the nineteenth century. This was facilitated by a strong retail trade that offered mail order to outlying areas and was subsequently supported by a healthy output from recording companies from the earliest decades of the twentieth century onwards.[239] In this way the melodeon, button and piano accordions found a special place in the rural Highlands, including Argyll.

In the twentieth century, local players of the button accordion adopted the distinct, Gaelic song and piping influenced, 'West Coast Style'[240] commonly associated with the Mull accordionist and bandleader Bobby MacLeod. A current accordionist in this manner is Graham Irvine of Dunoon, whose playing can be viewed online.[241] This style and repertory is also found in Scottish mouth organ playing as epitomised in the music of Donald Black, from Benderloch in Argyll.[242] While the accordion clearly has a following in Antrim, it is not known whether the West Highland style has permeated playing there to any degree. Antrim does have a tradition of accordion bands which has parallels in Scotland, but is not found in Argyll.

Conclusion

The foregoing evidence supports the presumption that there are concrete musical connections between Argyll and Antrim. Along with landscape, archaeology, built heritage and language, this music and song is highly important in defining the identities of the two areas and has great potential in the promotion of image the places for both residents and visitors. Shared elements and contrasts await further exploration by scholars and musicians alike and, subject to an appropriate degree of understanding and sensitivity, a precious store of material awaits future creative exploitation and enjoyment. We listen out for more resonances across the Moyle.

Acknowledgements

I am grateful to Prof. Hugh Cheape of Sabhal Mòr Ostaig for informally guiding me to important contextual sources and to Dr Katherine Campbell and Dr John Shaw of the University of Edinburgh for reading and commenting on drafts of this paper.

Notes

1 Hamish Henderson, 'Willie Mitchell', *Tocher*, 31 (Summer 1979) reproduced in Hamish Henderson, *Alias MacAlias. Writings on songs, folk and literature* (Edinburgh, 1992), pp 181–9 at p. 181.

2 For example, Ireland is given little attention in Francis Collinson, *The Traditional and National Music of Scotland* (London, 1966). Similarly, Scotland is mentioned only in passing in Tomás Ó Cannainn, *Traditional Music in Ireland* (London, 1978).

3 Hugh Cheape, *Bagpipes. A National Collection of a National Instrument* (Edinburgh, 2008), p. 44.

4 J. H. Delargy, *The Gaelic Story-Teller with some Notes on Gaelic Folk Tales* (London, 1945), p. 29.

5 Wilson McLeod, *Gaelic Cultural Identities in Scotland and Ireland c. 1200–c. 1650* (Oxford, 2004), p. 221.

6 Ibid., p. 6.

7 Marion Campbell, 'A farm manager's cashbook, 1843–1854', *Review of Scottish Culture*, 5 (1989), pp 41–50 at p. 47.

8 J. E. Handley, *The Irish in Scotland, 1798–1845* (Cork, 1945), p. 81.

9 Maureen Donnelly, *The Nine Glens. A Personal Look at the History, Folklore and Poetry of the Nine Glens of Antrim* (Antrim, 1987), p. 110. It has been suggested by Donald Meek that the Islay poet William Livingston (1808–70), who wrote so sensitively about Ireland in his poem *Eirinn a' Gul*, may have had first-hand knowledge of Antrim through visits to the Ballycastle fair: D. E. Meek, *Caran an t-Saoghail* (Edinburgh, 2003), p. 460.

10 T. M. Devine, *Scotland's Empire. The Origins of the Global Diaspora* (London, 2004), p. 147. See also T. M. Devine, *The Scottish Nation, 1700–2000* (London, 2000), pp 486–512.

11 Devine, *Scotland's Empire*, p. 124.

12 Joan Blaeu, 'Cantire' in *Atlas* (Amsterdam, 1654), p. 58.

13 N. M. Holmer, *The Irish language in Rathlin Island, Co. Antrim* (Dublin, 1942), pp 1–2.

14 John MacKechnie (ed.), *The Dewar Manuscripts. Scottish West Highland Folk Tales Collected Originally in Gaelic by John Dewar* (Glasgow, 1964), p. 24.

15 Martin Dowling, *Traditional Music and Irish Society: Historical Perspectives* (Farnham, 2014), pp 107–08, 143–46.

16 Kerry Bletch, 'In the Field – An interview with Mark Wilson' *The Old-Time Herald*, 7:6 (Winter 2000/01), published online at: www.oldtimeherald.org/archive/back_issues/volume-7/7-6/mark_wilson.html. See the recent measured and tactful review by Michael Newton of Fiona Ritchie and Doug Orr, *Wayfaring Strangers: The Musical Voyage from Scotland and Ulster to Appalachia* (Chapel Hill, 2014) in *E-Keltoi Book Reviews*, vol. 1, pp 67–74 (10 June 2015), published online at: www4.uwm.edu/celtic/ekeltoi/bookreviews/vol01/newton13.html. See also Peter Gilmore, 'Rebels and Revivals: Ulster Immigrants, Western Pennsylvania Presbyterianism and the Formation of Scotch-Irish Identity, 1780–1830', PhD thesis, Carnegie Mellon University (2009), and Peter Gilmore, 'Irish Tunes and Scotch-Irish Myths in Early Western Pennsylvania' in *Celebrating Northern Appalachia in Word and Song* (California University of Pennsylvania, 2011), published online at: www.academia.edu/779702/Irish_Tunes_and_Scotch-Irish_Myths_in_Early_Western_Pennsylvania.

17 '*Do Mhac Dhomhaill*' in J. Carmichael Watson, *Gaelic Songs of Mary MacLeod* (Edinburgh, 1965), p. 81.

18 '*Bidh Clann Ulaidh*' in Valerie Bryan (ed.), *Ceòl nam Feis* (Portree, 1996), p. 27.

19 John Shaw, 'Oral traditions/folklore of Argyll' in Donald Omand (ed.), *The Argyll Book* (Edinburgh, 2004), pp 213–22 at p. 216.

20 Eoin Mac Néill, 'Irish in the Glens of Antrim', *Leabhar na Gaedhilge*, 6 (1895), pp 106–10 at p. 107.

21 Arthur Geddes, '"Craig and Ben" – Their life and song: A study of response to environment', *Geography*, 37:1 (Jan. 1952), pp 32–6. See also Peter McIntosh, *History of Kintyre* (Campbeltown, 1861; 1929 edition), p. 39.

22 NLS, Adv. MS 72.2.3.

23 Leslie V. Grinsell, *Folklore of Prehistoric Sites in Britain* (Newton Abbot, 1976).

24 Neil Ross, *Heroic Poetry from the Book of the Dean of Lismore* (Edinburgh, 1939), p. xxi.

25 Shaw, 'Oral Traditions', p. 213.

26 Patrick McDonald, *Highland Vocal Airs* (Edinburgh, 1784), published as *The Patrick McDonald Collection* (Skye, 2000), pp 36–7.

27 John Purser, *Scotland's Music* (Edinburgh, 1992), p. 72.

28 Collinson, *Traditional and National Music of Scotland*, p. 49.

29 McDonald, *Highland Vocal Airs*, pp 37, 72 n.

30 Ross, *Heroic Poetry*, p. 251.

31 Ibid.; Ethel Basin, *The Old Songs of Skye. Frances Tolmie and Her Circle* (London, 1977), pp 47–52.

32 See: http://www.tobarandualchais.co.uk (search: '*Laoidh Fhraoich*').

33 '*Laoidh Fhraoich*' (www.tobarandualchais.co.uk/en/fullrecord/17302/20).

34 Purser, *Scotland's Music*, p. 73. He also discusses Patrick McDonald's air *Manus* and the collected versions of '*Laoidh Mhanuis*'.

35 A James McDonnell graduated MD from the University of Edinburgh in 1784. David Dobson, *Later Scots-Irish Links, 1725–1825* (Baltimore, 2003), p. 67.

36 Donal O'Sullivan (ed.), *Bunting's Ancient Music of Ireland* (Cork, 1983), pp 209–10.

37 Edward Bunting, *The Ancient Music of Ireland arranged for the Pianoforte* (Dublin, 1840), p. 7

38 Ibid.

39 O'Sullivan, *Bunting's Ancient Music*, pp 209–10. See also 'A song of the Antrim Glens and Scottish Isles', *Journal of the Irish Folk Song Society*, 8 (1910), pp 6–9.

40 O'Sullivan, *Bunting's Ancient Music*, p. 212.

41 Bunting, *Ancient Music of Ireland*, p. 88.

42 O'Sullivan, *Bunting's Ancient Music*, pp 211–12. Also published as 'Dan Ossian – Fingalian Air' in Simon Fraser, *Airs and Melodies Peculiar to the Highlands of Scotland and the Isles* (Edinburgh, 1815), p. 19.

43 Alexander Campbell, *Albyn's Anthology* (2 vols, Edinburgh, 1816–18), vol. 1, p. 71.

44 University of Edinburgh Library, MS Gen. 614.

45 See also the modern edition, *The Angus Fraser Collection of Scottish Gaelic Airs* (Skye, 1996).

46 Fraser, *Airs and Melodies,* p. 20.

47 Ibid., p. 61.

48 Ibid., p. 107.

49 Ibid.

50 Ibid., pp 21, 108. The Fraser's settings must be approached with caution on account of their modernisation of the music.

51 Ibid., p. 3.

52 Collinson, *Traditional and National Music*, p. 49.

53 John Bowie, *A Collection of Strathspey Reels & Country Dances* (Edinburgh, 1789), p. 32.

54 Niel Gow & Sons, *Fourth Collection of Strathspeys and Reels etc.* (Edinburgh, 1800), p. 17.

55 Niel Gow & Sons, *Fifth Collection of Strathspeys and Reels etc.* (Edinburgh, 1809), p. 12.

56 Alexander Mackay, *A Collection of Reels, Strathspeys and Slow Tunes* (Glasgow, *c.* 1802). NLS, Glen.344. See: http://www.campin.me.uk/Music/McKay.abc.

57 *A Collection of Celtic Melodies* (2 vols, Edinburgh, *c.* 1830). Published online as a facsimile at: http://www.cl.cam.ac.uk/~rja14/musicfiles/manuscripts/celticmelodies1.pdf and http://www.cl.cam.ac.uk/~rja14/musicfiles/manuscripts/celticmelodies2.pdf. Vol. 2 is dedicated to Lady Ellinor Campbell of Islay.

58 Cheape, *Bagpipes*, p. 116.

59 http://www.earlygaelicharp.info/sources/maclean-clephane.htm. NLS, MS 14949 a, 7. Includes '*Failte Chlarsaich*' which is reproduced in Keith Sanger and Alison Kinnaird, *Tree of Strings* (Temple, 1992), p. 189. The National Library of Scotland holds a complete photocopy of three volumes (NLS, MS 14949 a, b and c) and copies of other material are said to be held by the University of Edinburgh. See also K. E. McAulay, 'The accomplished ladies of Torloisk', *International Review of the Aesthetics and Sociology of Music*, 44:1 (2013), pp 57–78, and Keith Sanger, *Echlin O'Cathain*, published online at http://www.wirestrungharp.com/harps/harpers/o-cathain-echlin.html) (2014 and 2015.

60 Peter Cooke, Morag Macleod and Colm Ó Baoill (eds), *The Elizabeth Ross Manuscript – Original Highland Airs Collected at Raasay in 1812*, published online at: http://www.ed.ac.uk/files/imports/fileManager/RossMS.pdf, note and item 55, 114 and 44.

61 Ibid., note and item 56, 114 and 44.

62 Ibid., note and item 57, 115 and 45.

63 Ibid., note and item 101, 37 and 38.

64 P. O'Farrell, *O'Farrell's Pocket Companion for the Irish or Union Pipes* (4 vols, Dublin, 1804–16), vol. 3, p. 37.

65 Stanford, Charles Villiers (ed.), *Complete Collection of Irish Music as Noted by George Petrie* (3 vols, London, 1902–05), vol. 2, p. 259.

66 Francis O'Neill *Waifs and Strays of Gaelic Melody* (Boston, 1922).

67 Samuel Thomson, *The Hibernian Muse* (London, *c.* 1790).

68 J. F. Morison, *Highland Airs and Quicksteps* (Inverness, 1882).

69 Collinson, *Traditional and National Music*, p. 49.

70 A. L. Gillies, *Songs of Gaelic Scotland* (Edinburgh, 2005), p. 325.

71 As with the setting of '*Am bròn binn*' in Gillies, *Songs of Gaelic Scotland,* pp 322–5.

72 'Experimental Workshops Comparing the Musical Performance of Vernacular Bardic Poetry in Medieval Wales, Ireland and Scotland' held at University of Edinburgh in April 2009. See also Gillies, *Songs of Gaelic Scotland,* p. 324.

73 J. L. Campbell, *Songs Remembered in Exile* (Edinburgh, 1999), pp 182–4.

74 See Virginia Blankenhorn, 'The Rev. William Matheson and the Performance of Scottish Gaelic "Strophic" Verse', *Scottish Studies*, 36 (2013), pp 15–44. Matheson can be heard on the CD *Gaelic Bards and Minstrels* (Scottish Tradition Series, vol. 16) (Greentrax, CDTRAX9016D) and at the *Tobair and Dualchais* website (search: 'William Matheson').

75 John Purser, *Scotland's Music* (Edinburgh, 1992), p. 73, example 4. This can be heard, sung by Mary Macmaster to her wire-strung harp accompaniment on the CD *Scotland's Music* (Linn Records, CKD008), track 7.

76 See for example the pages of the website (www.wirestrungharp.com).

77 Published online at http://pipehacker.com/2014/03/14/small-tunes-podcast-deirdres-lament.

78 Alison Kinnaird and Keith Sanger, 'Harps in Scotland' in John Beech, Owen Hand, Mark Mulhern and Jeremy Weston (eds), *Scottish Life and Society, Volume 10: Oral Literature and Performance Culture* (Edinburgh, 2007), pp 274–87 at p. 280. Much that is reliably known about the early harp and its players in Argyll is dependent on the thorough and thoughtful research of Keith Sanger and Alison Kinnaird.

79 See, for example, Keith Sanger and Michael Billinge Keills, *'Harp Key' on the Keills Grave Slab*, published online (2012) at: www.wirestrungharp.com/harps/other_images/keills_grave_slab.html.

80 Keith Sanger, *Final Chords – The Last Scottish Harpers* (2012). Published online at: www.wirestrungharp.com/harps/harpers/final_chords.html.

81 William Matheson, *The Blind Harper (An Clarsair Dall)* (Edinburgh, 1970).

82 Keith Sanger, 'The McShannons of Kintyre: Harpers to Tacksmen'*, The Kintrye Antiquarian and Natural History Society Magazine*, 28 (Autumn 1990) published online at: www.ralstongenealogy.com/number28kintmag.htm.

83 Sanger, *Final Chords.*

84 Kinnaird and Sanger, 'Harps in Scotland', p. 282.

85 Keith Sanger, 'Fresh leaves on the Tree of Strings', paper given to The Historical Irish Harp Society Summer School, Kilkenny (Aug. 2009) published online at: www.academia.edu/7994298/Fresh_Leaves_on_the_Tree_of_Strings.

86 Keith Sanger, *A Harper, Some Young Ladies and the Minister: The Background to the Maclean Clephane MS*, paper given at the Irish Harp School in Kilkenny (August 2007), published online at: www.academia.edu/12830969/A_Harper_Some_Young_Ladies_and_The_Minister.

87 John Magee, *The Heritage of the Harp* (Belfast, 1992), p. 20.

88 Bridget Mackenzie, *Piping Traditions of Kintyre* (Glasgow, 2004), p. 3.

89 Michael Newton and Hugh Cheape, 'The keening of women and the roar of the pipe: From Clàrsach to Bagpipe, *ca.* 1600–1782', *Ars Lyrica Celtica*, 17 (2008), p. 85 fn.47.

90 Newton and Cheape, The keening of women', pp 75–95.

91 Mackenzie, *Piping Traditions of Kintyre,* p. 5.

92 As suggested in an article online at Wikipedia (https://en.wikipedia.org/wiki/Pibroch#Irish_Ce.C3.B2l_M.C3.B3r).

93 From Angus MacKay, *A Collection of Ancient Piobaireachd* (Edinburgh, 1838), p. 8, quoted in William Donaldson *The Highland Pipe and Scottish Society 1750–1950* (East Linton, 2000), p. 157.

94 Peter McIntosh, *History of Kintyre* (Campbeltown, 1929), p. 32.

95 William Donaldson, '"Entirely at the pleasure of the performer": a further exploration of piobaireachd', *Piper & Drummer* (2001–02), published online at www.pipesdrums.com/wp-content/docengines/A51191C54453471192974BB509421138.pdf.

96 Mackenzie, *Piping Traditions of Kintyre,* pp 7–8. She suggests that the McMurchy family were from the Irish weaver community at Garvachy, Campbeltown. See also Keith Sanger, *William McMurchy,* published online at www.ralstongenealogy.com/number13kintmag.htm.

97 Mackenzie, *Piping Traditions of Kintyre,* p. 29.

98 Ibid., p. 7.

99 Ibid., p. 9.

100 Keith Sanger, 'Patronage – or the price of the piper's bag', *Common Stock,* 24:1 (June 2009), pp 14–19. Published online at www.academia.edu/11166278/Patronage_or_the_price_of_the_pipers_bag.

101 McIntosh, *History of Kintyre,* p. 41.

102 Thomas Pennant, *A Tour of Scotland* (London, 1796), p. 239.

103 Handley, *Irish in Scotland,* p. 81 n.2.

104 Arnold Morrison, *Some Scottish Sources on Militias, Fencibles and Volunteer Corps, 1793–1830,* p. 1 (published online at www.scribd.com/doc/68100606/The-Defence-of-Scotland-Militias-Fencibles-and-Volunteer-Corps1793-1820). See also www.knapdalepeople.com/am04.html on the Argyll Militia.

105 Morrison, *Some Scottish Sources on Militias,* p. 5. Devine, *Scotland's Empire,* p. 304, notes that '… Scots were among the most ruthless and feared of the crown forces which routed the Irish rebellion of 1798. Thirteen of the twenty regiments stationed in Ireland on the eve of the rebellion were Scots and later reinforcements drew heavily on Scottish reserves.'

106 Neil Stewart, *Collection of the Newest & Best Reels or Country Dances for Violin* (Edinburgh, 1761). The Scots song and tune 'Highland Harry' would appear to be of the same family and may be further evidence that the air had an older pedigree and wider currency. Interestingly, the Donegal fiddler Tommy Peoples plays as a prelude to the Irish reel a slow strathspey version of the tune on the gramophone record *The High Part of the Road* (Shanachie, 29003) (1977), track 11.

107 Collected from Mary MacDonald, 1976. Released on long play record *Cape Breton Scottish Fiddle* (Topic, 12TS354).

108 AFS 04939 A05, Traditional Music and Spoken Word Catalog, American Folklife Center, Library of Congress. Released on long play record *Emmet W. Lundy – Fiddle Tunes from Grayson County, Virginia* (String Records, STR802).

109 Fraser, *Airs and Melodies,* p. 46.

110 Ibid., p. 111 n.95.

111 See: www.78thfrasers.org/history/genealogy.

112 J. G. Gibson, *Traditional Gaelic Piping, 1745–1945* (Montreal, 1998), p. 92.

113 MacKenzie, *Piping Traditions.*

114 Alastair Campbell, *A History of Clan Campbell, from the Restoration to the Present Day* (Edinburgh, 2000), pp 280–81.

115 Cooper, *Musical Traditions,* p. 66.

116 Ríonach ui Ógáin and Tom Sherlock, *The Otherworld,* (Dublin, 2012), p. 119; Padraic Cléireacháin, 'Feiseanna Remembered' in Eamon Phoenix, Padraic Ó Cléireacháin, Eileen McCauley and Nuala McSparran (eds), *Feis Na nGleann: A Century of Gaelic Culture in the Antrim Glens* (Belfast, 2005) pp 141–3.

117 'Irish Pipe Music', *Journal of the Irish Folk Song Society,* 7 (Jan.–June 1909, p. 32.

118 See also Derick Thomson, 'Gaelic learned orders and literati in medieval Scotland', *Scottish Studies,* 12 (1968), pp 57–78; Derick Thomson, *An Introduction to Gaelic Poetry* (Edinburgh, 1974), pp 57–98; Derick Thomson, 'Scottish Gaelic traditional songs from the 16th to the 18th century', *Proceedings of the British Academy,* 105 (London, 2000), pp 93–114.

119 Donald Meek, 'Gaelic language and literature in Argyll' in Donald Omand (ed.), *The Argyll Book* (Edinburgh, 2004), pp 232–42 at p. 239.

120 Shaw, 'Oral traditions', p. 214.

121 Gillies, *Songs of Gaelic Scotland*, p. 289.

122 McIntosh, *History of Kintyre*, p. 22.

123 *Faileasan* (*Reflections*) (SRM004) (2013).

124 This can be auditioned online at: www.tobarandualchais.co.uk/fullrecord/27107/1.

125 There is also an arrangement of this song by Islay Gaelic Choir on the CD *Sruth air a' Charraig* (SKU, 10000). The CD comprises a collection of songs associated with the island and its songsmiths.

126 Gillies, *Songs of Gaelic Scotland*, p. 341. This song can be heard sung by William Matheson on the CD *Bards and Minstrels*.

127 J. D. Marshall, 'Notes on the statistics and natural history of the island of Rathlin', *Transactions of the Royal Irish Academy*, 17, (1837), p. 54, quoted in *Ceol Tíre*, 20 (1981), p. 13.

128 McIntosh, *History of Kintyre*, p. 37.

129 McLeod, *Gaelic Cultural Identities*, p. 6.

130 See, for example, www.smo.uhi.ac.uk/~oduibhin/daoine/aoidhmin2.htm.

131 Holmer, *Irish Language in Rathlin*, p. 127.

132 Alan Stivel Cochevelou, *Telenn Geltiek: Harpe Celtique* (Mouez Breiz, 4597), 1964; Skara Brae, *Skara Brae* (Gael-Linn Records, CEF 031), 1971; Kevin Burke and Michael O'Domhnaill, *Portland* (Green Linnet, SIF-1041), 1982.

133 Viewable online at www.youtube.com/watch?v=NssuVkvwq8A&feature=youtu.be.

134 See: www.irishharpschool.com/griogair.htm. The singer recorded the song on the CD *Dail-rìata* (DUN0701) in 2007.

135 Gillies, *Songs of Gaelic Scotland*, pp 65–7.

136 Viewable online at www.youtube.com/watch?v=TA_d8WkUGv0.

137 Cléireacháin, 'Feiseanna Remembered', p. 143.

138 'Parish of Carnmoney' in Angélique Day and Patrick McWilliams (eds), *Ordnance Survey Memoirs of Ireland. Vol. 2, Parishes of County Antrim I, 1838–9* (Belfast, 1990), p. 63.

139 'Parish of Mallusk' in Day and McWilliams, *Ordnance Survey Memoirs*, p. 113.

140 John Moulden, *Songs of the People: Songs from the Sam Henry Collection, part one* (Belfast, 1979); Gale Huntington and Lani Hermann with John Moulden (eds), *Sam Henry's 'Songs of the People'* (Athens, GA, 1990).

141 Fintan Vallely, *Companion to Irish Traditional Music* (2nd edition, Cork, 2011), p. 716.

142 Len Graham, *Joe Holmes. Here I am Amongst You* (Dublin, 2010), p. 234.

143 Lawrence Holden, *John Kennedy: By the Banks of the Maine* (Belfast, 2012) (CD with booklet).

144 David Cooper, *The Musical Traditions of Northern Ireland and its Diaspora. Community and Conflict* (Farnham, 2009).

145 John Moulden, *Songs of Hugh McWilliams, Schoolmaster, 1831* (Portrush, 1992), and other works.

146 John Hewitt, *Rhyming Weavers & Other Country Poets of Antrim and Down* (Belfast, 1974).

147 Carol Baraniuk, 'Ulster's Burns? James Orr, the Bard of Ballycarry', *Review of Scottish Culture*, 19 (2007), pp 54–62.

148 John Moulden, 'One singer, two voices: Scots and Irish style song in the work of the mid-Antrim poet and song maker Hugh McWilliams (fl. 1816–1831)' in Thérèse Smith and Mícheál Ó Súilleabháin (eds), *Blas. The Local Accent in Irish Traditional Music* (Limerick, 1997), p. 75. Scotland too had weaver poets such as Robert Tannahill of Paisley (1774–1810) and James Thomson (1763–1832) of Currie. Devine, *Scotland's Empire*, p. 147, suggests that prior to Burns the works of Scottish poet and song publisher Allan Ramsay were highly popular in Ulster.

149 Gavin Sprott, *Robert Burns. Farmer* (Edinburgh, 1990), pp 52–3.

150 Henderson, 'Willie Mitchell', pp 181–2. See Andrew McKerral, *Kintyre in the 17th Century*, (Edinburgh, 1948) for a discussion of the variants of the name Shannon and the history of that line. The pedigree and changed status of the McShannons of Lephenstrath are explored in Sanger, 'The McShannons of Kintyre'. Extensive field recordings of Willie Mitchell, the McShannon family and others are held in the School of Scottish Studies Archive, University of Edinburgh.

151 Published online at: www.tobarandualchais.co.uk/fullrecord/83067/1.

152 Hugh Shields, *Shamrock, Rose and Thistle: Folk Singing in North Derry* (Belfast, 1981), p. 51. See: www.itma.ie/digitallibrary/book/shamrock-rose-and-thistle-songs.

153 Argyll and Bute Council, *Gaelic in Kintyre* (n.d.) (leaflet published online at www.argyll-bute.gov.uk/sites/default/files/Gaelic%20in%20Kintyre%20leaflet.pdf). The Ordnance Survey Name Book entry for the site can be viewed at: www.scotlandsplaces.gov.uk/digital-volumes/ordnance-survey-name-books/argyll-os-name-books-1868-1878/argyll-volume-13/96.

154 Henderson, 'Willie Mitchell', p. 184. For an example of a Scottish building worker carrying traditional song into Ulster, see the case of 'Down by the Mellon Green' in Robin Morton *Folk Songs Sung in Ulster* (Cork, 1970), pp 26–7.

155 Agnes Stewart, 'A Sang at Least: The Life of Willie Mitchell', *The Kintyre Antiquarian and Natural History Society Magazine*, 51 (Spring 2002). Republished online at: www.ralstongenealogy.com/number51kintmag.htm.

156 Paddy Tunney, *The Stone Fiddle. My Way to Traditional Song* (Dublin, 1979), p. 161.

157 Paddy Tunney, *Where Songs do Thunder* (Belfast, 1991), pp 180–81.

158 'Ardmore Green' sung by Paddy Hegarty, *Irish Traditional Music Archive* (475-ITMA-MP3), online at www.itma.ie/digitallibrary/sound/ardmore_green_paddy_hegarty.

159 Nigel Gatherer, *Songs and Ballads of Dundee* (Edinburgh, 2000), pp 125–6 n.63, 132–3.

160 John Moulden, 'One singer, two voices', p. 73.

161 Cooper, *Musical Traditions*, pp 52–6; Gillies, *Songs of Gaelic Scotland*, p. 295.

162 Gillies, *Songs of Gaelic Scotland*, p. 413.

163 Gavin Grieg, 'Folk-Song in Buchan', *Transactions of the Buchan Field Club*, 9 (1906–07), reproduced in Gavin Grieg, *Folk Song in Buchan and Folk-Song of the North East* (Hatboro, 1963), p. 58. Devine, *Scotland's Empire*, p. xxvi, stresses the often unacknowledged large number of Irish recruits who served in the British army.

164 Marion Campbell, *Argyll. The Enduring Heartland* (Edinburgh, 1977, 2001 edition), pp 157–8, 169–70.

165 McIntosh, *History of Kintyre*, p. 39.

166 Shaw, 'Oral traditions', p. 221.

167 Timothy Neat, *The Voice of the Bard. Living Poets and Ancient Tradition in the Highlands of Scotland* (Edinburgh, 1999), pp 237–68. See also Hamish Henderson's introduction to Duncan and Linda Williamson, *A Thorn in the King's Foot: Stories of the Scottish Travelling People* (Harmondsworth, 1987), reproduced in Henderson, *Alias MacAlias*, pp 217–28.

168 John Moulden, '"Clodhopper". Alexander Crawford, Leck, Ballymoney, County Antrim, His Songs, Life and Philosophy', *Béaloideas*, 77 (2009), pp 37–57, and ui Ógáin and Sherlock, *The Otherworld*, p. 114.

169 Henderson, *Alias MacAlias*, pp 95–6, 179–80.

170 Dick Gaughan, *No More Forever* (Trailer LER, 2072), 1972.

171 For example, Willie Williamson, *School of Scottish Studies Archive* (SA1967.152.A8b) and Duncan and Jock Williamson, *School of Scottish Studies Archive* (SA1976.34.A3).

172 From Robert Ford, *Vagabond Songs and Ballads of Scotland* (Paisley, 1904), pp 49–51.

173 Vic Smith, 'Len Graham', *Musical Traditions*, Article MT294 (interview of 31 Oct. 2013) published online at: http://mustrad.org.uk/articles/l_graham.htm (published 27 March 2014).

174 David Murray, *Music of the Scottish Regiments* (Edinburgh, 2001), p. 9.

175 Ibid., p. 9.

176 Ibid., p. 7.

177 Gary Hastings, 'Ag Ciceáil Leis an Dá Chos (Kickin' with both feet)' in Smith and Ó Súilleabháin, *Blas*, p. 103.

178 George Miller, *The Military Band* (London, 1912), p. 9. The tune 'Hills of Glenorchy' is named after a place in Argyll and in Ireland it is associated with the song 'The Boys of Tanderagee'.

179 Murray, *Music of the Scottish Regiments*, p. 15 n.8.

180 NLS, MSS 21739–21744.

181 For example, *Aird's Selection of Scotch, English, Irish and Foreign Airs for Fife, Violin or Flute* (Glasgow, *c.* 1782). For a note on tunes known in Ulster that are found in the Aird collections see in David Cooper, '"With Fife and Fiddle": Protestants and Traditional Music in Northern Ireland' in John Morgan O'Connell and Salwa El-Shawan Castelo-Branco (eds), *Music and Conflict* (Illinois, 2010), pp 89–106.

182 For example, the published collections of Niel Gow & Sons.

183 Colette Moloney (ed.), *The Irish Music Manuscripts of Edward Bunting (1773–1843): An Introduction and Catalogue* (Dublin, 2000), p. 193.

184 Cooper, *Musical Traditions*, p. 79.

185 Gary Hastings, *With Fife and Drum* (Belfast, 2003).

186 Peter MacIntyre, *Odd Incidents of Olden Times, or, Ancient Records of Inveraray* (Glasgow, 1904), pp 44, 53, 55, 57–8.

187 Ian Russell, 'Flute bands and their annual walks in north-east Scotland: music, tradition, and community', *Review of Scottish Culture*, 15 (2002–03), pp 99–111.

188 Katherine Campbell, 'George Riddell of Rosehearty: Fiddler and Collector' in Ian Russell and Mary Anne Alburger (eds), *Driving the Bow: Fiddle and Dance Studies from Around the North Atlantic 2* (Aberdeen, 2008), pp 35–56; Katherine Campbell, 'Masonic song in Scotland: folk tunes and community', *Oral Tradition*, 27:1 (2012), pp 85–108.

189 'Parish of Mallusk' in Day and McWilliams, *Ordnance Survey Memoirs*, p. 113.

190 NLS, MS 21738.

191 Unpublished research by the author.

192 NLS, MS 3346/Inglis.153. Jack Campin's website (www.campin.me.uk/Flute/Webrelease/Flute/09Duet/09Duet.htm) states: 'Carrick Fergus is a duet setting of the tune included in the variation section as Rural Felicity. This arrangement is from a big set of commonplace books compiled by the Edinburgh music publisher John Brysson between the 1790s and about 1820; this volume, the earliest and best-known, is often known as the *Sharpe of Hoddom* manuscript, after one of its owners.'

193 'Parish of Mallusk' in Day and McWilliams, *Ordnance Survey Memoirs*, p. 113.

194 Dowling, *Traditional Music and Irish Society,* pp 104–08. The writer speculated whether or not this was part of the wave of enthusiasm for fiddle in Scotland. It should be noted that, at the time, Scottish dance music was highly popular in the north of England also as demonstrated by manuscripts and published collections from Newcastle-upon-Tyne, Northumberland and Cumbria.

195 Cooper, *Musical Traditions*, pp 76–100.

196 *Statistical Account of Scotland. Gigha and Cara, County of Argyle* (1791–9), published online at: http://stat-acc-scot.edina.ac.uk/link/1791-99/Argyle/Gigha%20and%20Cara.

197 Shaw, *Oral Traditions,* p. 215, quoting Campbell, *Albyn's Anthology,* pp 17–18, 21–2, 27–9.

198 Shaw, *Oral Traditions,* p. 215.

199 Sanger, *Echlin O'Cathain.*

200 Mary Anne Alburger *Scottish Fiddlers and Their Music* (London, 1983), p. 147.

201 From Robert Burns' poem 'The Brigs of Ayr'.

202 MacKenzie, *Piping Traditions of Kintyre*, p. 117.

203 From Wilson, MacLean collected the tales 'The Young King of Easaidh Ruadh', 'Connall Cra-bhuidhe' and 'The Slim Swarthy Champion'.

204 McIntosh, *History of Kintyre*, p. 37.

205 National Records of Scotland, GD170/2103. This must have been a musical household. The National Records of Scotland holds an account for a Broadwood piano sent to Barcaldine by the Union Canal and Oban, in 1825, and an account for a new patent double action harp, light tinted sounding board from Erard, Paris, 1834.

206 Letters from Archibald Campbell of Kilberry, quoted in J. P. Flett and T. M. Flett, *Traditional Dancing in Scotland* (London, 1964), pp 40–41.

207 Mackenzie, *Piping Traditions of Kintyre*, p. 7.

208 McIntosh, *History of Kintyre*, p. 32.

209 Alexander Fraser, *The Royal Burgh of Inveraray* (Edinburgh, 1977), p. 31.

210 Such as the Kintyre musician who used to 'fiddle at all the dancing weddings round about' but who "immediately gave up when his eyes were opened" during a religious revival of the early nineteenth century. Alexander Haldane, *Lives of Robert Haldane of Airthrey and James Alexander Haldane* (London, 1852), p. 290.

211 Dancing masters made burgesses of Inveraray included Daniel McGibbon (3 Sept. 1726), Duncan McGibbon (20 May 1729), William Paterson (10 Oct. 1743) and John Tarbet (19 May 1752). Elizabeth Beaton and Sheila MacIntyre, *Burgesses of Inverary 1665–1963* (Edinburgh, 1990), pp 29, 45, 63, 176; MacIntyre, *Odd Incidents*, p. 54; letter of John Campbell, Inveraray, to his uncle Patrick Campbell of Barcaldine noting, 'We have got a dancing master' (19 Feb. 1790), National Records of Scotland, GD1/1050/3; Lachlan McEachen (*c.* 1799–1871), Teacher of dancing at Killearn and Kilchenzie, 1861 Census, Campbeltown, 507/00/4/00/17.

212 McIntosh, *History of Kintyre*, p. 37.

213 'Parish of Mallusk' in Day and McWilliams, *Ordnance Survey Memoirs*, p. 113; 'Parish of Culfeightrin', *Ordnance Survey Memoirs*, published online at: http://antrimhistory.net/ordnance-survey-memoir-for-the-parish-of-culfeightrin.

214 Nigel Boullier, *Handed Down Country Fiddling and Dancing in East and Central Down* (Belfast, 2012), pp 23–32.

215 Mackenzie, *Piping Traditions of Kintyre*, pp 7–8. See also Sanger, *MacMurchy*.

216 Mackenzie, *Piping Traditions of Kintyre*, p. 37.

217 Ibid., p. 208.

218 Ibid., pp 202–03.

219 See: www.scottishfiddle.org/angusgrant and www.fiddle.com/Articles.page?ArticleID=17983&Index=12.

220 McDonald, *Highland Vocal Airs*, pp 64–5. Ardchattan is near Oban in Argyll. The tune is edited and discussed in David Johnson, *Scottish Fiddle Music in the Eighteenth Century* (Edinburgh, 1984), pp 125, 134–5, 142.

221 Johnson, *Scottish Fiddle Music*, pp 123, 131, 141.

222 i.e. *Canntaireachd*, the traditional chanting of traditional bagpipe music using a system of vocables. Angus Martin, *Kintyre. The Hidden Past* (Edinburgh, 1984), p. 76.

223 MacKenzie, *Piping Traditions*, lists these by area.

224 NLS, MS 14949 b.; Trinity College Dublin, MS 10615. See: www.earlygaelicharp.info/sources/maclean-clephane.htm; Sanger, *Echlin O'Cathain* and Sanger, *A Harper*.

225 Dowling, *Traditional Music and Irish Society*, p. 143.

226 As listed in Charles Gore, *The Scottish Fiddle Music Index* (Musselburgh, 1994).

227 MacKay, *Collection of Reels, Strathspeys and Slow Tunes*, p. 14. Mackay was from the island of Islay.

228 Nigel Boullier, *Handed Down*.

229 Gerard Michael O'Connor, 'Luke Donnellan's Dance Music of Oriel: A graphic and aural interpretation, realisation and critical representation of the work of an early-twentieth century music collector', MA dissertation, Dundalk Institute of Technology (2008); Pádraigín Ní Uallacháin, *A Hidden Ulster* (Dublin, 2003).

230 Allen Feldman and Eamonn O'Docherty, *The Northern Fiddler* (Belfast, 1979).

231 Cooper, *Musical Traditions*, pp 70–72.

232 Fintan Vallely, *Tuned Out. Traditional music and identity in Northern Ireland* (Cork, 2008), p. 61; Kevin McCann, 'Scottish fiddle playing and its Scottish connections', *Treoir*, 25:1 (1993), pp 27–9 at p. 29; Stuart Eydmann, 'On first hearing. The John Junner collection of Scottish and Irish fiddle music', paper presented at the North Atlantic Fiddle Convention, Derry/Donegal (June 2012), awaiting publication. There are references to Antrim fiddlers at: www.seanreidsociety.org/SRSJ3/3.16/William%20Hope.pdf.

233 J. Murray Neil, *The Scots Fiddle. Volume 3. Tunes, Tales and Traditions of the Western Highlands* (Castle Douglas, 2005), p. 47.

234 There was an ensemble named The Argyll Reel and Strathspey Band that recorded for Parlophone in the 1920s, but little is known of them.

235 Murray Neil, *Scots Fiddle*, p. 46.

236 See: www.youtube.com/watch?v=__ce6d0YLxM.

237 *Mark Wilson's Scottish Musical Journey. Stage 6 – Campbeltown* (broadcast on 2 Nov. 2011), online at: www.bbc.co.uk/ulsterscots/library/mark-wilsons-scottish-musical-journey-stage-6-campbeltown.

238 Liner notes from CD: Dominic McNabb, *Traditional Fiddle Music from the Glens of Antrim* (Glens Music). See: http://homepage.ntlworld.com/sean_quinn/glensmusic/dominic.htm.

239 Stuart Eydmann, 'As common as blackberries. The first hundred years of the accordion in Scotland, 1830–1930', *Folk Music Journal*, 7:5 (1999), pp 595–608.

240 Stuart Eydmann, 'From the wee melodeon to the big box. The accordion in Scotland since 1945', *Musical Performance*, 3:2–4, (2001), pp 107–25.

241 For example, the traditional Argyll pipe tunes 'Hills O' Glenorchy' and 'The Campbell's are Comin' played at www.youtube.com/watch?v=VX1SSNT5oO4 and the pipe marches 'Colonel McLean of Ardgour' and 'The Cowal Gathering' played for a Dunoon Barn Dance at www.youtube.com/watch?v=jSFFlMVkrEE. See also the CD by piano accordionists Colin Campbell and Colin Forgrieve, *Men of Argyll* (Feorlin CCCDR06) (www.feorlin-oban.co.uk/cd/).

242 See: www.tremoloharmonica.com/donald-black.shtml.

5

Argyllshire Emigrants to North Carolina and the Antrim Flaxseed Traders

Eric J. Graham

In late August 1775 two former transatlantic flaxseed traders from the port of Larne in County Antrim – the *Lord Dunluce* (Captain Richard Shutter) and the *Jeannie* (Captain John McNeill) – dropped anchor in Ardminish Bay on the eastern shore of Gigha. This small, remote island lies a few miles off the Atlantic facing west coast of the Mull of Kintyre, Argyllshire. They had arrived at this exposed, open anchorage under charter to uplift organised parties of emigrants, led by their clan tackmen, from the immediate area and convey them across the Atlantic to Cape Fear River, North Carolina.[1] As knowledge of their appearance in Ardminish Bay eventually reached Edinburgh it triggered a direct response from a deeply concerned Scottish establishment. On 2 September, William Nelthorpe – the Secretary to the Customs Commissioners of Scotland – wrote to inform his Collector at Campbeltown – Ronald Campbell – in whose precinct the island fell:

> We are informed from the Western Isles that there are two vessels lying at Gigha ready to take in emigrants for Cape Fear from Kintyre, Knapdale and circumjacent islands. They are to set sail as soon as beds can be fitted which amount to 150 to each vessel.

Underpinning their concern was the rapid deterioration of security in the American colonies where the British forces were struggling to contain the rebellion and a spiralling cycle of armed clashes. None of which seemed to dissuade the would-be emigrants:

> The people engaged to go over in these ships are in high spirits and seem in no way intimidated on account of the many informations they received concerning the commotions in the British Colonies and the danger [of] emigrating at this time.[2]

Collector Campbell was well aware of what was afoot in his precinct as the *Lord Dunluce* – a regular passengers and linen 'out' and flaxseed 'in'

Excerpt from 'A new & accurate map of Scotland … ', 1752 (Library of Congress)

carrying transatlantic trader of 200 tons burthen – had been in Campbeltown Bay earlier in August where Captain Shutter made his customs declaration on her cargo of '300 chests & 100 casks of used bedding, clothing, table linen and household goods – the belongings of passengers', along with a large stock of barrelled molasses, bread and biscuits.[3] Later that month, two Campbeltown herring busses (turned coasters) arrived at their home port from Belfast and Larne with 153 chests and 1,000 casks of used bed clothing and wearing apparel. This was, most certainly, the personal stock of those passengers who were currently embarking on the newly refitted *Jeannie* lying off Gigha.[4]

Why their bedding and personal possessions were delivered by such a convoluted route via the Ulster ports is of interest. It would seem more than likely that this was a ploy to avoid their seizure by customs officers or the Argyllshire lairds intent on deterring their tenants from giving up their lease or wadset (mortgage) on their lairds' farms – many taking their servants with them – for a better life in America. This form of obstruction had been deployed before. On one occasion, a few years earlier, an 'utterly frustrated' Archibald Campbell, Laird of Jura, had secured warrants from his now aged namesake Archibald Campbell of Stonefield – then the

142

Sheriff Substitute at Inveraray – to impound the bedding and arrest the eighteen heads of household of emigrants from the Keils area of that island. He claimed that by 'relinquishing and deserting their possessions at such an unseasonable time as this in the year' (before the harvest was in) he would be losing 'silver rent' (cash) and 'like rent' in addition to incurring additional losses from his land being left before the harvest was brought in or new tenants found.[5]

The would-be emigrants had signed articles with Neil Campbell (one of the 'Black River Jamaica Campbells') to be taken to Cape Fear River – sailing no later than 25 June.[6] By late May 1754 they were preparing to load their 50 chests of clothing, bedding and workman's tools onboard the brig *Mary* of Glasgow (Captain Alexander McLarty), then lying in Small Isles Bay, Jura.[7] As she had been fully vittled for the transatlantic passage by the Belfast merchant James Getty, there was nothing, bar adverse weather, to stop her sailing as scheduled other than legal action.[8] The matter was, however, resolved when Campbell was given assurance on any outstanding rents owed to him being forthcoming, whereupon he withdrew his objection to their departure.

Government intervention in Highland emigration

The start of the 1770s saw the largest surge in emigration of tenantry and servants driven out from the Highlands and Islands to the Carolinas and Georgia by the rapid and dramatic rise in rents and the changes in agricultural methods and management imposed by their lairds.[9] They left, not only with their skills, but also with cash from selling their leases, agricultural equipment and livestock. All of which was increasing perceived as detrimental to the interest of the landowner and, ultimately, the security of the nation. The Lord Chief Justice Clerk of Scotland – Thomas Millar – had profound misgivings as to the exodus, having been alerted to the problem in 1773 by the illegal activities of the Irish speculator Thomas Desbrisay whose agents had been recruiting settlers in Ayrshire for the St John's Island, Newfoundland, scheme. Millar succeeded in having Desbrisay officially warned off – though not before some 170 settlers had left for the island from Campbeltown on the Mull of Kintyre and Lamlash Bay on Arran in 1770–71.[10]

Millar had recruited the Earl of Suffolk to press his cause with the London administration to take notice of the haemorrhage of people from 'North Britain'. So prompted, Suffolk wrote to the Colonial Secretary – the Earl of Dartmouth – in November 1773, requesting that: 'Every check within the power of government, should be given to plans which tend, so fatally, to depopulate a considerable part of the dominions.'[11] Such concerns had been duly passed on to the Secretary of the Treasury – John Robinson – in London. His initial response, in December 1773, was to request that

Excerpt from 'A compleat map of North Carolina', 1770 (Library of Congress)

the Commissioners of Customs in Scotland instruct their local customs officers to 'board all emigrant vessels in their ports and creeks, make a list of the passengers and their previous domicile and to enquire as to their reasons for emigrating'.[12] This order fell short of an outright ban on such sailings; he left it to his Scottish legal authority the Lord Advocate – John Montgomery – to resolve by obstructive means other than an embargo.

On such case of obstruction was experienced by a group of Highland emigrants embarking for New York at the mainland port of Greenock in early June of that year. They were stopped at the quayside and stripped of their personal weapons – firearms, knives and swords – by the customs officers who claimed they were saving the vessel's master and owners from being charged under the old Gunpowder Act which forbade the export of firearms without an official licence.[13]

As the number of emigrants soared the following year, pressure for stronger action was brought to bear by a group of major Scottish landowners led by the Member of Parliament for Inverness-shire – Colonel James Grant of Ballindalloch. In mid April 1775, Grant wrote to Montgomery ostensibly concerned: 'for the preservation of His Majesty's Subjects & more immediately of those poor deluded people, who in great numbers, I am informed, proposed sailing with their wives & families this Spring.' It was his recommendation:

… that the government may never have a more proper opportunity of chequing the Emigration Disposition without force, particularly if closure of the ports was followed by steps to employ this valuable set of people, who are always ready to fight for their King & Country when required.

In effect, he was emphasising the inherent danger of large groups of potentially disaffected Highlanders leaving with arms and cash for the colonies which were then on the point of open rebellion.

Such warnings had the desired effect on the Scottish administration. By the time the two Larne vessels – the *Lord Dunluce* and the *Jeannie* – anchored off Gigha in August 1775 moves were in hand. Ronald Campbell in Campbeltown was instructed by his superiors – in the second half of their letter dated 2 September 1775 – to intervene and be obstructive to this scheme:

> The Lord Advocate has thereupon represented to the Board that, though the Government has not taken any coercive measures to prevent such emigration, it may be highly proper from the present situation of America to discourage or even prevent the same as much as possible. You are therefore to postpone the clearing out of such ships and to use your best endeavours to prevent their sailing, conducting yourselves in this important business in a private manner as may be.

Two days later, a follow up letter from the Scottish Board of Customs was sent to him conveying a new resolution by the government to stop all sailings of emigrants to the colonies in rebellion. The change in sentiment was due to a new hand at the helm in Edinburgh, the rising star in Scottish politics Henry Dundas, who had just taken over from Montgomery as Lord Advocate. Campbell's new orders were now unequivocal:

> The Lord Advocate having acquainted us that he has been informed of many embarkations of His Majesty's subjects of this country for America and some with money, arms and ammunition and signified that if a check is not given thereto it may afford aid and support to His Majesty's Rebellious subjects in the several colonies in America, that he is therefore determined as far as lies in his power to prevent the same and has desired that no vessel may be cleared from the ports of Scotland for the continent of America with more persons on board than their proper complement of men, and from the present state of the Colonies it appears to us highly necessary to discourage and prevent as much as possible, emigration from this country, we direct you till further orders not to clear out

any ship or vessel from your Port for the colonies of America with more persons on board than their proper crew.

Collector Campbell at Campbeltown probably never received the final communiqué in time to act on Dundas' instructions as the postal service conveyed by coach took between five and nine days to reach Campbeltown from the capital. Even if he had acted immediately on its receipt, there would have been a further day or two lost before he could inform his officers on Gigha to stop them sailing. In two successive letters (8–9 September 1775) he informed their Lordships that he had failed to deter or detain either of the two Larne vessels:

> In our letter of the 8th inst we acquainted your Honours that the ship *Jeannie,* John McNeill master, was lying at the island of Gigha ready to sail with the first fair wind with passengers for North Carolina and the surveyor with the boatmen there attending her. The vessel sailed yesterday afternoon from Gigha having onboard 245 passengers viz 88 men, 78 women and 79 children. The numbers onboard the *Lord Dunluce* lately sailed was 93 men, 94 women and 113 children making in all 300.

A report from his brother customs officer at Fort William around the same time suggests that the Ulster masters had a forewarning of the ban as only a couple of days before the departure of the *Jeannie*, a sister vessel from Larne – the *Jupiter* (Captain Samuel Brown) – had cleared out for Cape Fear River from the isolated anchorage of Dunstaffnage – taking a party of 136 of emigrants gathered from Appin, Glen Orchy and Lismore in Argyllshire.[14] Like most uplifts of Highland migrants, the master did so without the approval or knowledge of the local customs officers. As the Collector at Inverness – Roderick McKenzie – had earlier stated to Secretary Nelthorpe in Edinburgh, such chartered passenger vessels: 'having no business at the Customs house left for distant ports … without [I] knowing anything of them but by report.'[15] These were the last large organised parties of emigrants to sail from Scottish waters before Dundas' embargo formally came into effect on 21 September 1775. This ban remained in place for the duration of the war.

The 'Argyll Colony of 1739'
The employment of flaxseed vessels from across the North Channel to transport Presbyterian Argyllshire Highlanders to the Scots and 'Scotch Irish' settlements in North Carolina dates back some four decades. Indeed, it was the earlier exodus of Presbyterian Ulstermen from Londonderry, Belfast and Larne to the Americas that greatly influenced the would-be Argyll colonists of the same religious persuasion. They were encouraged by

the Irish authorities' abandonment of attempts to block group departures by 1729.[16] In that year, one of the agents of Dowager Countess of Argyll – a young Archibald Campbell of Stonefield – reported to her:

> … that several persons in Kintyre in imitation of there neighbours in Irland show a great Inclination to go to New England to settle there … Mr McNeill – I mean Niell oge – is very active in carrying on the project he is forst to [go] himself upon the expense of the adventurers to see a proper place for the Colony and according to his Report they are to be Determine.[17]

Eight years later he reported to a 'Mr Smith':

> the same disposition of going to America, which has for some years prevailed in Irland, is at length come over the water and Seiz'd our people in Arygleshire to the degree that some of our landed men are about to sell their concerns and determined to try their fortunes in that Country.[18]

The success of such schemes depended wholly on the integrity of the tacksmen (or, in the case of Lowlanders, the promoters of their society) organising the uplift. It was a dangerous business for the more gullible emigrants. In the same year as the founding of the 'Argyle Colony' (as they referred to it) in Bladen (later Cumberland) County, North Carolina, one promoter promised free passage and six months provisions to any local tenantry of mid Argyll (1739) willing to settle in Jamaica. This scheme was the brainchild of the 'n'er-do-good' Sir James Campbell of Auchinbreck and was strenuously denounced by the clan chief – John, 2nd duke of Argyll. Writing from London to Archibald Campbell of Stonefield, the duke declared that this 'knavish trick' was a trap for 'poor ignorant folk' as he was certain that Auchinbreck's intention was to sell 'the poor wretches as slaves' on landing on the island.[19]

Which was almost certainly the fate awaiting the 111 *de facto* 'prisoners' forcibly incarcerated in the hold of the *William* of Donaghadee – which had been ostensibly chartered to carry convicts – when she put back to her home port to refit for the Atlantic crossing in October 1739. In that scandalous affair the poor wretches under hatches had been coerced or forcibly kidnapped from Loch Bracadale in Skye and from Harris by a gang led by Norman McLeod of Berneray with the tacit knowledge of some the major chiefs on the islands. After this human cargo been landed at Donaghadee they managed to break out of the barns near the town where they had been handcuffed and lock up, only to be hunted down and beaten by the crew led by their Captain William Davison, aided by one of the scheme's principal promoters from Skye – McLeod of Unish.[20]

Some 40 years later, Edward Long, the first historian of Jamaica, alluded to such unscrupulous methods of supplying white indentured servants:

> … great numbers used formerly to be brought from Scotland where they were actually kidnapped by some man traders in or near Glasgow and shipped for this island to be sold for four or five years term of service. On their arrival they used to be ranged in a line like new Negroes for the planters to pick and chose. But this traffic has ceased for some years since the despotism of clanship was subdued and trade and industry drove out laziness and tyranny from the North of Scotland.[21]

'Spiriting' – as kidnapping of servants for the Americas was known – remained rife in Scotland well beyond the mid century.[22] At one point the Earl of Suffolk, came close to stationing soldiers on Skye to deter 'the business', but did not – in deference to the local population's aversion to red coats. As he reluctantly acknowledged, their presence could only serve to fan the embers of smouldering Jacobite sentiment and promote further emigration.

This was in marked contrast to the Ulster servant recruitment model at around the same time. Shipping owners at the ports relied wholly on newspaper advertisements and pamphlets and agents touring the countryside, to drum up individuals and family groups as fee paying or indentured and 'redemptionist' passengers to augment the outgoing cargo of linen and household goods.[23]

It followed that most Gaelic-speaking Highlanders emigrating from Argyllshire and Skye to North Carolina were recruited by trusted tacksmen or local promoters and uplifted from a close at hand coastal location far removed from Glasgow. In the case of the Argyll Colony of 1739, the two promoters were former tacksmen and brothers-in-law – Coll McAlister of Ballinakill in Knapdale and Neil 'Dubh' McNeill of Ardelay in Gigha. The seed of the idea for this settlement was probably sown by their kinsman – Captain Hector McNeil (son of Lachlan of Tirfergus) – a master mariner who regularly sailed between America, Africa and Bristol and recently settled in Boston.[24] Three years previously, Hector wrote to his brother – Neil 'the Baron' – residing in Losset, Argyllshire:

> I should be glad to know if I could have any encouragement to get 200 or 250 passengers from the North of Ireland to New England, who could pay for their passage if a ship was sent there to take them abroad. You may easily be informed of this from our friends in Belfast. No doubt the Highlands could also spare many who, if industrious and versed in husbandry, might with little change procure lands capable of improvement …

148

He raised this proposal for an Ulster-Kintyre uplift twice over the next two years before his advice was sought on another scheme via his brother:

> You mentioned several of our relations that designed to come to America and settle in North Carolina. I wish they may have the desired success but I can assure you that Province is remarkable for knaves and villains of all sort ... however Neill Du[bh] of Gigha has been there no doubt he is a better judge of both people and country than I can be.[25]

Neill Dubh returned to Argyllshire via Ulster and convinced his family of the merits of a settlement in North Carolina, the prime being the benevolent attitude of the Scots-born governor of the province – Gabriel Johnston – towards allocating land grants and remission of ten years' taxes to incoming 'foreign Protestants'.[26] In June 1739 McNeill led the first contingent of settlers that sailed from Campbeltown on the *Thistle* of Saltcoats – Captain Robert Brown – calling at Gigha.[27] The *Belfast News Letter* around the same time states that a further party followed, swelling the number landed to *c.* 350 by 1740. By then their leaders – now five in number – were petitioning the General Assembly of North Carolina for financial assistance and land grants to establish the 'Scotch Gentlemen and several poor people brought onto this province'. The three new leaders signing were Duncan Campbell of Kilduskland (Ardrishaig) Dugald McNeill of Losset (Machrihanish) and Daniel (or Donald) McNeill of Taynish (Vayvallich). Most had sold or mortgaged their Scottish estates to ensure the success of their new venture. All were closely related by blood or marriage to Neill Dubh's father – Hector McNeill of Losset, Machrahanish – who died in 1730. Their contacts with Ulster were also particularly strong as three of Hector's brothers had previously settled in Northern Ireland.[28]

The second wave

Over the next 30 years this tight network linking North Carolina with Kintyre and Gigha welcomed their kinsman. The second wave followed with the end of the Seven Years' War – 'the French and Indian War' as they are known in America. Governor William Tryon's emigrant £15 bounty scheme introduced in 1767 added a further inducement to both the shippers and poor emigrants escaping rack renting at home. Furthermore, a considerable number of Highlanders who served in Lord Fraser's and Lord Eglinton's regiments fighting the French and their Indian allies chose to be discharged in America, receiving of a land grant in gratuity.[29]

Unfortunately, only a few vessels and masters carrying the earlier waves of Highlanders from Argyllshire across the Atlantic before Secretary

Robinson's edict of December 1773 are named. The *Scots Magazine* alludes to some 19 uplifts of which ten were destined for North Carolina. The customs records of the Ulster ports for the colonial period have not survived and what has been compiled of passages from Ulster to North Carolina has come from advertisements in such newspapers as the *Belfast News Letter*.[30] On the other side of the North Channel the Customs records of the Firth of Clyde – Campbeltown, Ayr, Irvine, Greenock and Port Glasgow – are available from the mid 1740s onwards. They occasionally record trading to Charleston and Wilmington – mainly in rice, indigo, barrel staves, pitch and turpentine, but rarely mention passengers.

Both Ulster and Scottish vessels are known to have engaged in coastal trading along the eastern American seaboard and the West Indies before returning home, as with the *Edinburgh* of Campbeltown – a small brig which carried emigrants from its home port to North Carolina and Prince Edward Island, Nova Scotia during the summers of 1770 and 1771 respectively. One that second trip the captain – John McMichael – failed to secure a cargo of dried fish for Lisbon so he returned via Charleston to Newry with flaxseed.[31] All of which provided the opportunity for the Scots network to pass on individuals and parties. As happened with the Gigha uplift, emigrants on the *Lord Dunluce* who were landed at Norfolk, Virginia, after a 13-week passage and were provided with provisions and cartage to move on to North Carolina by Lord Dunmore.[32]

Likewise, only fragments have survived of the 'Naval Office Accounts' (Customs Accounts) for Brunswick. This was the legal port of entry half way up the Cape Fear River before Wilmington was developed in the later in the century. The records of the port of Charlestown, South Carolina on the other hand have largely survived and reveal the regular shuttling across the Atlantic of Irish flaxseed traders. Some arrived by a more convoluted way via West Indies for rum and molasses

Unfortunately, the uplifting and landing of groups of passengers was of little interest to customs officers either sides of the Atlantic until the 1770s and the emergence of government concerns over emigration to America. However, it can be assumed that the Ulster ports, with their close proximity across the North Channel and regular use of Campbeltown as the port of compliance with the British Navigation Acts, and the proven expertise of their masters in the safe navigation to the Carolinas – were the preferred choice of emigrants leaving from Argyllshire.

The final wave

Propelling this dramatic leap in emigrants was cattle blight in the late 1760s and a major deterioration in weather patterns across most of western Scotland in the early 1770s. The wet, cold summer in 1771 adversely affected the harvest, followed by a severe autumn of wind and rain and a harsh winter with snow on the ground for two months. During that 'black Spring' – as it was known in Skye – the black cattle which traditionally paid the rent, died in large numbers. Thomas Pennant who toured Skye and the Hebrides that year reckoned that 5,000 beasts had perished on Skye alone, reducing the rural population to carrion eating and mollusc scavenging to stave off starvation.[33] Unable or unwilling to pay the new high rents, many were forced off the land – often to make way for sheep runs.

Capitalising on this 'push' to emigrate was the 'pull' of a stream of complimentary letters home from America and a pamphlet that it was widely circulated in the distressed areas – *Information Concerning the Province of North Carolina Addressed to Emigrants from the Highlands and Western Island of Scotland by an Impartial Hand* – which extolled the virtues of the land and climate awaiting settlement. Published in Glasgow 1773 under the pseudonym 'Americanus Scotus' it was it most likely the work of Alexander Campbell of Balole on Islay – a nephew of Neil Dudh who had returned home to organise a new party of emigrants.[34] Collector Campbell at Campbeltown noted this upsurge in propaganda in his area in his correspondence with his superiors that 'these gentlemen (the tacksmen) were chaffed and published their resolution to go to America and were, it is said, at a great deal of pains to induce people to take the same resolution.'[35] So much so, that Campbell of Balole returned to North Carolina the following year having chartered an unnamed vessel to uplift a party of Highlanders.

Their reasons for emigration

Secretary Robinson's request that the local Customs officers should interview emigrants to establish their reasons for emigrating was only complied with when their vessel was moored in the main harbour of the precinct port. With very few exceptions the answer was the increase in rents over the past three years – double or tripling in some cases. At that time many lairds in western and northern Scotland were striving to maximise their revenue from their Highland estates by discarding the old feudal system of military service in part rent – in favour of market driven capitalism managed by the professional 'estate factor'. With this change the clan tacksman – the middleman in the old land management system – was, to all intents and purposes, redundant. It followed that it was these well connected and educated men who organised and led the large parties of their neighbours that had been leaving Argyllshire and the islands in successive waves since the late 1730s. How many made the crossing to North Carolina before 1776 has been a matter of speculation by historians, although the consensus has settled at no more than 20,000.

The end of an era

The outbreak of the American War of Independence marked the end of an era in the maritime activity across and from the North Channel. Retaliatory embargoes on trading with British merchants and masters passed in the opening months of the conflict by the 'non importation – non exportation' patriot committee of Wilmington and New Hanover in North Carolina, effectively terminating the American flaxseed (out) and passengers and linen (in) trade in January 1775. This had been the mainstay of the Ulster ports transatlantic trade since the beginning of the century who had been excluded from all other direct trade in colonial produce by the Navigation Acts (effectively from 1694 onwards). Thereafter, flaxseed was imported directly and separately into Ulster and Scotland from the Baltic.

Even before the outbreak of war, the Ulster transatlantic traders had lost their West Indies trade in linen and herring in exchange for sugar and rum (which they had been legally landing at Campbeltown to conform to the British Navigation Acts). This was the direct result of an orchestrated campaign led mainly by Bristol merchants to have that Scottish precinct stripped of its status as an 'enumerated port' following allegations of widespread smuggling of American tobacco and West Indian rum at the quay side and landings in the creeks of the precinct facing the North Channel.

The final erosion of regular maritime connections between the Ulster ports and Campbeltown came with the termination of the herring bounty in 1785. This expensive government scheme was based on the barrel count of the suitably equipped herring buss as inspected and measured at Campbeltown. This generous subsidy system had provided the Antrim ports with large quantities of barrelled herring for their West Indian trade. Thereafter, Campbeltown was relegated to an outpost of the Firth of Clyde. After the war ended in 1783, however, the uplift of emigrants resumed from the west coast and islands of Scotland, but this trade was now much more in the hands of shipping agents (rather than local tackmen) who worked mainly out of Port Glasgow and Greenock. It was also more controlled by the agents of government after the passing of the Passenger Act of 1805. These Clyde ports joined Leith, Bristol, London and Liverpool to dominate the British West Indies trades while the British Navigation Acts still applied.

Notes

1 *The Scotsman Magazine*, 37 (1775), p. 690.

2 NRS, CE 82/2/79: Letterbook 1, Collector to the Board to the Collector at Campbeltown.

3 NRS, Customs Quarterly Returns for Campbeltown, entries dated 4 and 9 Aug. 1775.

4 Ibid., entries dated 22 (the *Stonefield*) and 30 Aug. (the *Mains*).

5 NRS, GD 64/5/21–2: petition by Archibald Campbell of Jura, 17 June 1754. They eventually arrived at Cape Fear on 2 Oct. 1754. The *Mary* returned to Dumfries via St Kitts carrying Carolina tar the following year. See also Duane Meyer, *The Highland Scots of North Carolina* (Raleigh, NC, 1963).

6 For the Jamaican Campbell connection, see Eric J. Graham, 'The Scots penetration of the Jamaican plantation business, 1700–1834' in T. M. Devine (ed.), *Revisiting Scotland's Slavery Past* (Edinburgh, 2015) pp 83–6.

7 For a detailed examination of the lists, see Alexander Murdoch, 'Two Scottish documents concerning emigration to North Carolina in 1754', *The North Carolina Historical Review*, 93 (Oct. 2016), pp 361–85.

8 NRS CS 230/Mc/4/4: McNeil v. Campbell, Court of Session, unextracted processes, as quoted by Alexander Murdoch, 'Hector McAllister in North Carolina, Argyll and Arran: family and memory of return migration to Scotland in the eighteenth century', *Journal of Scottish Historical Studies*, 33:1 (2013), p. 10.

9 In 1771, two gentlemen from the Isle of Skye had petitioned the Board of Trade for a grant of 40,000 acres of land in North Carolina on which to settle servants they would recruit in the Highlands and Islands (The National Archives (TNA), CO 391/78). While this was refused, it would seem that the scheme went ahead.

10 R. J. Dickson, *Ulster Emigration to Colonial America, 1718–1775* (1966; reprinted Belfast, 2016), p. 161.

11 TNA, CO 5/138, pt 2, f. 741.

12 TNA, Treasury 11/30m, p. 450.

13 This was the *Monimia*, one of four vessels that sailed for America from Port Glasgow and Greenock with 700 emigrants mostly from the 'North Highlands': *The Scotsman Magazine*, 37 (1775), p. 340.

14 TNA, T 47/12.

15 TNA, T 1/500/ 1: letter dated 3 Jan. 1774.

16 The usual method was for customs officers to claim that the woollen bedding taken onboard constituted a breach on the ban on exporting wool.

17 NRS GD 14/10/1, pp 224–5: Archibald Campbell of Stonefield to your Grace, 13 Feb. 1729, Campbell of Stonefield Letter Book.

18 Campbell of Stonefield died in 1777.

19 NRS GD 14/12: letter from John, 2nd duke of Argyll, to Archibald Campbell of Stonefield, 22 Mar. 1740.

20 This well known episode of 'slavery' in Scotland seriously implicated two of the leading lairds on Skye – McLeod of Slate and McDonald of Dunvegan – and threatened to become a national scandal had not the Machiavellian skills of the influential Duncan Forbes of Culloden orchestrated a hush up.

21 Edward Long, *History of Jamaica* (3 vols, London, 1774), vol. 2, pp 287–8.

22 One of the most notorious rings was led by officials of the town of Aberdeen who carried away *c*. 600 children and young adolescents to America in the early 1740s. This was legalised by inducing them to sign indentures while being kept in an isolated warehouse or onboard away from their parents.

23 Dickson, *Ulster Emigration to Colonial America*, p. 161.

24 His later voyages in the slave trade are listed in the Transatlantic Slave Trade Database (www.slavevoyages.org).

25 Family papers of MacNeal of Ugadale and Lossit, as quoted by A. I. B. Stewart, 'The North Carolina Settlement of 1739', *The Kintyre Antiquarian & Natural History Society*, 15 (Spring 1984).

26 Born in Southdean, near Hawick, in the Borders, Johnston studied at St Andrews later becoming Professor of Hebrew there. Prior to becoming governor, he was secretary to the Earl of Wilmington for seven years.

27 Saltcoats harbour (1700) in Ayrshire was the first developed coal port on the Firth of Clyde serving Ireland mainly. The anchorage accounts for the harbour for 1737–40 indicate that the tonnage of the *Thistle* was *c.* 101 tons burthen; Eric J. Graham, 'Saltcoats: a pre-railway coal port', *Scottish Industrial History*, 2:1 (1978), p. 28. Tonnage burthen was a very flexible term in the eighteenth century and often varied by as much as 100 per cent depending on what the master decided to declare – low for customs and harbour duties, but high for advertising cargo and passenger capacity. See 'Tonnage Measurements' in Eric J. Graham, *A Maritime History of Scotland* (Edinburgh, 2015), pp 335–7.

28 The eldest brother John acquired the estate of Faughart in County Louth. Neil Buie, the second brother, acquired the estate of Killoquin in County Antrim. He married Rose, daughter of Captain Stewart of Garve, a family descended from Archibald Stewart of Ballintoy, of the Bute Stewarts, factor to the earl of Antrim, who was much involved in the attempt of the seventh earl of Argyll to settle Kintyre on his younger son. The third brother, Archibald, married an Irish McNeill, while Malcolm, the sixth brother, went to Ireland as a 'Tory hunter' and it was said that he was given the estate of Ballymascanlon in gratitude. See A. I. B. Stewart, 'Lachlan McNeil Buidhe', *The Kintyre Antiquarian & Natural History Society*, 19 (Spring 1986).

29 One such was the leader of the Appin band of emigrants onboard the *Ulysses* of Larne on her final wave passage to Cape Fear from Dunstaffnage in Sept. 1775. He was the 44-year-old Captain Allan Stewart, formerly a Lieutenant in Fraser's Regiment, returning to take up his land grant before the troubles escalated. A. R. Newsome (ed.), *Records of English and Scottish Emigrants to North Carolina, 1774–1775* (Raleigh, NC, 1989), p. 29.

30 See Richard K. McMaster, *Scotch-Irish Merchants in Colonial America* (Belfast, 2009).

31 Frank Bigwood, 'Two lists of intending passengers to the New World, 1770 and 1771', *The Kintyre Antiquarian & Natural History Society*, 41 (Spring 1997).

32 *Edinburgh Advertiser*, 22 Mar. 1776. The same intelligence states that two other emigrant vessels that had left the Highlands at the same time as the *Lord Dunluce* – named the *Jupiter* and *Fanny* – had safely reached Wilmington with 'all well' on board. It may well be that the *Fanny* is the *Jeanie* in the August Campbeltown Customs report or vice versa.

33 The best contemporary account of conditions on Skye and the Islands is that of Thomas Pennant *A Tour in Scotland and Voyage to the Hebrides, 1772* (2 vols, Chester, 1774).

34 Murdoch, 'Hector McAllister in North Carolina, Argyll and Arran'.

35 NRS, Campbelltown Letterbook Class I, entry of 23 Feb. 1774.